Mum*life*

WITTY AND PRETTY MUSINGS ON *the Truth* ABOUT MOTHERHOOD

PAULA KUKA

TILLER PRESS

NEW YORK LONDON TORONTO SYDNEY NEW DELHI

TILLER PRESS

An Imprint of Simon & Schuster, Inc.
1230 Avenue of the Americas
New York, NY 10020

First Tiller Press hardcover edition September 2020

This publication contains the opinions and ideas of its author. It is intended to provide helpful and informative
material on the subjects addressed in the publication. It is sold with the understanding that the author
and publisher are not engaged in rendering medical, health, or any other kind of personal, professional services in
the book. The reader should consult his or her medical, health, or other competent professional before
adopting any of the suggestions in this book or drawing inferences from it.

The author and publisher specifically disclaim all responsibility for any liability, loss, or risk, personal or
otherwise, that is incurred as a consequence, directly or indirectly, of the use and application of any of the
contents of this book.

For information about special discounts for bulk purchases, please contact Simon & Schuster
Special Sales at 1-866-506-1949 or business@simonandschuster.com.

The Simon & Schuster Speakers Bureau can bring authors to your live event.
For more information or to book an event, contact the Simon & Schuster Speakers Bureau
at 1-866-248-3049 or visit our website at www.simonspeakers.com.

Interior design by Paula Kuka

Manufactured in the United States of America

3   5   7   9   10   8   6   4   2

Library of Congress Cataloging-in-Publication Data
Names: Kuka, Paula, author.
Title: Mumlife : witty and pretty musings on (the truth about) motherhood / by Paula Kuka.
Description: First Tiller Press hardcover edition. | New York : Tiller Press, 2020. | Identifiers: LCCN 2020016769
(print) | LCCN 2020016770 (ebook) | ISBN 9781982155322 (hardcover) | ISBN 9781982155346 (ebook) |
Subjects: LCSH: Kuka, Paula. | Kuka, Paula—Family. | Mothers—Australia—Biography. | Motherhood—Australia—
Anecdotes. | Motherhood—Australia—Humor. | Mother and child—Australia.| Classification:
LCC HQ759 .K835 2020 (print) | LCC HQ759 (ebook) | DDC 306.874/3—dc23
LC record available at https://lccn.loc.gov/2020016769
LC ebook record available at https://lccn.loc.gov/2020016770

ISBN 978-1-9821-5532-2
ISBN 978-1-9821-5534-6 (ebook)

To Hugo & Leni

Sorry I never filled in your baby books.
This is for you instead.

It's all for you.

TO MY CHILDREN, THANK YOU:

FOR YELLING AT ME ALL DAY.

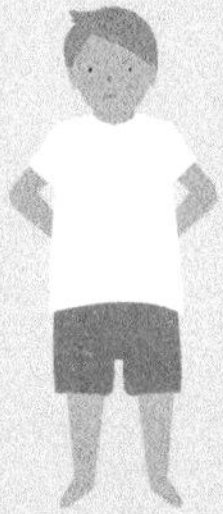

I KNOW NO ONE WILL EVER
TAKE ADVANTAGE OF YOU.

FOR KEEPING ME UP ALL NIGHT.

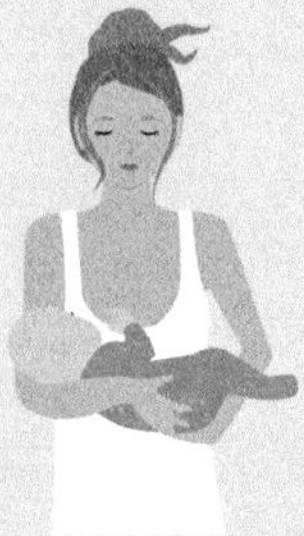

BEING NEEDED BY YOU IS
MY MOST FULFILLING DUTY.

FOR THE INTENSE EXPERIENCE
OF CHILDBIRTH.

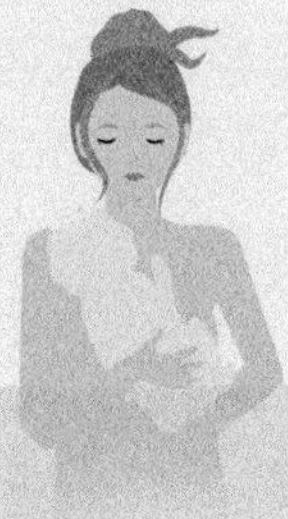

BECAUSE NOW I KNOW
NOTHING WILL BREAK ME.

FOR FILLING MY HEAD WITH WORRY.

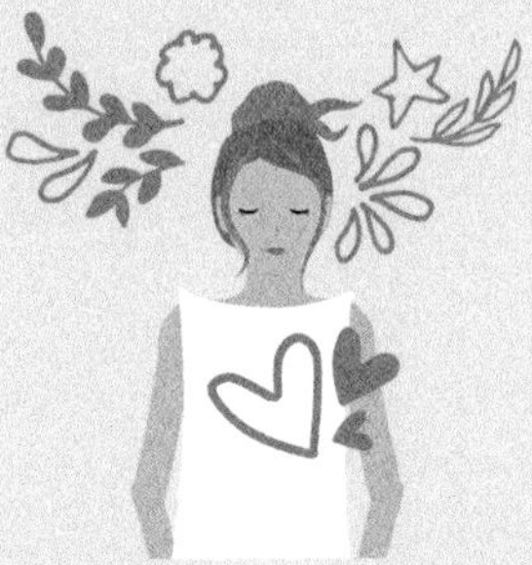

MATCHED ONLY BY A HEART
OVERFLOWING WITH LOVE.

INTRODUCTION

I was completely prepared for my son's arrival. Or so I thought. Hospital bag packed. Breathing techniques down pat. Vintage woodland fabric curtains sewn and hung. Physically, I was as prepared as you can be. Nothing, however, can prepare you for the surreal moment you walk through the door of your home carrying your newborn baby—a whole new life that days earlier wasn't here. The burden of responsibility is enormous. The emotional shift is palpable. Nothing will ever be the same again.

Creativity has always been a big part of my life. I'm a landscape architect and have worked in some incredible places on diverse and interesting projects. I've sat in design meetings at Cambridge University trying to find an equally long-lasting replacement for four-hundred-year-old paving stones. I've discussed underground swimming pool details with a Russian oligarch for their Central London townhouse. I've worked through the night on a Malaysian waterfront precinct presentation before boarding an eight-hour flight and launching straight into that presentation to a boardroom full of slightly disengaged businessmen who were smoking, sleeping or discussing what was for lunch. I spent a chaotic and enchanting year living in Shanghai, where I designed bizarrely themed housing developments in far-flung mountainous cities of China. I always threw myself into work with great gusto.

It was with this same enthusiasm and dedication that I entered motherhood. All the energy that went into my career needed a new home. I researched. I baked. I read the books. I obsessed. I regrettably read the articles. *All* of the articles. My son, a placid bundle of sweeping blond hair and fat rolls, filled my heart with joy. But suddenly the world seemed to have shrunk to the size of our inner-city Sydney terrace house. And as for my baby, I wondered how someone so small could take up so much space. I thought motherhood would completely fulfill me. I thought it would be crafts and sing-alongs and baking organic cookies. No one warned me about the boredom. I had no idea I would feel so consumed. I didn't know it was possible to spend an entire day with another person—a person that you created—and yet feel so lonely. I was full of self-doubt; there were no positive reinforcement or performance reviews. With my family living on the other side of the country and my husband working long hours, I was incredibly isolated.

With slight reluctance I started freelance landscape architecture and illustration when my son was just over a year old. Torn between my desire to be the best possible mum (and surely that means always being there) and my own emotional needs for mental stimulation, I set up an illustration business, working in the evenings and during his nap time on my digital creations. I started selling art prints through my online store and at local art markets. And slowly the world started opening up again. It was a huge sense of relief when I realised that working on my small creative projects, even though it meant time away from my son, made me more fulfilled and, subsequently, a happier and more engaged mum.

Our family grew again when our daughter was born, and during that early hazy and intense time as a mother to two under three, I started drawing cartoons as a way to document our days. I knew I was never going to get around to filling in their baby books, and I wanted a way to remember this very strange but magical chapter. Initially it was going to be a project for and about my children, but it didn't take long till I noticed that the cartoons that were more about my emotional experience of being a mother garnered the most interest. When I posted a drawing about my overwhelming feelings of guilt, comments flowed in, and my burden suddenly felt lighter. I realised what a powerful thing it was to acknowledge and express these feelings. People told me they felt validated by seeing their own emotions represented.

I had always compared myself to the perfect image of motherhood that dominates social media. Unintentionally, my drawings were starting to celebrate a different view of motherhood. It wasn't about the bubble of bliss and contentment, and it wasn't necessarily about the darker side of motherhood and postnatal mental health issues. It was about the messy middle ground that most of us occupy, and the fact that we can go from intense frustration, boredom and loneliness to hilarity and overwhelming love in a matter of seconds.

The juggle of working and raising children is immensely challenging. My kids are now two and five, and I often feel like I'm being pulled in every possible direction. There is a constant tug-of-war among all my responsibilities: my children's emotional needs, my work, looking after myself, looking after the house, watering my plants, feeding us all nutritious food, dressing us in clean clothes and making sure we all have the correct balance of bacteria in our guts. I often feel like I have a million balls in the air at once, but I also know how incredibly lucky I am that I've found something that fulfills me and also allows me to be at home with my kids.

A far cry from my independent days of working and travelling around the world, my life now revolves around these two small but mighty people. We live in a cute mid-century cottage in Perth, nestled among trees and filled to the brim with the obscene amount of stuff children seem to require: kitchen cupboards bursting with snacks and sippy cups; an overflowing laundry basket; a profusion of children's art pinned to every available vertical surface. I'm surrounded by things and I'm surrounded by people. Moments alone are now very rare.

As my children grow and gain independence, I feel my freedom slowly creeping back, but unlike before I had children, there is now a thread tethering me to my family, and just like a spider's web, it's almost invisible but unthinkably strong. I used to see motherhood as an obstacle. I didn't want to be defined by the role of mother, as if this would somehow hold me back. But it hasn't held me back. It has anchored me to an indomitable force that has propelled me forward. Free from ten-year plans and expectations of what I should have achieved. Free from judgement. Free from regrets. How can I possibly regret anything when every single decision I ever made led me to them?

My drawings represent my own personal experience of motherhood. Hiding behind my drawn alter ego enables me to share things online that I would previously have struggled to share with my closest friends. Being so open and vulnerable can be scary, but by my doing so, maybe other people will feel that they have permission to do the same.

It's certainly made me feel less alone. I hope it does the same for you.

I NEED SPACE

INHALES THEIR CLOTHES

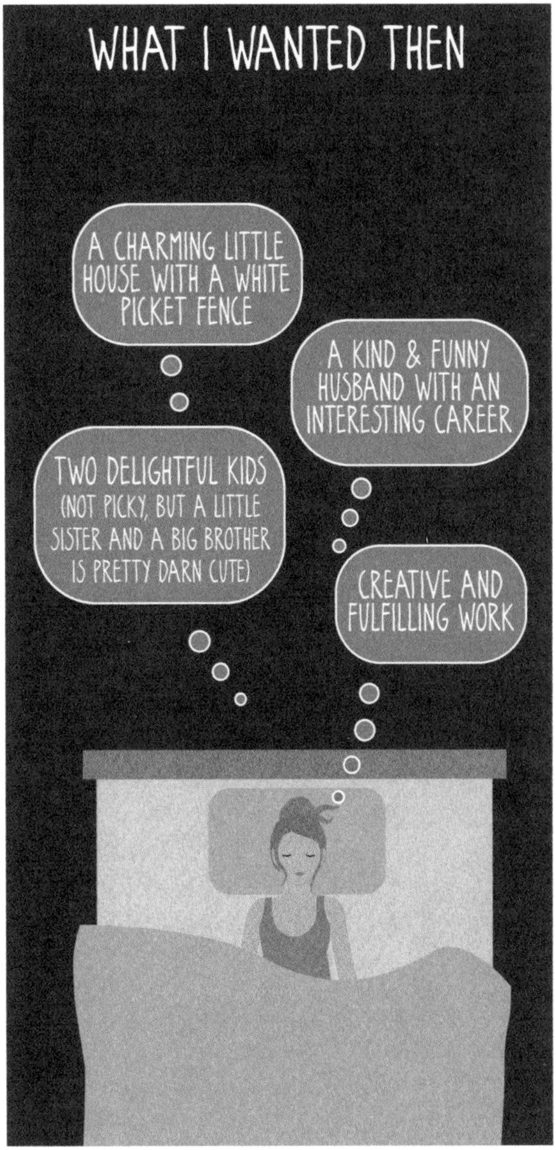
WHAT I WANTED THEN
A CHARMING LITTLE HOUSE WITH A WHITE PICKET FENCE
A KIND & FUNNY HUSBAND WITH AN INTERESTING CAREER
TWO DELIGHTFUL KIDS (NOT PICKY, BUT A LITTLE SISTER AND A BIG BROTHER IS PRETTY DARN CUTE)
CREATIVE AND FULFILLING WORK

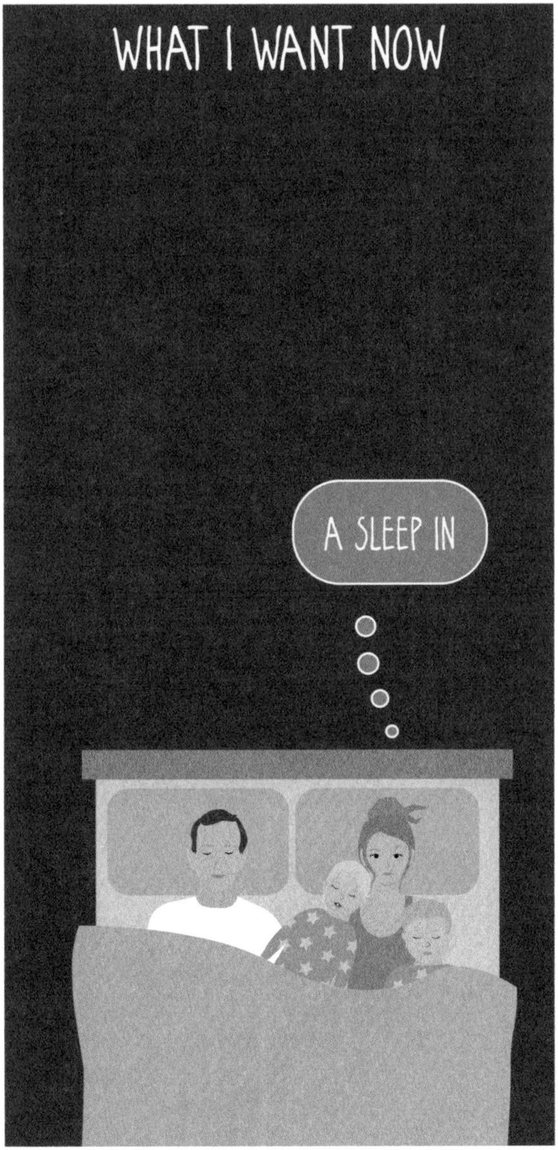
WHAT I WANT NOW
A SLEEP IN

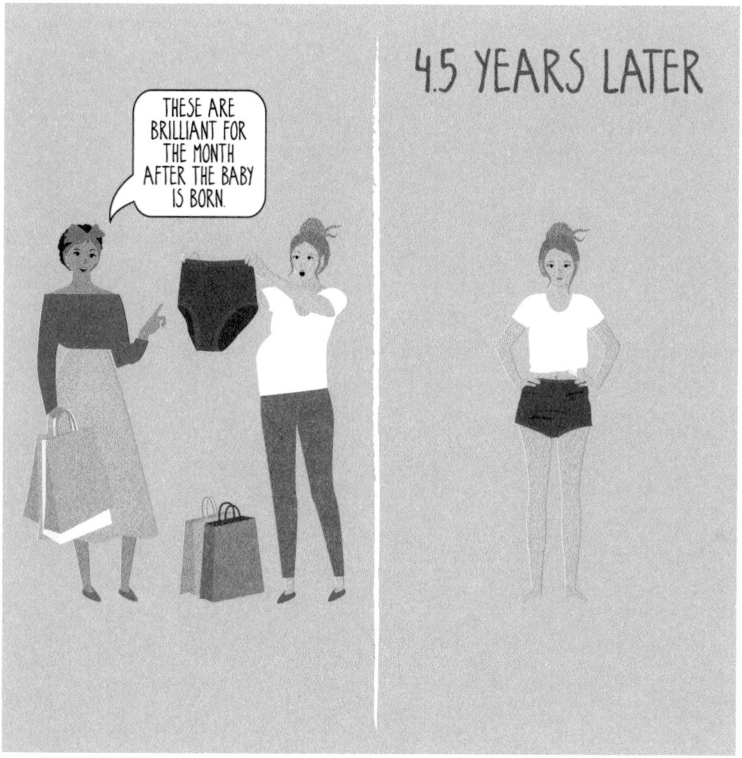
THESE ARE BRILLIANT FOR THE MONTH AFTER THE BABY IS BORN.
4.5 YEARS LATER

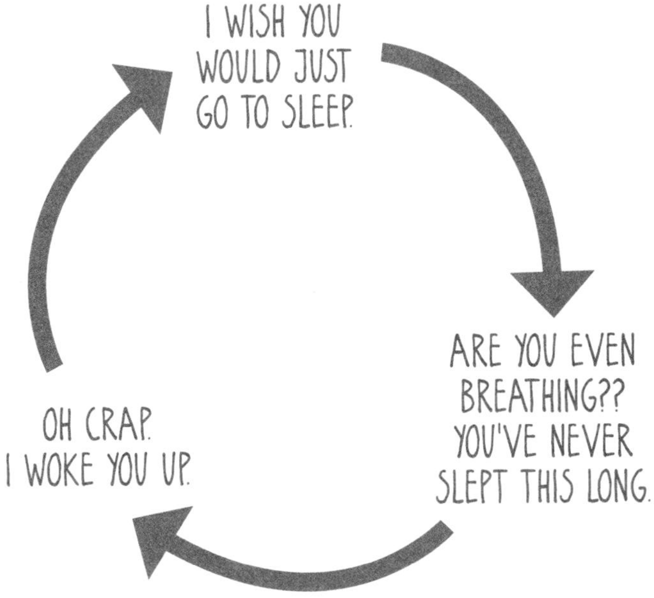
I WISH YOU WOULD JUST GO TO SLEEP.
ARE YOU EVEN BREATHING?? YOU'VE NEVER SLEPT THIS LONG.
OH CRAP. I WOKE YOU UP.

WAYS TO SHOW LOVE
(THAT MIGHT NOT WORK IF YOU ARE A GROWN UP)

WAKE THEM UP IN THE MIDDLE OF THE NIGHT TO TELL THEM A STORY.

ASK TO BRUSH THEIR HAIR AND THEN YANK IT, YELL AT THEM AND TELL THEM THEY LOOK SILLY.

SAY YOU DEFINITELY DON'T WANT ANY FOOD BUT THEN EAT EVERYTHING ON THEIR PLATE.

STEAL SOMETHING OF THEIRS, WRAP IT UP BADLY AND PRESENT IT TO THEM.

VOMIT ON THEM. REPEATEDLY.

BEG TO STAY WITH THEM. BUT THEN CRY EVERY TIME THEY LOOK AT YOU.

ASK FOR THEIR HELP AND THEN SCREAM AT THEM WHEN THEY TRY TO GIVE IT.

PICK THEM SOME FLOWERS FROM THEIR GARDEN.

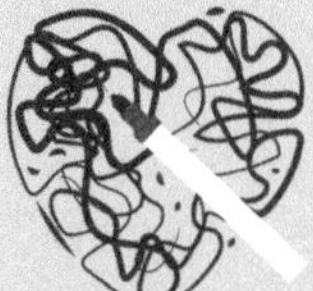

DRAW A HUGE ABSTRACT PICTURE ON THEIR WALL IN PERMANENT MARKER.

DO NOT TAKE YOUR EYES OFF THEM ALL DAY. EVEN WHEN THEY USE THE BATHROOM.

INSPECT THEIR FACE AND EXCITEDLY POINT OUT THEIR FLAWS.

WONDER WEEKS FOR MUMS

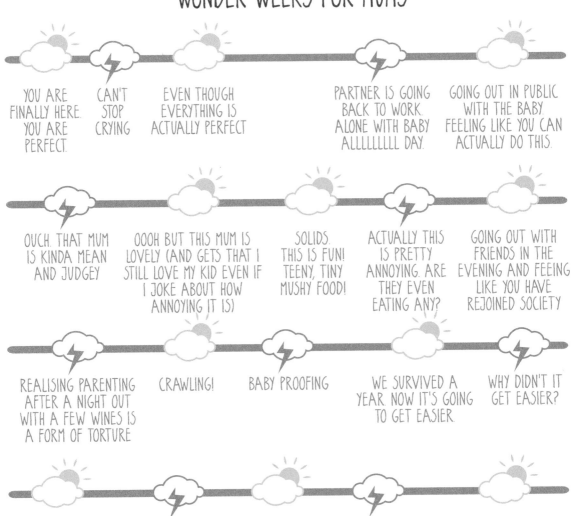

YOU ARE FINALLY HERE. YOU ARE PERFECT.

CAN'T STOP CRYING

EVEN THOUGH EVERYTHING IS ACTUALLY PERFECT

PARTNER IS GOING BACK TO WORK. ALONE WITH BABY ALLLLLLLLL DAY.

GOING OUT IN PUBLIC WITH THE BABY. FEELING LIKE YOU CAN ACTUALLY DO THIS.

OUCH. THAT MUM IS KINDA MEAN AND JUDGEY

OOOH BUT THIS MUM IS LOVELY (AND GETS THAT I STILL LOVE MY KID EVEN IF I JOKE ABOUT HOW ANNOYING IT IS)

SOLIDS. THIS IS FUN! TEENY, TINY MUSHY FOOD!

ACTUALLY THIS IS PRETTY ANNOYING. ARE THEY EVEN EATING ANY?

GOING OUT WITH FRIENDS IN THE EVENING AND FEEING LIKE YOU HAVE REJOINED SOCIETY

REALISING PARENTING AFTER A NIGHT OUT WITH A FEW WINES IS A FORM OF TORTURE

CRAWLING!

BABY PROOFING

WE SURVIVED A YEAR. NOW IT'S GOING TO GET EASIER.

WHY DIDN'T IT GET EASIER?

FINALLY ARRANGED A CATCH-UP PLAY DATE WITH A GOOD FRIEND

DIDN'T MANAGE TO FINISH ONE CONVERSATION AT SAID CATCH-UP

YOU ARE WALKING

NOW YOU CAN RUN AWAY FROM ME

CATCHING A GLIMPSE OF YOUR CHILD AND REALISING "I MADE YOU"

LET'S PLAY HIDE-AND-SEEK

GIFTS FROM AN IMPERFECT MOTHER

My imperfection is my gift to my children. I haven't always felt that way. As a first-time pregnant mother, I would have had trouble distinguishing a "good mum" from a "perfect mum," but I now know they are not one and the same.

I had a major turning point when I was pregnant with my second child. Struck down with debilitating nausea and unable to face the contents of my fridge without heaving, I lay on the floor and ordered McDonald's delivery for my toddler's dinner, sobbing as the *Thomas and Friends* theme song played more times than I care to admit. I felt like a complete and utter failure, but the next day when I was feeling better something strange happened. My son didn't demand takeaway and TV. We just got on with things, as if the day before hadn't existed.

In my son's second week of Kindy, at 2:45 p.m., I received a call from the school asking where I was. I was engrossed in work at home and had forgotten that they finished early that day. I knew this was an inevitable parenting milestone; I just hadn't anticipated it would happen on his third day of school. When I rushed to collect him, he was happily tidying the room with the teacher, enjoying the one-on-one attention, blissfully unaware of my emotional turmoil.

It's hard to let go of aspiring for the unattainable standard of perfection, but it is in our less-than-perfect moments that our children might gain the most. My children can learn a lot from seeing me struggle and then persevere. I want them to see me asking for and accepting help. I would love to show them how to be less self-conscious about making mistakes and not consumed with what other people think.

There will always be times when I have nothing left to give, or for whatever reason I'm not around. While I'm in no rush for my kids to be thrust into the dizzying world of adulthood, it is very reassuring to see my children gaining in confidence and independence, comforting each other or learning to lean on other people.

Despite what their grandparents think, my children aren't perfect. Just as their lives will be full of successes, they will also be full of failures. The least I can do is show them how to fail with grace and wit.

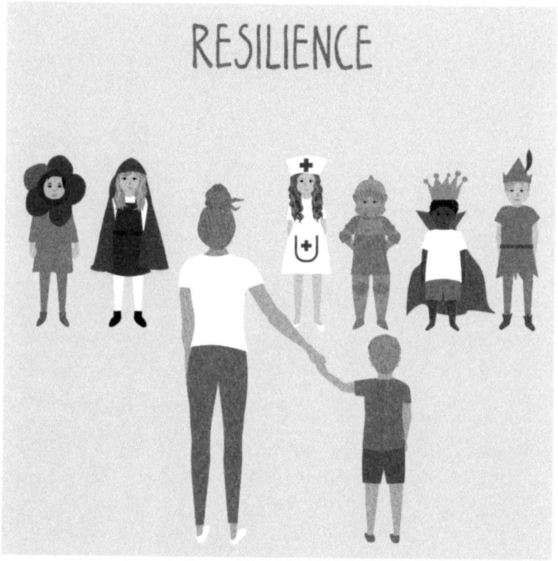
RESILIENCE

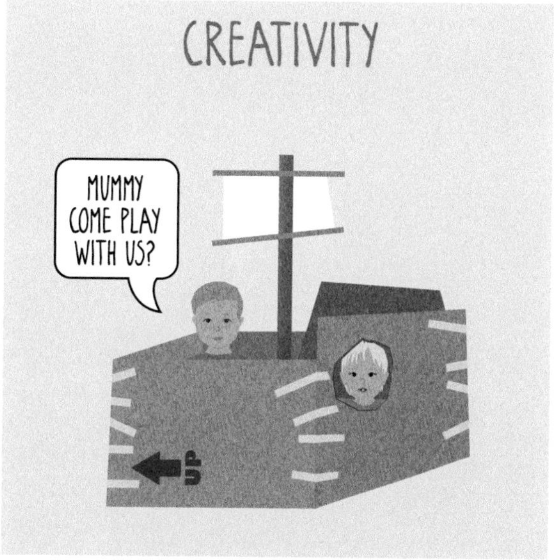
CREATIVITY
MUMMY COME PLAY WITH US?
UP

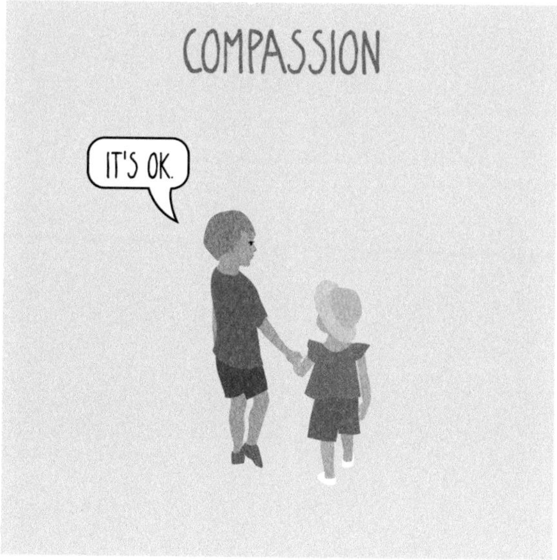
COMPASSION
IT'S OK.

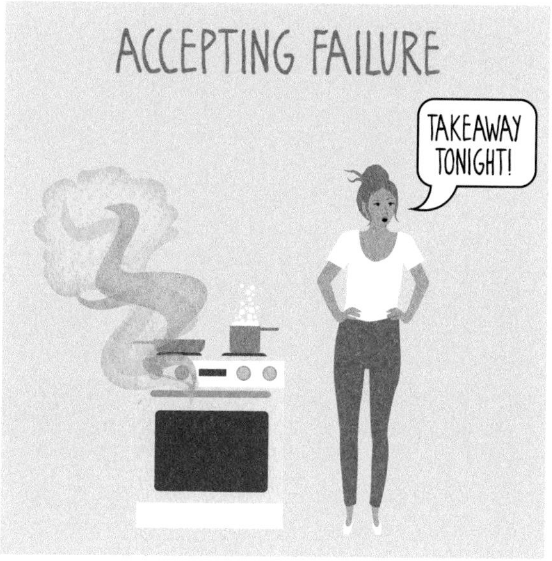
ACCEPTING FAILURE
TAKEAWAY TONIGHT!

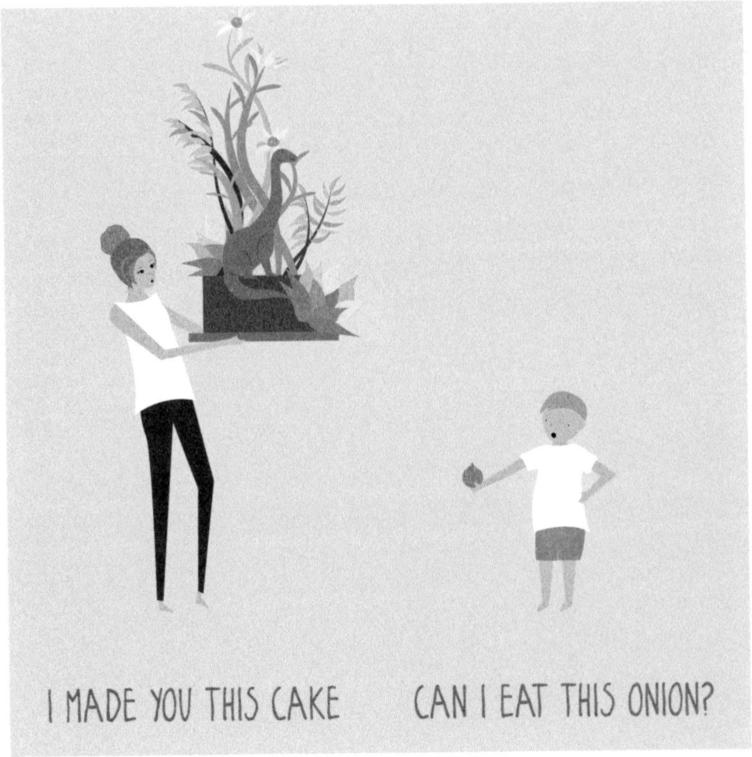
I MADE YOU THIS CAKE
CAN I EAT THIS ONION?

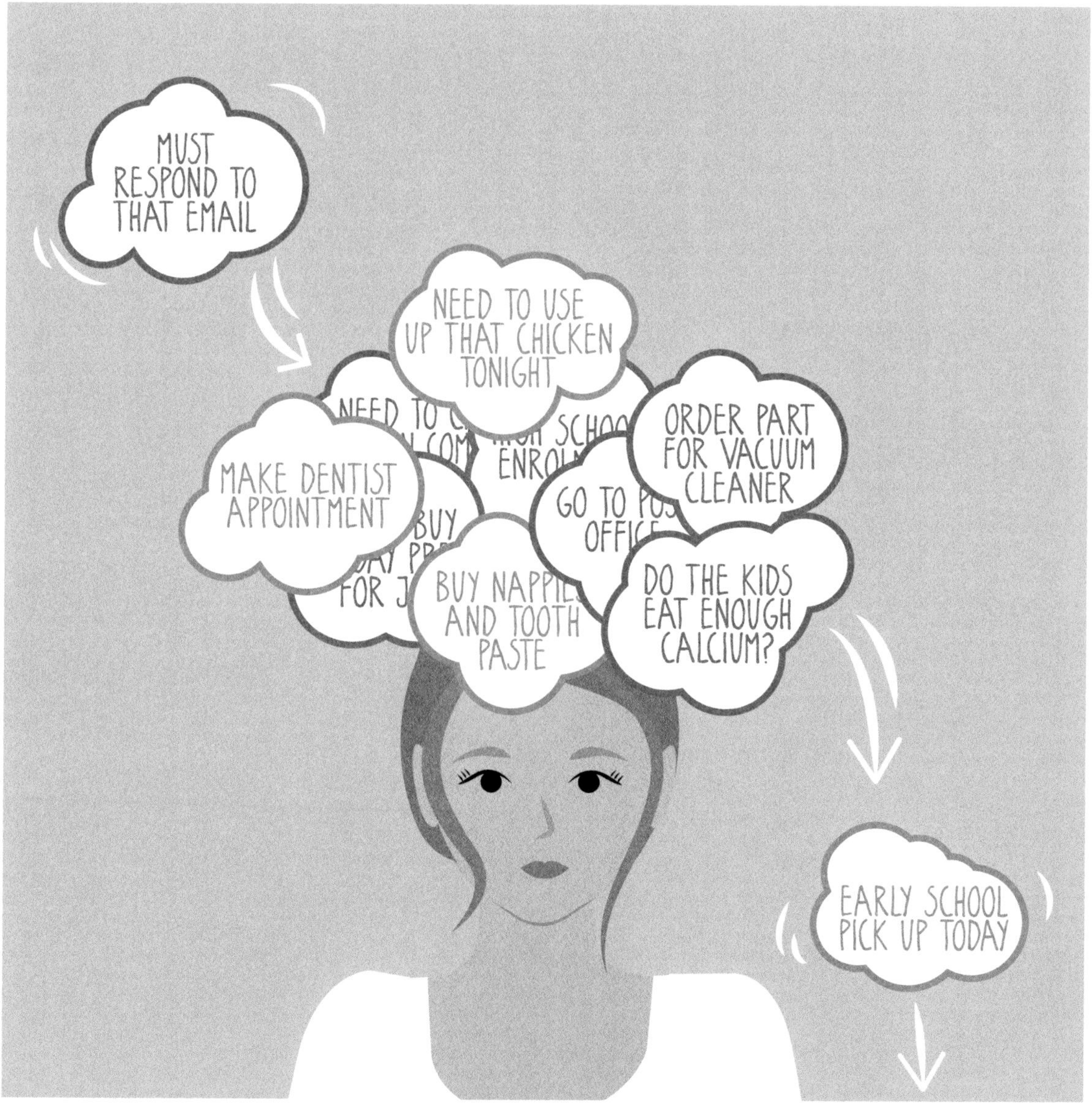
MUST RESPOND TO THAT EMAIL
NEED TO USE UP THAT CHICKEN TONIGHT
MAKE DENTIST APPOINTMENT
ORDER PART FOR VACUUM CLEANER
BUY NAPPIES AND TOOTH PASTE
DO THE KIDS EAT ENOUGH CALCIUM?
EARLY SCHOOL PICK UP TODAY

When I was pregnant I walked out the front of our house and discovered someone had crashed into our car. I sent a series of photos and emotional text messages to my husband. After a few very stressful minutes he wrote back, "That's not our car." —Paula

During my first pregnancy I got to work and got manic that I left the stove on with a pot of boiling water. Paid $30 for a cab ride home (because public transit would be way too slow) just to see that I had turned the stove off and removed the pot of water, and then paid another $30 to get back to work, all before 9:30 a.m. —Claudia

After three weeks of leave I went back to work, arrived at 8 a.m. and discovered I had left my laptop at home. I called my boss and arranged to go home and work from there. My boss called back later in the day and told me that I was still on leave for another week! —Rachel

I put the electric kettle on the stove. I didn't realise until my husband smelled burning plastic. I have never owned a stovetop kettle, so I have no idea where my brain came up with that idea! —Veronica

I called my husband on my cell phone to tell him not to call me because I left my cell phone at home. —Shanny

After spending the night at my mum's place I drove down the street with the steriliser full of bottles on the top of the car. A very confused motorcycle rider informed me when I was stopped at a red light. —Monie

Heavily pregnant and with my daughter in the car, I drove to a friend's house to drop something off. As I pulled into their driveway her husband came out so I jumped out to give him the package. My car started rolling forward towards their garage. I had left it in drive! I stood there confused for a moment before trying to hold the car back with my massive pregnant belly and somehow managed to get my foot onto the brake to stop the car 5 cm from their garage. I was so embarrassed I drove home bawling my eyes out. —Kelly

I ran the coffee maker with no pot underneath it and then walked away. I came back into the kitchen to a flood of coffee on the counter and the floor. I spent the next 20 minutes cleaning everything up. When I went to make the next pot of coffee (so I could finally have a cup) I did exactly the same thing again. —Alicia

I used hair mousse instead of deodorant. Literally skooshed it directly onto my armpit. I also used black eyeliner on my eyebrows. I have red hair and fair skin so I looked like a pirate! —Sarah

My sister had been out running errands and returned home late in the afternoon. She brought some things inside and got distracted puttering around. A few hours pass, it's dark out now, and she notices car lights in the driveway. "Who's here?" she wonders. No one comes to the door. After a few minutes, she goes outside and discovers it's her car. Still running. Doors still open. The rest of her groceries still waiting to come in.
—Christine

I forgot to collect my friend's son from school. I picked up my own daughter, who was in the class next door, and was half way around the supermarket before I remembered! This was actually the second time; the first time I was home for more than an hour before it clicked. I called my friend, left a message saying I had forgotten and felt terrible, then called back to say I realised I had the wrong day, then realised I actually had the right day after all (luckily she had called someone else to collect him when the school rang her). —Carla

I drove to my son's orthodontist appointment, and when I arrived I discovered that he wasn't in the car. I had loaded two kids in and told him to get in himself because we were running late. It turns out that he had walked over to the neighbour's property to say hi and I had accidentally driven away without him.
—Erin

When I was pregnant I tried to make a pavlova and forgot to separate the egg whites. And literally just then, hubby asked me to grab his glasses to watch tellie and I just came back with his sunnies. —Kate

While pregnant I arrived at work one day and pulled my lunch out of my bag only to discover I had packed my pyjama bottoms instead. I thankfully found my lunch on the bench when I got home and not in the washing machine. —Kim

It was raining one day when I was pregnant, and I decided I couldn't face public transport so I drove into town. That night I left work, got the train to where I usually park and was wandering the car park hysterical because my car had been stolen. I rang the police, and it wasn't until I was searching my bag to get a pen out to write down some details that I found my parking token for where my car was actually parked in the city. I sheepishly caught a train back into the city to collect my car. —Lucy

I let myself into a friend's house to pick her up for lunch. I made it all the way to her lounge room before I figured out it wasn't her house. The owner and her children were just as surprised as I was.
—Rhiannon

I put rice and water in the rice cooker and then put the rice cooker on the stove top and tuned on the burner. I melted the feet right off and filled our house with noxious burning rubber odours.
—Tracey

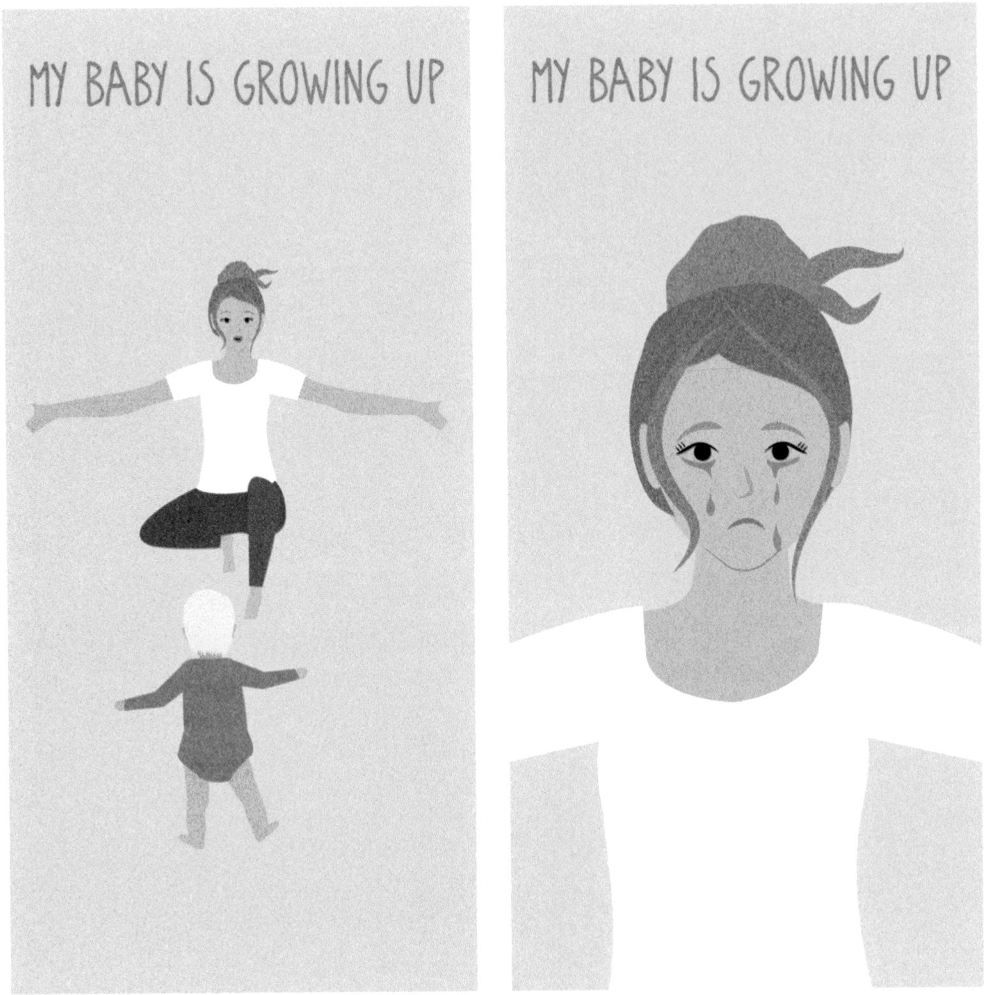
MY BABY IS GROWING UP
MY BABY IS GROWING UP

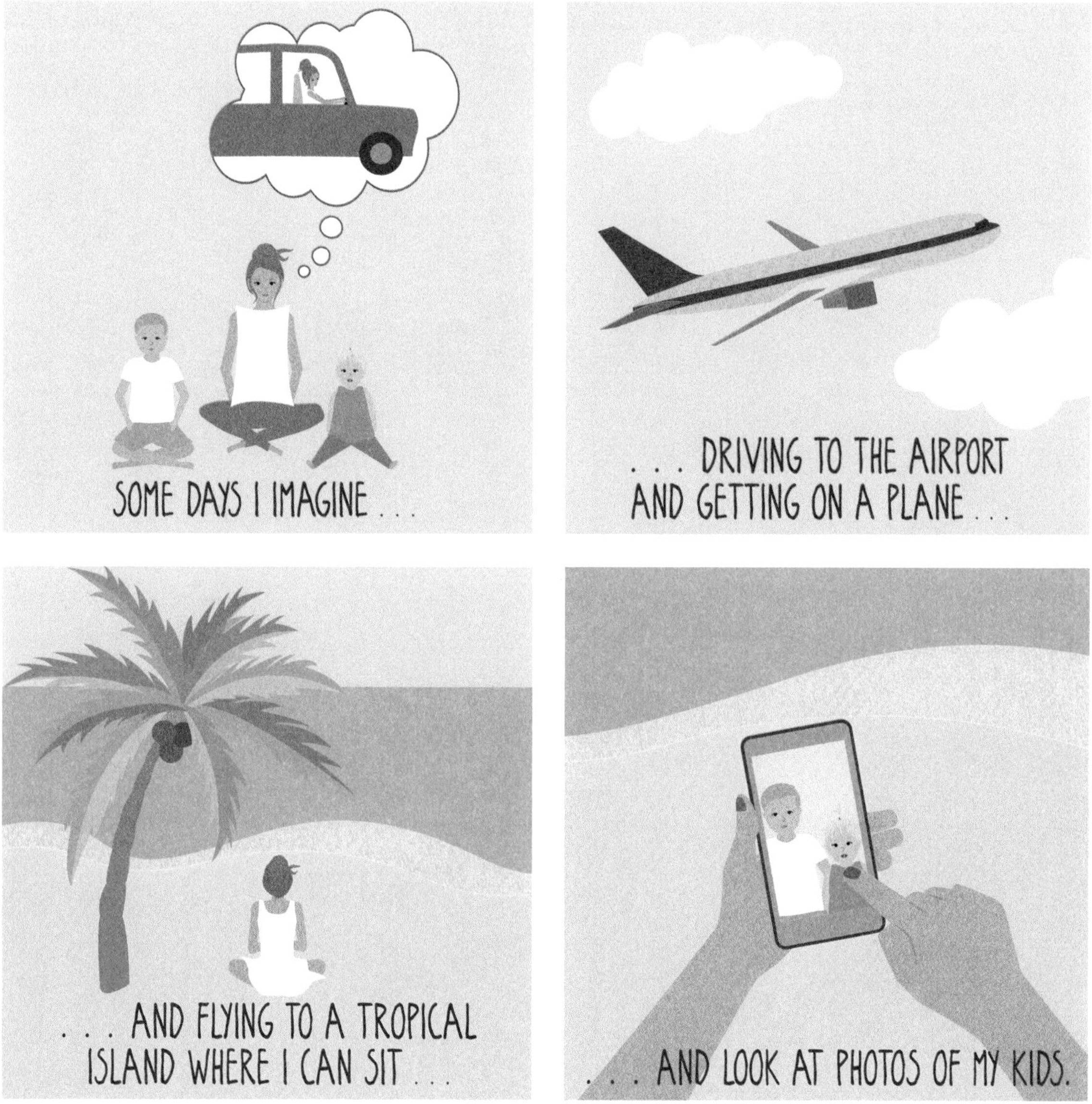
SOME DAYS I IMAGINE . . .
. . . DRIVING TO THE AIRPORT AND GETTING ON A PLANE . . .
. . . AND FLYING TO A TROPICAL ISLAND WHERE I CAN SIT . . .
. . . AND LOOK AT PHOTOS OF MY KIDS.

WHAT I DID

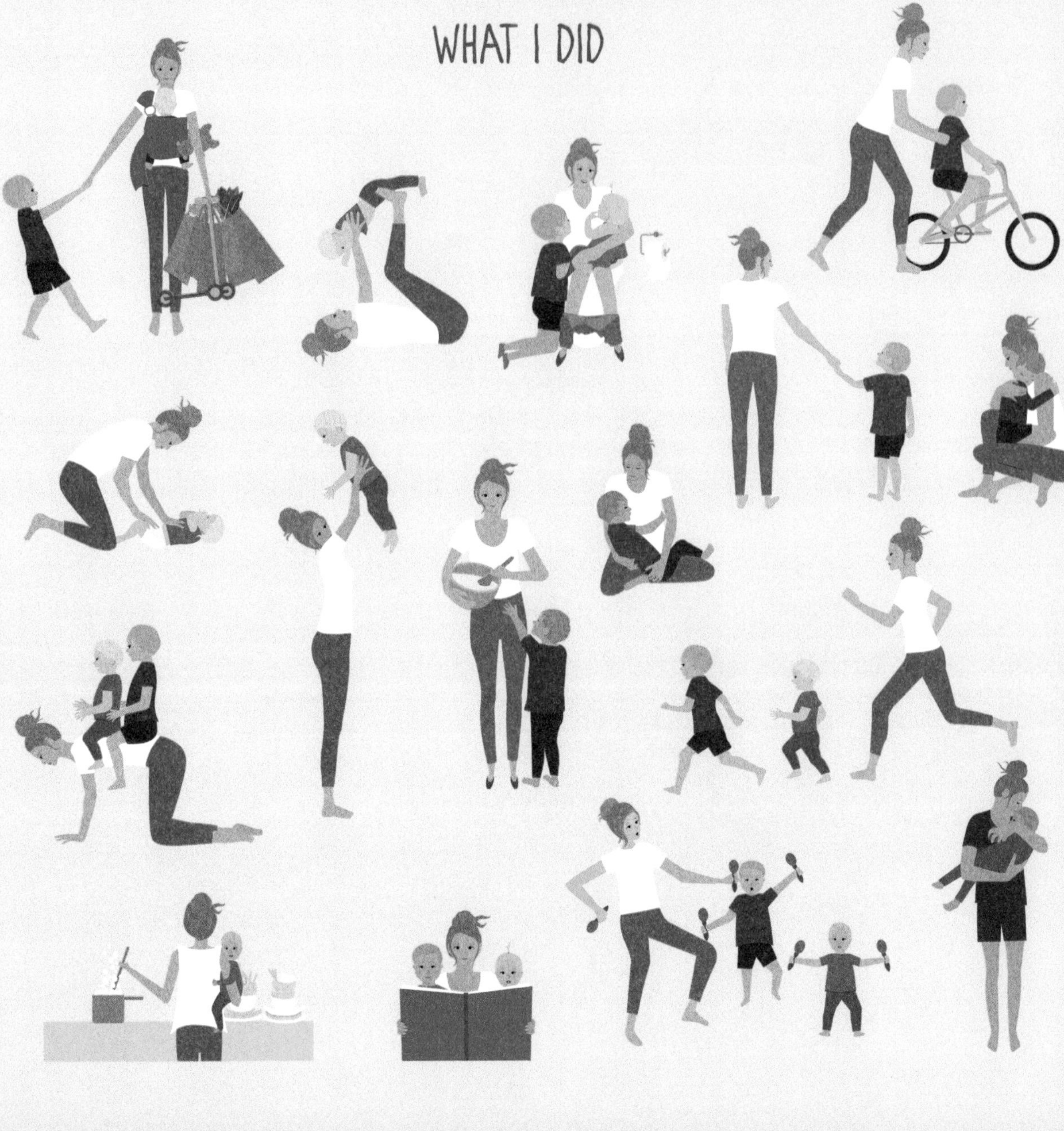

WHAT YOU SAW

WHAT THEY SAY	WHAT I HEAR	WHAT THEY MEAN
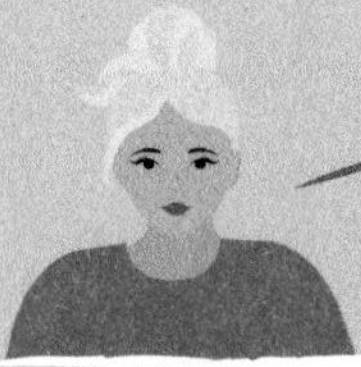 WE ARE DOING GYM, SWIMMING AND MUSIC CLASSES	YOU ARE HOLDING YOUR KIDS BACK BY NOT PUTTING THEM IN ALL THESE CLASSES	WE ARE DOING GYM, SWIMMING AND MUSIC CLASSES
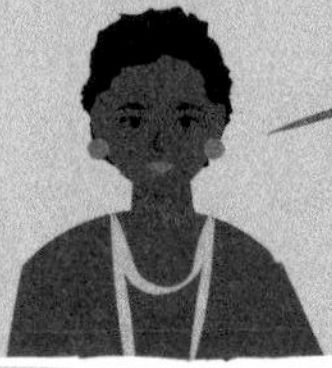 WE HAD BARRAMUNDI TACOS FOR DINNER LAST NIGHT	YOUR CHILDREN'S DIET ISN'T VARIED OR NUTRITIOUS ENOUGH	WE HAD BARRAMUNDI TACOS FOR DINNER LAST NIGHT
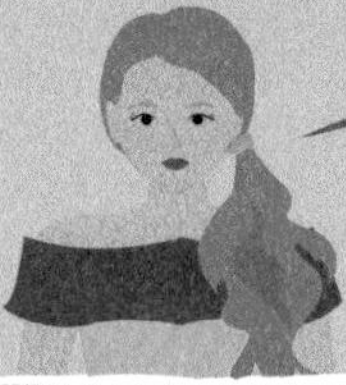 SHE'S WRITING HER NAME PERFECTLY AND LEARNING TO READ	YOUR CHILD SHOULD BE DOING THOSE THINGS TOO. THEY ARE BEHIND.	SHE'S WRITING HER NAME PERFECTLY AND LEARNING TO READ
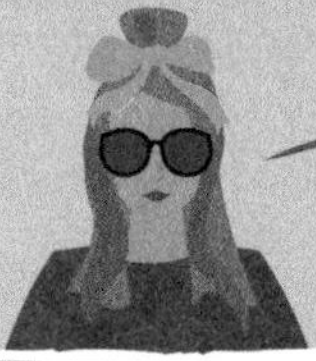 MY KIDS DON'T WATCH ANY TV	YOU LET YOUR KIDS WATCH WAY TOO MUCH TV	MY KIDS DON'T WATCH ANY TV
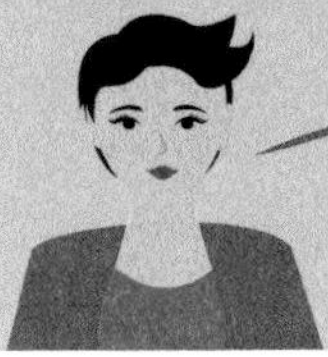 I'VE BEEN MUCH STRICTER LATELY AND HIS BEHAVIOUR HAS IMPROVED	YOU ARE NOT STRICT ENOUGH AND YOUR CHILD'S BEHAVIOUR IS APPALLING	I'VE BEEN MUCH STRICTER LATELY AND HIS BEHAVIOUR HAS IMPROVED

SOUND LEVELS

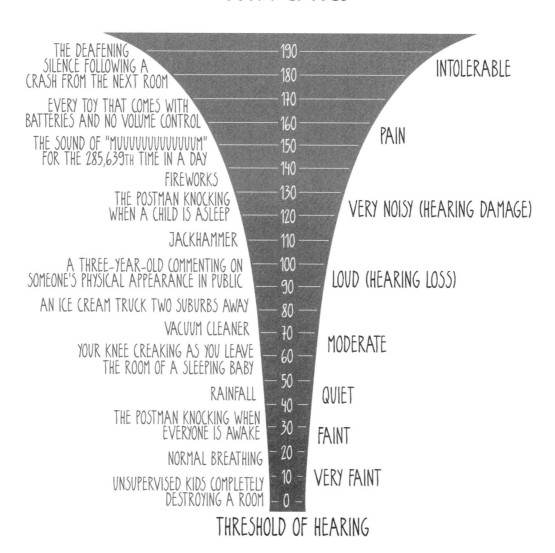

THE DEAFENING SILENCE FOLLOWING A CRASH FROM THE NEXT ROOM — 190

180 — INTOLERABLE

170

EVERY TOY THAT COMES WITH BATTERIES AND NO VOLUME CONTROL — 160

150 — PAIN

THE SOUND OF "MUUUUUUUUUUUUUM" FOR THE 285,639TH TIME IN A DAY — 140

FIREWORKS — 130

THE POSTMAN KNOCKING WHEN A CHILD IS ASLEEP — 120 — VERY NOISY (HEARING DAMAGE)

JACKHAMMER — 110

A THREE-YEAR-OLD COMMENTING ON SOMEONE'S PHYSICAL APPEARANCE IN PUBLIC — 100

90 — LOUD (HEARING LOSS)

AN ICE CREAM TRUCK TWO SUBURBS AWAY — 80

VACUUM CLEANER — 70

YOUR KNEE CREAKING AS YOU LEAVE THE ROOM OF A SLEEPING BABY — 60 — MODERATE

50

RAINFALL — 40 — QUIET

THE POSTMAN KNOCKING WHEN EVERYONE IS AWAKE — 30 — FAINT

NORMAL BREATHING — 20

10 — VERY FAINT

UNSUPERVISED KIDS COMPLETELY DESTROYING A ROOM — 0

THRESHOLD OF HEARING

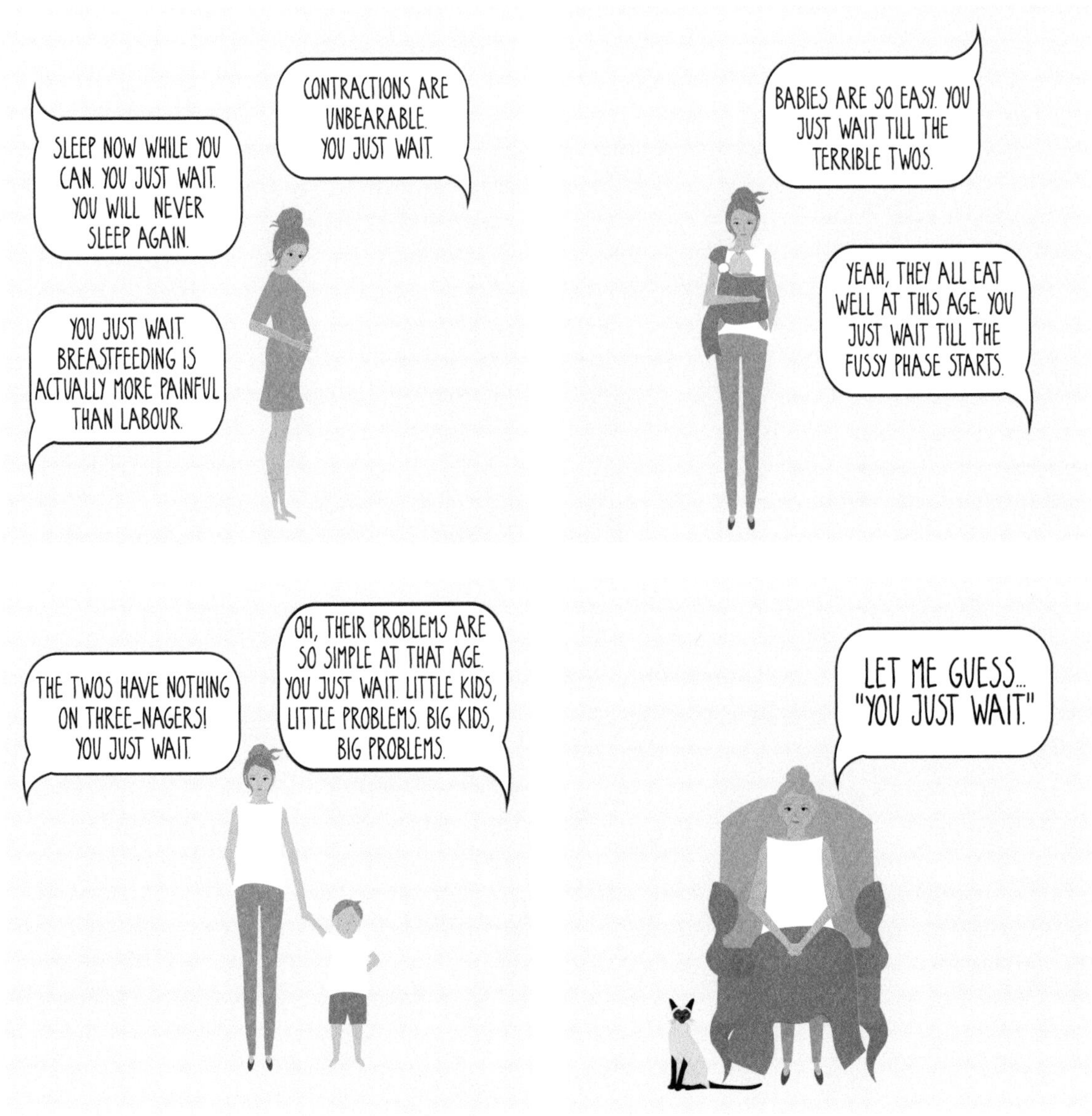
SLEEP NOW WHILE YOU CAN. YOU JUST WAIT. YOU WILL NEVER SLEEP AGAIN.
CONTRACTIONS ARE UNBEARABLE. YOU JUST WAIT.
YOU JUST WAIT. BREASTFEEDING IS ACTUALLY MORE PAINFUL THAN LABOUR.
BABIES ARE SO EASY. YOU JUST WAIT TILL THE TERRIBLE TWOS.
YEAH, THEY ALL EAT WELL AT THIS AGE. YOU JUST WAIT TILL THE FUSSY PHASE STARTS.
THE TWOS HAVE NOTHING ON THREE-NAGERS! YOU JUST WAIT.
OH, THEIR PROBLEMS ARE SO SIMPLE AT THAT AGE. YOU JUST WAIT. LITTLE KIDS, LITTLE PROBLEMS. BIG KIDS, BIG PROBLEMS.
LET ME GUESS... "YOU JUST WAIT."

YOU JUST WAIT

It starts when you're pregnant. "Get as much sleep as you can now."

We all know sleep doesn't work like that. It's not a tank you can fill up to draw on at a later, sleep-deprived stage.

But it doesn't stop there. "This is the easy part. All they do is sleep."

And my newborn son did sleep quite a lot. He slept for hours when he was upright, strapped to my chest, and I was walking at no less than 5 km per hour. One day I walked 21 km. A hard day was made harder by the thought that other people found this stage easy. It certainly didn't feel easy.

When we talk about the good parts of parenting, we tend to vaguely gloss over them. And yet when it comes to the challenges, we talk in certainties and specifics.

They warn us about sleep deprivation and cracked nipples and toddler tantrums. But they don't warn you that the first time your baby giggles you feel like your heart may actually explode.

The don't tell you that one-year-olds are a bundle of sloppy kisses and adorable mispronunciations. Two-year-olds are fascinated by the world around them. A three-year-old's love knows no bounds, and they aren't afraid to declare it. And a four-year-old's imagination can be wild, adventurous and intensely funny.

They warn you that sick kids don't sleep. But they don't tell you that in the middle of the night, not sleeping and wrapping your arms around a tired and sick little body makes you feel like the most important person in the world.

We know there will be challenges, but discovering them on our own and finding our own way to navigate them is all part of the journey. And if we're too busy fearing the next part of our journey, we just might forget to appreciate the magical chapter we're in.

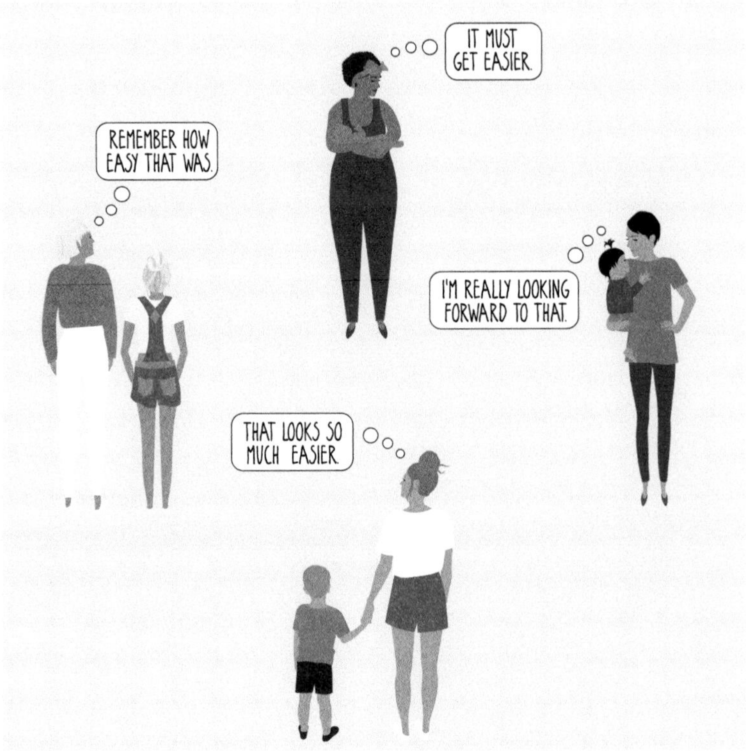
IT MUST
GET EASIER.
REMEMBER HOW
EASY THAT WAS.
I'M REALLY LOOKING
FORWARD TO THAT.
THAT LOOKS SO
MUCH EASIER.

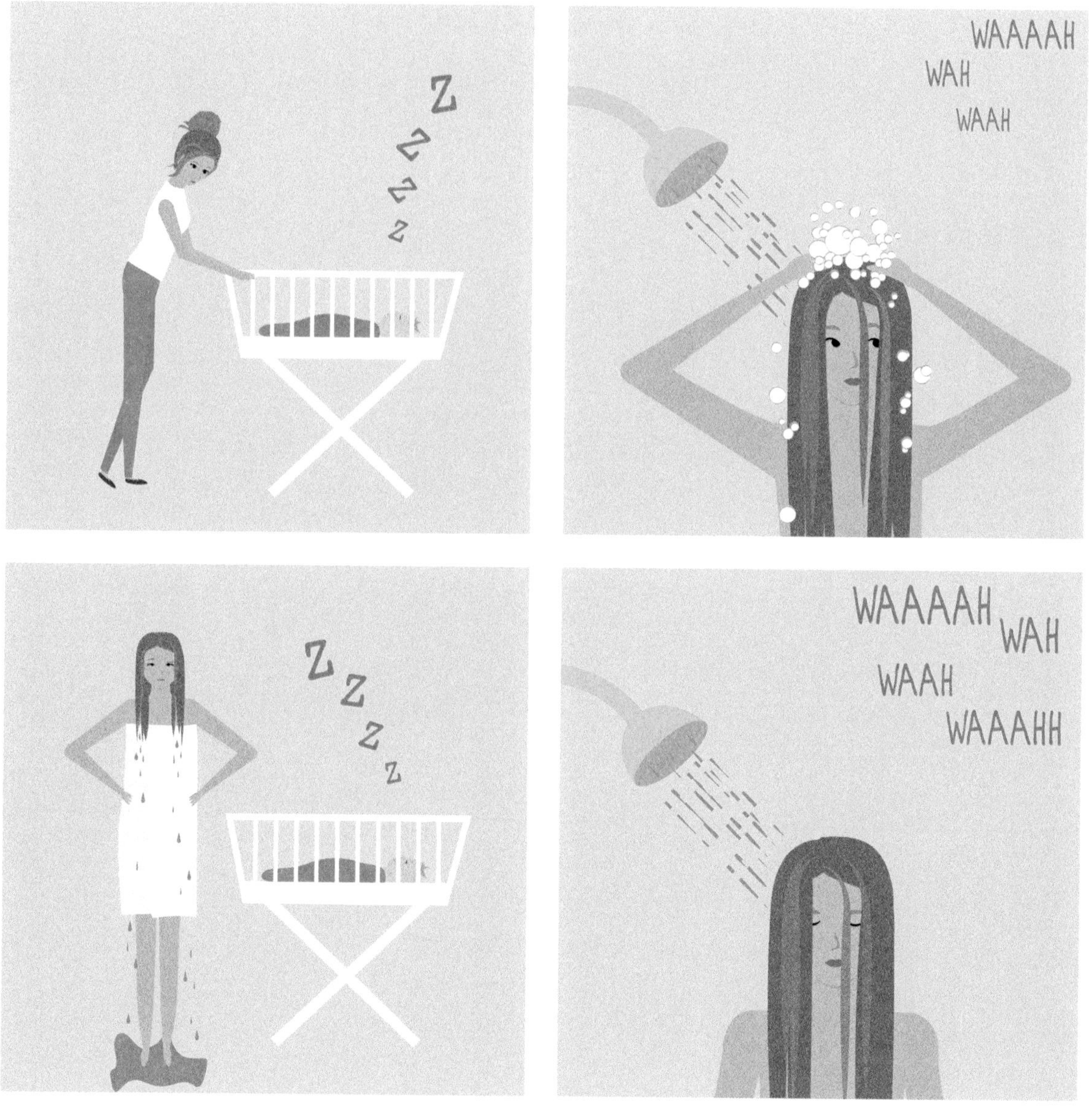
Z
Z
Z
Z
WAAAAH
WAH
WAAH
Z
Z
Z
Z
WAAAAH
WAH
WAAH
WAAAHH

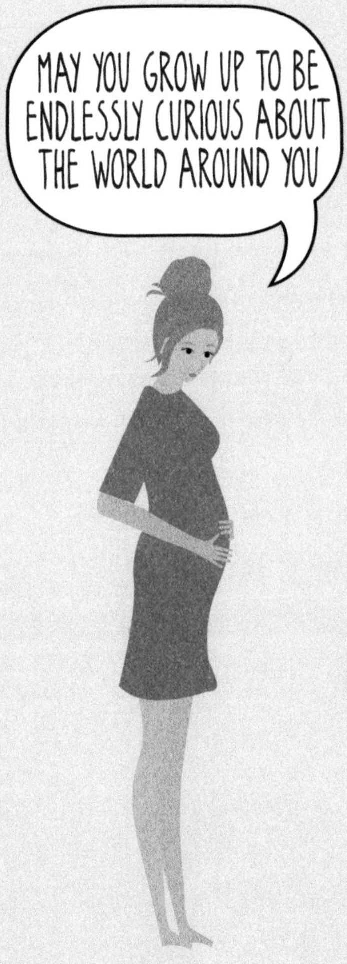
MAY YOU GROW UP TO BE ENDLESSLY CURIOUS ABOUT THE WORLD AROUND YOU

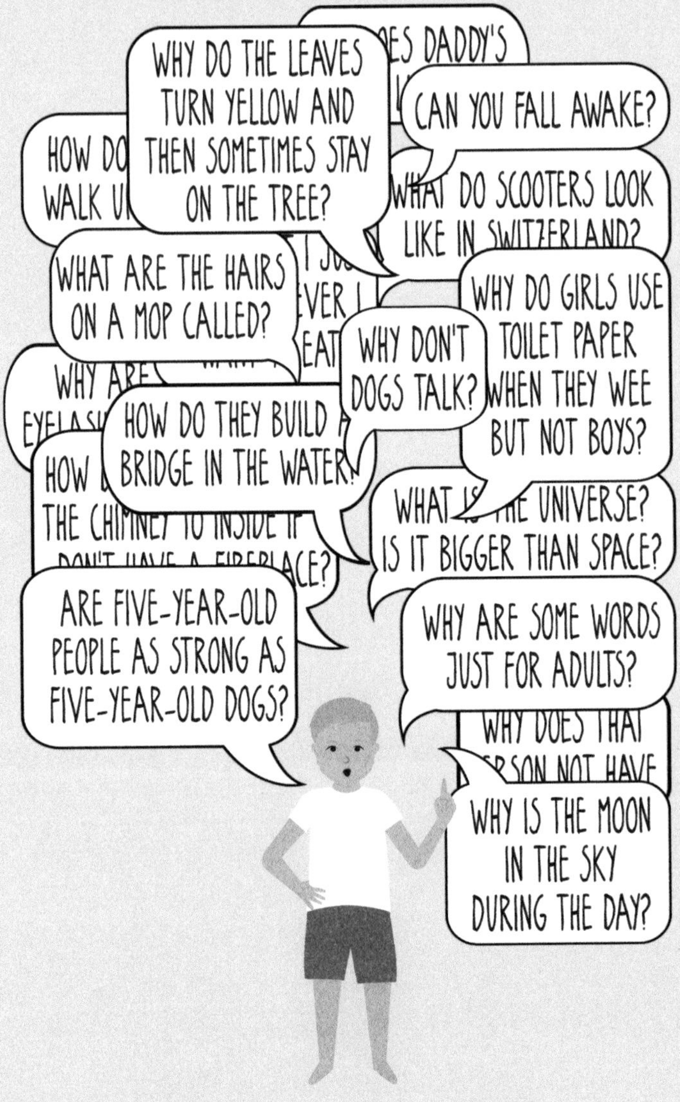
WHY DO THE LEAVES TURN YELLOW AND THEN SOMETIMES STAY ON THE TREE?
CAN YOU FALL AWAKE?
WHAT DO SCOOTERS LOOK LIKE IN SWITZERLAND?
WHAT ARE THE HAIRS ON A MOP CALLED?
WHY DO GIRLS USE TOILET PAPER WHEN THEY WEE BUT NOT BOYS?
WHY DON'T DOGS TALK?
HOW DO THEY BUILD A BRIDGE IN THE WATER?
WHAT IS THE UNIVERSE? IS IT BIGGER THAN SPACE?
ARE FIVE-YEAR-OLD PEOPLE AS STRONG AS FIVE-YEAR-OLD DOGS?
WHY ARE SOME WORDS JUST FOR ADULTS?
WHY IS THE MOON IN THE SKY DURING THE DAY?

READ ME THIS BOOK?

LET'S KEEP LOOKING

HOW MY FIRST BABY FELT
WHEN I BROUGHT THEM HOME
FROM THE HOSPITAL

HOW MY SECOND BABY FELT
WHEN I BROUGHT THEM HOME
FROM THE HOSPITAL

HOW MY TODDLER FELT WHEN
I BROUGHT MY SECOND BABY
HOME FROM THE HOSPITAL

HOW MY CHILDREN FEEL WHEN
THEY ARE SICK

HOW THEY FEEL WHEN THEY
ARE ANGRY

HOW THEY LOOK WHEN I SAY
GOODBYE IN THE MORNING

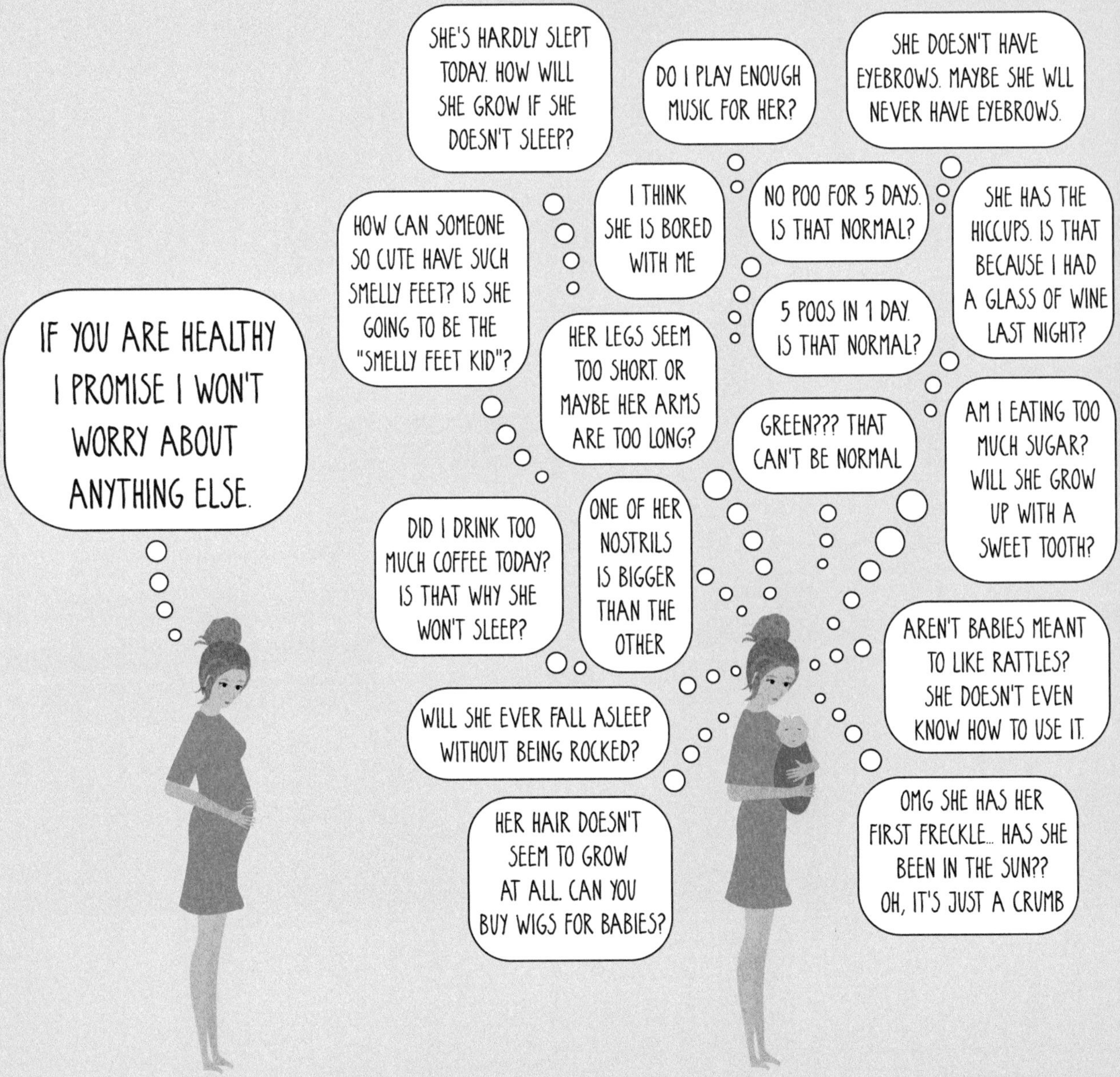
IF YOU ARE HEALTHY I PROMISE I WON'T WORRY ABOUT ANYTHING ELSE.
SHE'S HARDLY SLEPT TODAY. HOW WILL SHE GROW IF SHE DOESN'T SLEEP?
DO I PLAY ENOUGH MUSIC FOR HER?
SHE DOESN'T HAVE EYEBROWS. MAYBE SHE WLL NEVER HAVE EYEBROWS.
HOW CAN SOMEONE SO CUTE HAVE SUCH SMELLY FEET? IS SHE GOING TO BE THE "SMELLY FEET KID"?
I THINK SHE IS BORED WITH ME
NO POO FOR 5 DAYS. IS THAT NORMAL?
SHE HAS THE HICCUPS. IS THAT BECAUSE I HAD A GLASS OF WINE LAST NIGHT?
5 POOS IN 1 DAY. IS THAT NORMAL?
HER LEGS SEEM TOO SHORT. OR MAYBE HER ARMS ARE TOO LONG?
GREEN??? THAT CAN'T BE NORMAL
AM I EATING TOO MUCH SUGAR? WILL SHE GROW UP WITH A SWEET TOOTH?
DID I DRINK TOO MUCH COFFEE TODAY? IS THAT WHY SHE WON'T SLEEP?
ONE OF HER NOSTRILS IS BIGGER THAN THE OTHER
AREN'T BABIES MEANT TO LIKE RATTLES? SHE DOESN'T EVEN KNOW HOW TO USE IT.
WILL SHE EVER FALL ASLEEP WITHOUT BEING ROCKED?
HER HAIR DOESN'T SEEM TO GROW AT ALL. CAN YOU BUY WIGS FOR BABIES?
OMG SHE HAS HER FIRST FRECKLE... HAS SHE BEEN IN THE SUN?? OH, IT'S JUST A CRUMB

The day before my second child was born, I made a promise to myself: if the birth went smoothly and my baby was healthy, this time around, I would not obsess about the small things.

In some ways, I was more worried the second time because I was concerned about the impact it was going to have on my firstborn. "How would he cope if I had to stay in hospital? He needs me so much."

It all went as smoothly as these things can go, and not long after she was born, we took our chubby, pink, squeaking newborn home to meet her older brother.

Despite doing all the things the books tell you to do to prepare your toddler for a newborn, our son was stubbornly in denial that he was going to lose his only-child status. He refused to acknowledge my enormous belly that had made carrying him so much harder (on me, that is; he very much appreciated the armrest). The moment he saw his tiny sister and I saw his confused and wide-eyed face fall, I realised that no matter what happened, I would never stop worrying about these two little people.

Do I worry less the second time around? Absolutely. But do I still worry? All the time. Just as my children are a permanent part of my heart, my worries are a permanent part of my mind now. I'm learning to accept that.

It was 3 a.m. I had slept for an hour at most. Both my babies had colds and were craving my closeness. They tossed and turned in the bed next to me, taking it in turns to wake up and need comfort before drifting back to sleep.

My husband was on the other side of Australia, but he might as well have been on the other side of the world.

I had never been closer to anyone, and yet I had never felt so lonely. Exhaustion momentarily switched to anger, then went back to despair. Slipping in and out of consciousness. The morning felt impossibly far away, and while I longed for the comforting light of sunrise to signify the end of another seemingly endless night, I knew that if I didn't get a few hours of uninterrupted sleep, tomorrow would be even harder. They were just as demanding during the day.

THE NIGHTS MIGHT FEEL LONELY

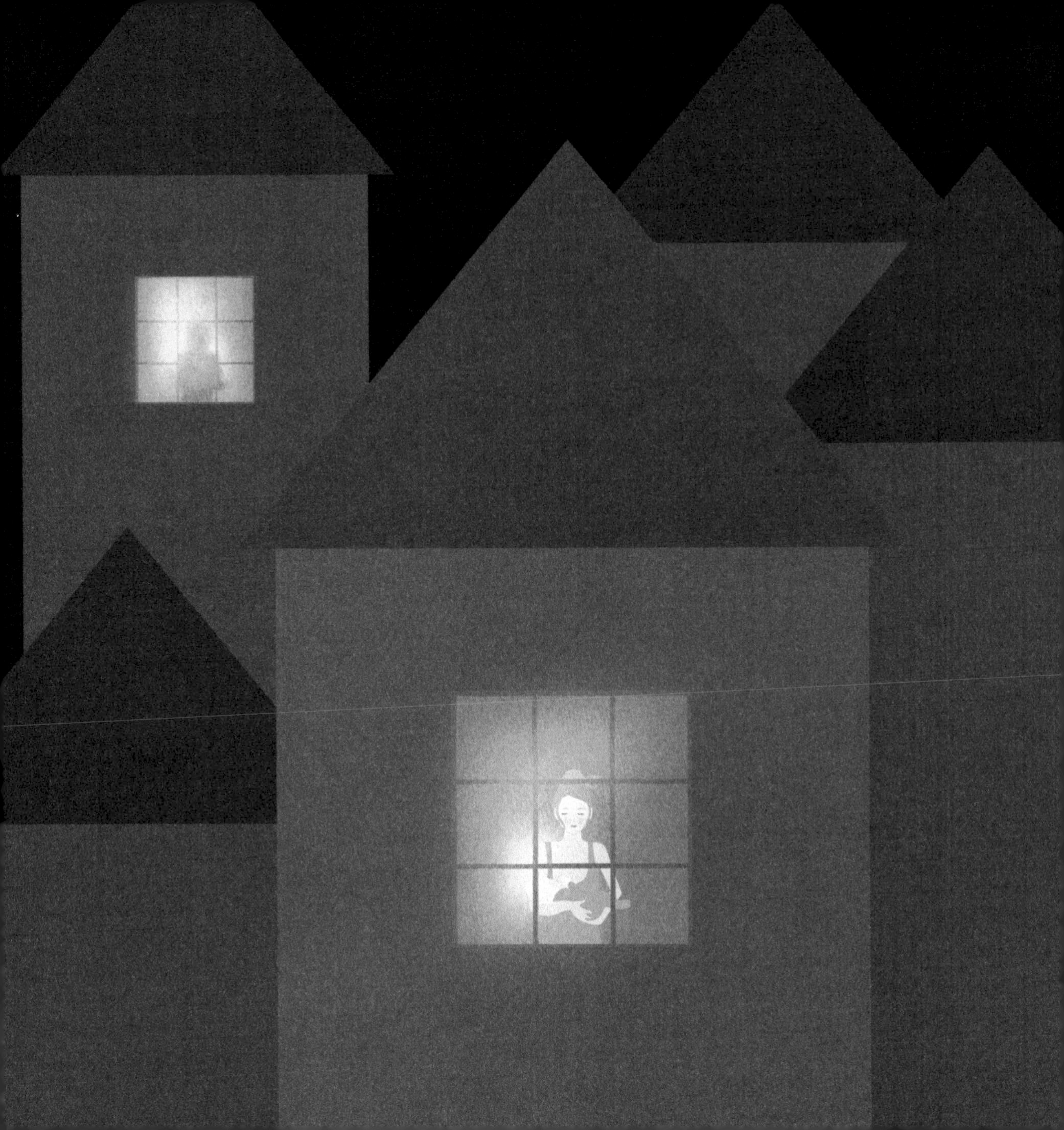

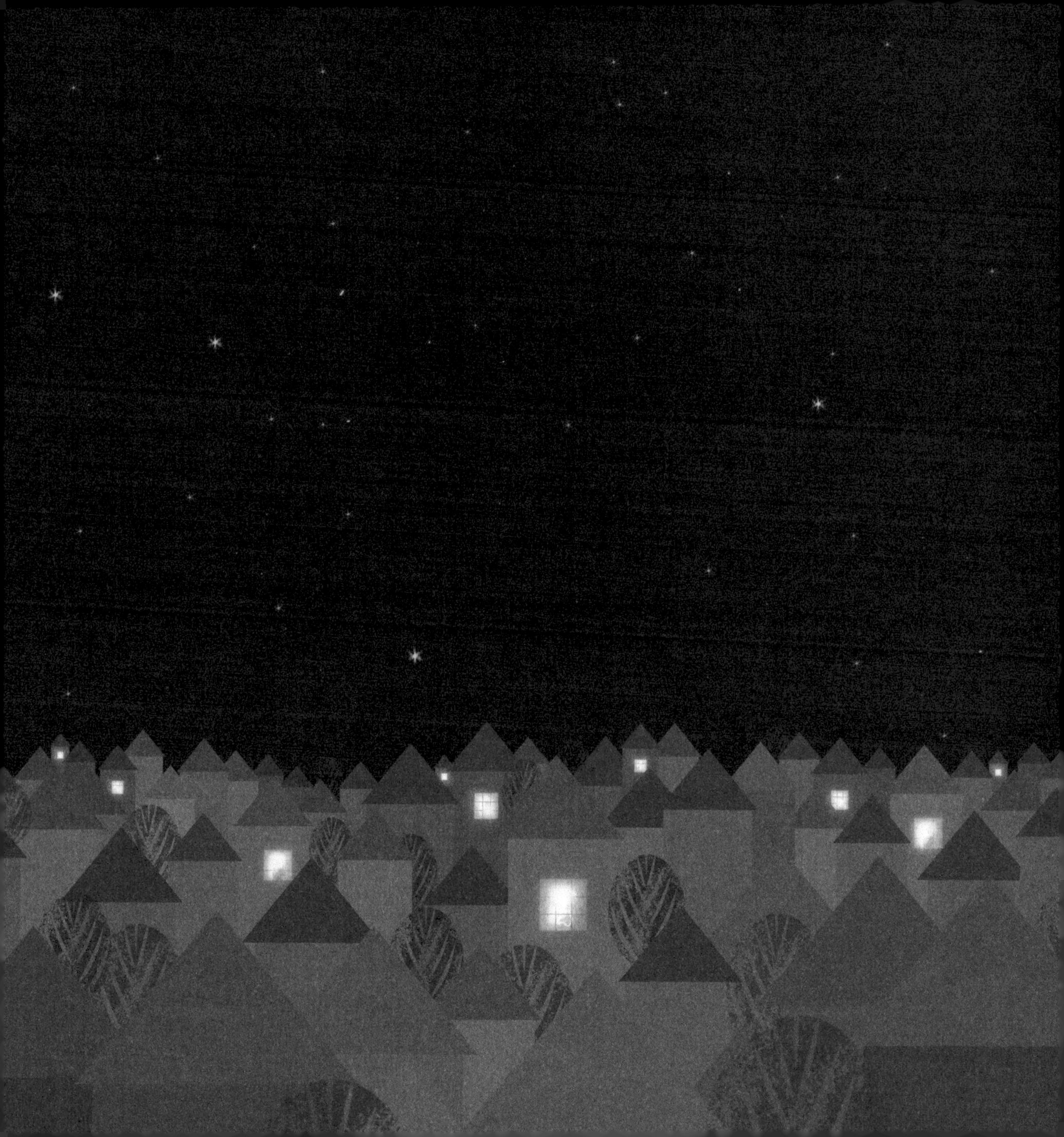

BUT YOU ARE NOT ALONE

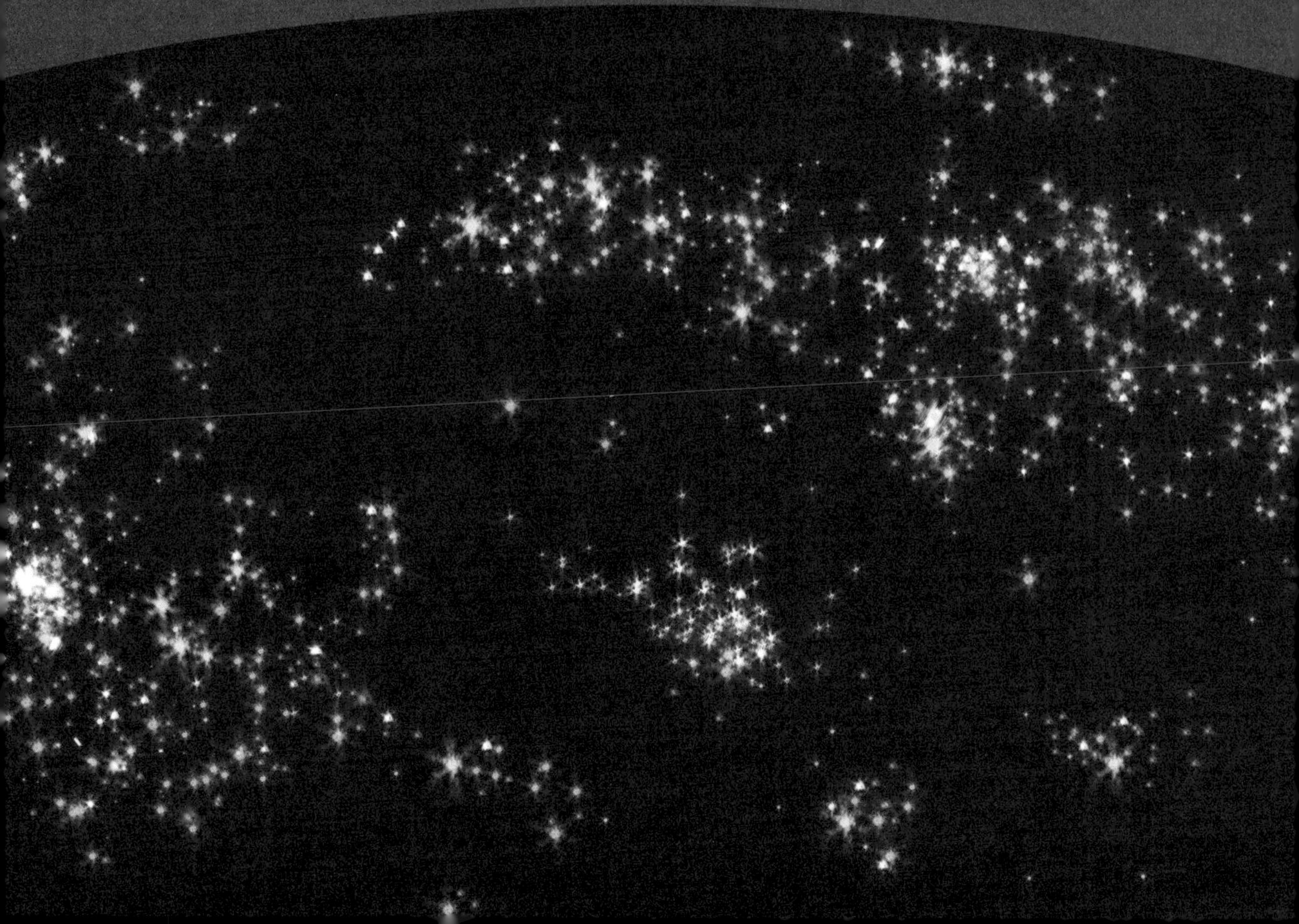

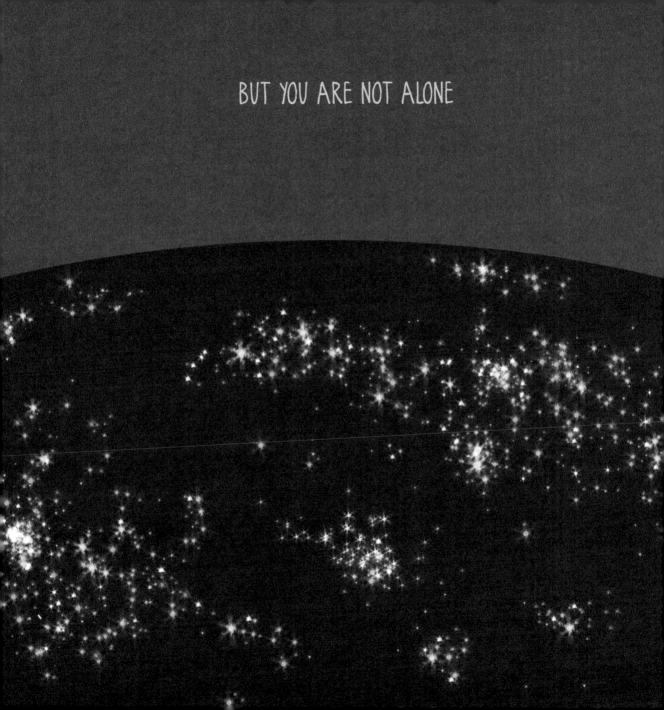

I held my restless child, warm and safe in my arms, and paced around the room. Looking out the window into the reassuring moonlight, I noticed a light flicker on upstairs in a house across the road. In that moment, I felt the weight of my loneliness lift. I wasn't the only one in the world awake right now.

The night sky was lit up by the radiating warmth of parents all over the world cradling children in their arms.

I no longer wished I could be somewhere else. My days with two small children at home were noisy and chaotic. The night was peaceful. Here in this moment, being the whole world to my child, was exactly where I needed to be.

Every time my little one calls for me in the night, I imagine him saying, "Thank you for picking me up, Mama, even when you can barely pick yourself up. You are my world, my everything, and I just want to be close to you always, like I used to be."

It's okay to not enjoy this stage. You don't have to enjoy everything parenthood entails. Not every single moment of every day. Let yourself feel your feelings, but don't let how you felt yesterday impact you now. You're learning. Be as kind to yourself as you are to your baby.

Please know that you are never truly alone, no matter how dark and quiet the world seems at 2:34 a.m. Your strength and selflessness may appear to go unnoticed but are seen and felt by thousands of mothers around the world. The exhaustion can be unbearable and the emotional roller coaster is nothing like you could ever imagine, but you are never alone. Don't ever be afraid to admit your struggles to another mum who you know and trust, because there is an incredible power in a shared experience. Empathy is the most beautiful gift for any new mother.

Hey there, Mama. You are up right now and a lot of other women are asleep. You are doing something your mind and body would like to you stop doing so you can get back to sleep. But your heart says, "Hey girl, get up and give life!" So in the quiet of the night when all you hear is the sound of your two hearts beating, you can know that the head is strong and the body wants what it wants, but really, it's the heart that always wins. And it's telling you that you're right where you need to be.

I hated every single night feed and am glad I no longer have to do them. I would have loved to have heard someone else say that too.

I feel your exhaustion, Mama, and I know the feeling of just wanting to be alone for a moment. To truly relax. But know that in this moment, you are strong. You are the epitome of love. And you, in your solitude, are everything to the little person you are holding. And that is all you need to be.

Don't listen to anyone. Listen to your instincts and do what is right for you and your baby. Every baby is different, and every mama is different. If that means co-sleeping just to get another hour of sleep when everyone says not to—do it! If that means going to comfort your baby every time he's crying because it breaks your heart to listen to him—do it. If that means letting your baby cry in a room you can't hear because you can't take another minute of it—do it. Motherhood is hard; so hard. You are not alone.

I don't know how positive or even profound this is, but a great friend told me that after every rough night she told herself, "I never have to do that night again. It's done." That helped me a lot more than "cherish every moment."

When you're up in the night with your baby, look out and see the other lights. Take strength from knowing you're not the only one, and remember and recognise that your light is sending strength to someone else up in the night.

When I was up for the fourth, fifth or sixth time that night and felt like I was losing my mind, the only thing that helped was imagining all those other women out there doing the same thing. I feel like part of a peaceful army. And that feeling of invisible comradeship helped me immeasurably.

It's okay (and completely normal) to both want the night to fly by and feel guilty for feeling that way. Not every moment is beautiful or perfect. You never see the hard times or the struggles in the photo album or the highlight reel, but they're what will get you from one wonderful memory to the next. You can do this, and you're doing a truly amazing job. You're never alone.

We are a club, a family, a powerful force that exists because of our ability to bring life into the world. These tiny humans who so desperately need us at all times can make us feel so very alone. But you are never alone, Mama. We are with you. We are fighting, loving and nurturing with you. It's beyond exhausting, I know. But you are one of us now, and never forget, we are awake with you.

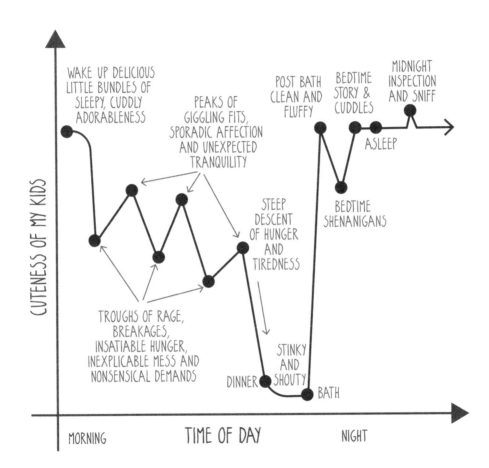

WAKE UP DELICIOUS LITTLE BUNDLES OF SLEEPY, CUDDLY ADORABLENESS

PEAKS OF GIGGLING FITS, SPORADIC AFFECTION AND UNEXPECTED TRANQUILITY

POST BATH CLEAN AND FLUFFY

BEDTIME STORY & CUDDLES

MIDNIGHT INSPECTION AND SNIFF

ASLEEP

STEEP DESCENT OF HUNGER AND TIREDNESS

BEDTIME SHENANIGANS

CUTENESS OF MY KIDS

TROUGHS OF RAGE, BREAKAGES, INSATIABLE HUNGER, INEXPLICABLE MESS AND NONSENSICAL DEMANDS

STINKY AND SHOUTY

DINNER

BATH

MORNING

TIME OF DAY

NIGHT

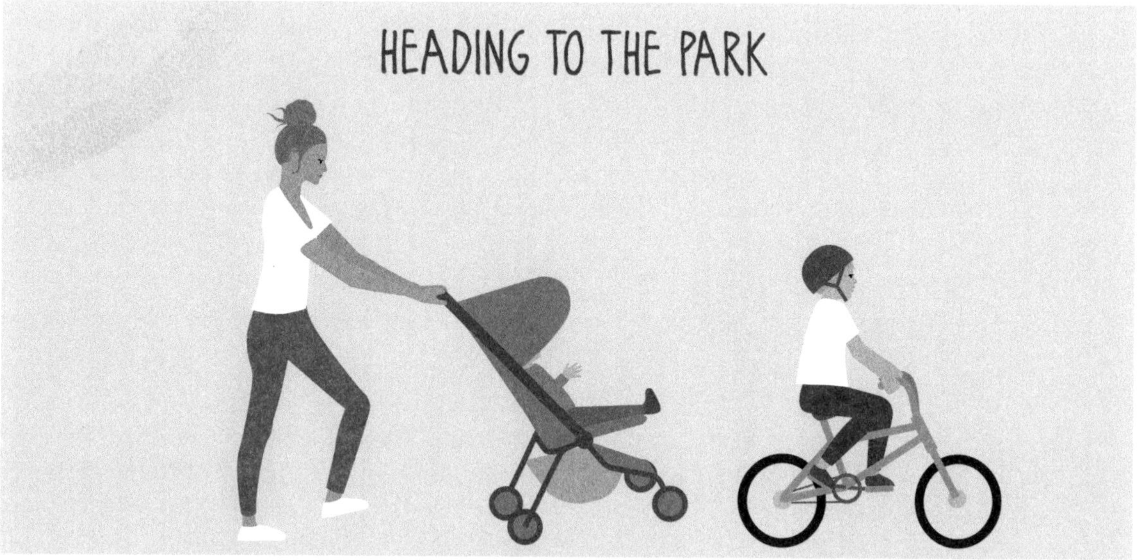
HEADING TO THE PARK

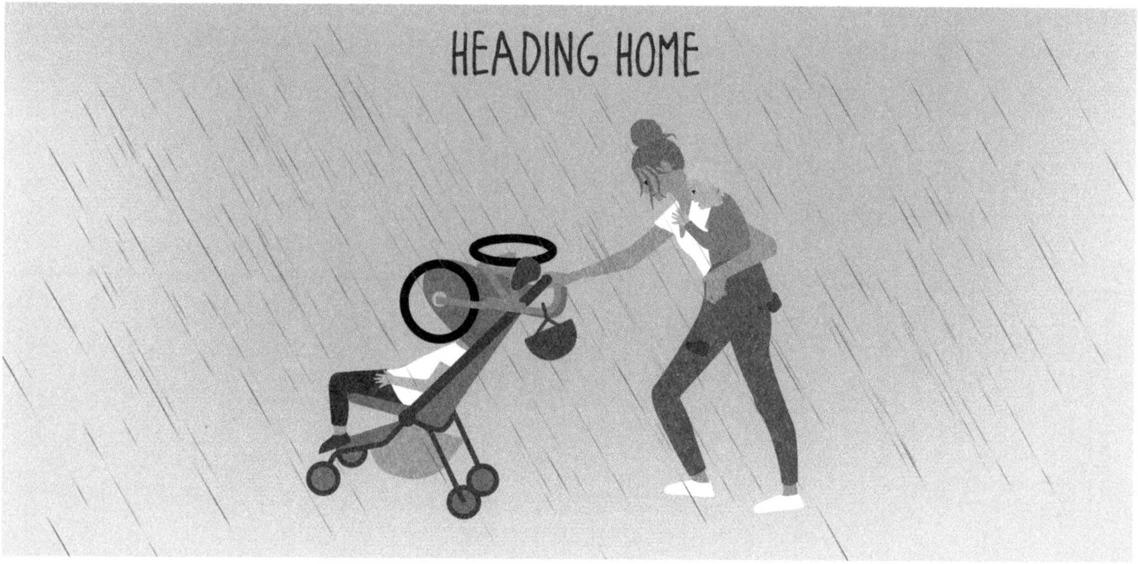
HEADING HOME

HOW THEY SEE US

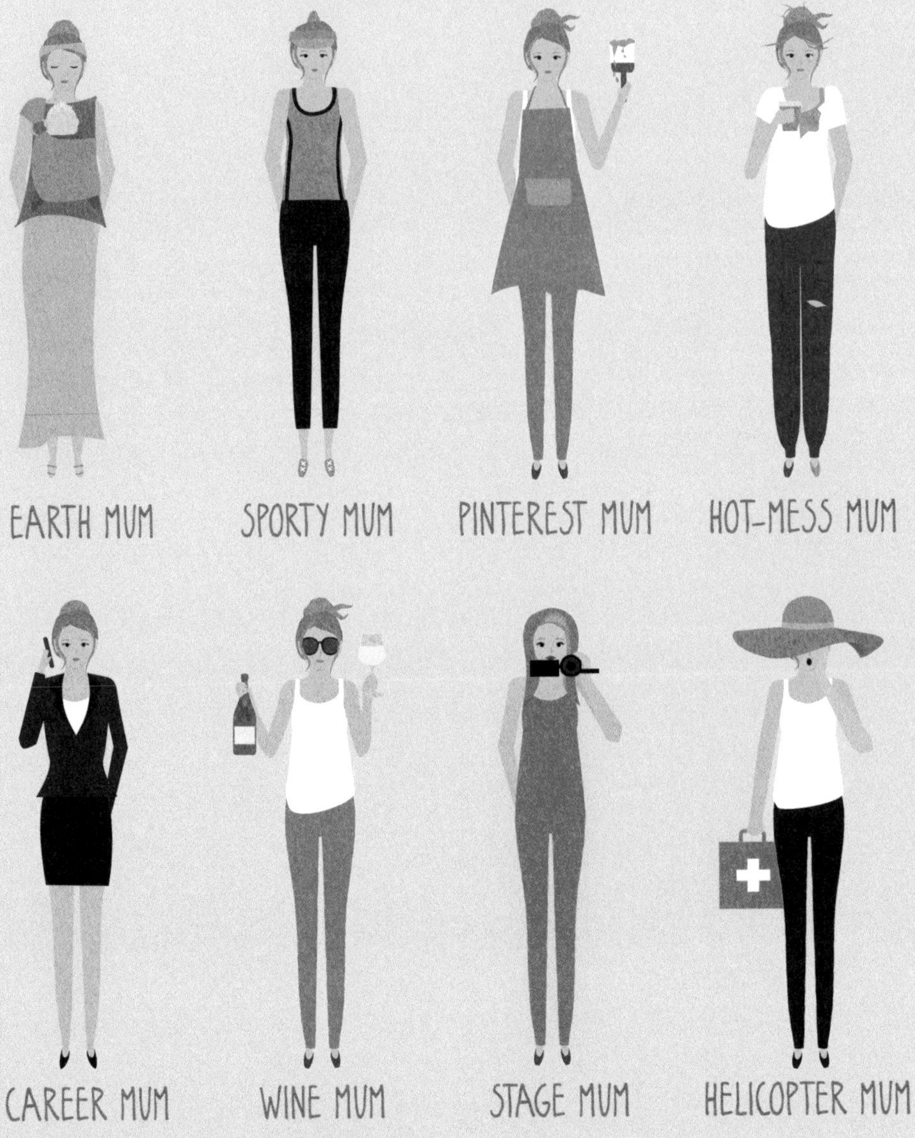
EARTH MUM
SPORTY MUM
PINTEREST MUM
HOT-MESS MUM
CAREER MUM
WINE MUM
STAGE MUM
HELICOPTER MUM

REALITY

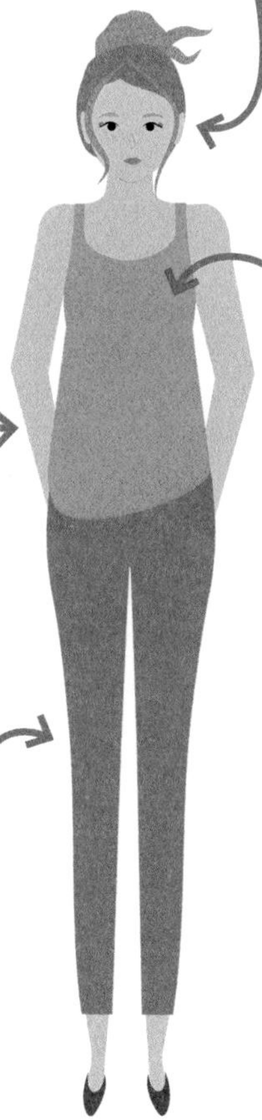

HOMEMADE SPROUTED MUNG BEAN FELAFEL FOR LUNCH. BURGERS & CHIPS FOR DINNER.

FAKE TAN & NAIL POLISH HIDE THE DIRT FROM DIGGING IN THE GARDEN.

TAKES COSTUME MAKING VERY, VERY SERIOUSLY.

ABSOLUTELY NEVER LATE (BUT THIS WEEK HAS BEEN ONE DAY EARLY FOR A MEETING, ONE WEEK EARLY FOR A CONFERENCE CALL AND SIX HOURS EARLY FOR AN APPOINTMENT)

EXCERCISES ONCE A WEEK (BUT IS IN ACTIVEWEAR ON AT LEAST TWO MORE OCCASIONS)

WILL BRIBE WITH CHOCOLATE. (USUALLY FAIR-TRADE, DAIRY-FREE, ORANGUTAN-FRIENDLY CHOCOLATE)

WOULD RATHER RUN OUT OF MILK THAN MASCARA.

CARRIED BABIES IN SLINGS BECAUSE IT WAS CONVENIENT. NEVER SAW IT AS "WEARING" THEM.

COFFEE. SO MUCH COFFEE.

BREASTFEEDS KIDS WHEN THEY ARE TODDLERS BECAUSE STOPPING WAS MORE EFFORT THAN CONTINUING.

WORKS 84 X 23 MINUTE SHIFTS A WEEK. WILL SOMETIMES SEAMLESSLY SLIDE FROM PLAYING TO WORKING WITHOUT EVEN NOTICING.

LOVES TO UNWIND IN THE EVENING WITH A GLASS (OR TWO) OF CHARDONNAY.

OVERWHELMINGLY EMOTIONAL AT SCHOOL PERFORMANCES. CONCLUDES CHILD IS IN THE TOP 10 PERCENT MOST SYNCHRONISED.

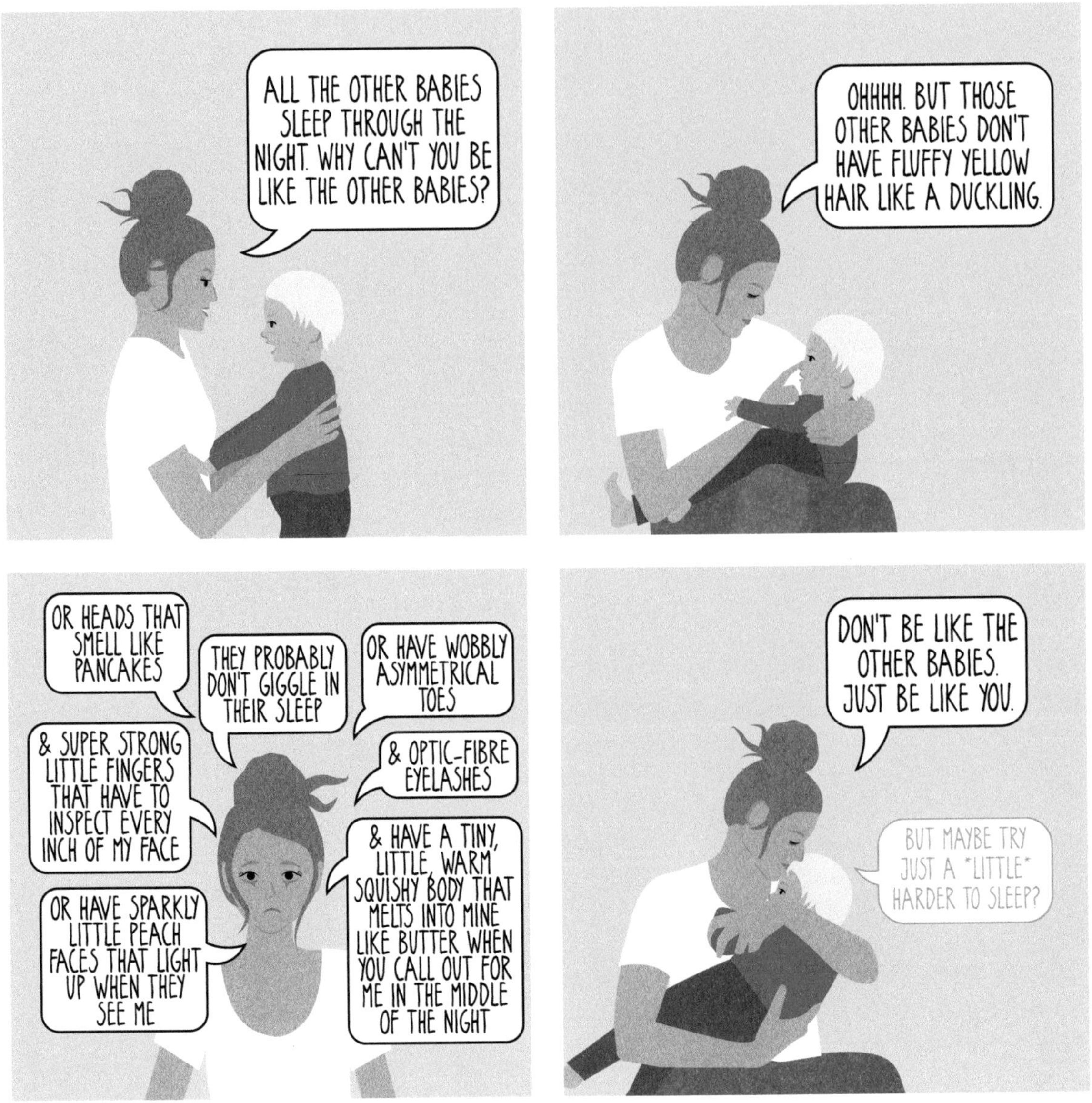
ALL THE OTHER BABIES SLEEP THROUGH THE NIGHT. WHY CAN'T YOU BE LIKE THE OTHER BABIES?
OHHHH. BUT THOSE OTHER BABIES DON'T HAVE FLUFFY YELLOW HAIR LIKE A DUCKLING.
OR HEADS THAT SMELL LIKE PANCAKES
THEY PROBABLY DON'T GIGGLE IN THEIR SLEEP
OR HAVE WOBBLY ASYMMETRICAL TOES
& SUPER STRONG LITTLE FINGERS THAT HAVE TO INSPECT EVERY INCH OF MY FACE
& OPTIC-FIBRE EYELASHES
& HAVE A TINY, LITTLE, WARM SQUISHY BODY THAT MELTS INTO MINE LIKE BUTTER WHEN YOU CALL OUT FOR ME IN THE MIDDLE OF THE NIGHT
OR HAVE SPARKLY LITTLE PEACH FACES THAT LIGHT UP WHEN THEY SEE ME
DON'T BE LIKE THE OTHER BABIES. JUST BE LIKE YOU.
BUT MAYBE TRY JUST A *LITTLE* HARDER TO SLEEP?

ALL THE OTHER BABIES

Not long after we are handed our baby, we are handed a little folder where we can record all the important things they are meant to do and a clever little graph that tracks exactly how big they are in comparison to all the other babies.

At every appointment, care providers obsessively pore over these charts. I had one baby who "shot up the chart" and one who "fell down it." Apparently both are no good.

We are told to watch for delays in meeting milestones because "early intervention is essential."

It really is no wonder we constantly find ourselves comparing our kids to other kids the same age. Comparison is a source of worry, inadequacy and even guilt. What is wrong with my baby? What am I doing wrong?

By day, my son was a placid bundle of sweeping blond hair and thigh rolls. Nighttime was a different story. No doubt, at our mothers' group meetups, while I was feeling slight resentment towards the babies who were sleeping through the night by eight weeks, their mums were wondering how easy it must be to have a baby who was just so chill.

As I reach the final pages in that little folder, I can see that in the scheme of things, none of it really mattered. Having a high-achieving baby probably isn't all it's cracked up to be.

The babies who started moving first were slightly terrifying. Agile babies cannot be contained by cots and will roam your house at night and hunt you down.

Early walkers become early runners, and early runners can run away from you.

When they learn to talk, they learn to ask questions, and when they learn to ask questions, they do not stop. Ever. Before you know it, you'll be googling "what are the hairs on a mop called" and trying to stay one step ahead of an endless stream of curiosities.

And as for sleep, well, recent studies show that babies who wake up a lot at night tend to be more intelligent—although I suspect this research was fabricated by a very sleep-deprived parent who just wanted to give other exhausted parents something to cling to.

One thing is for sure: your baby will always be the best at one thing—being your baby. And that's all we can really ask of them.

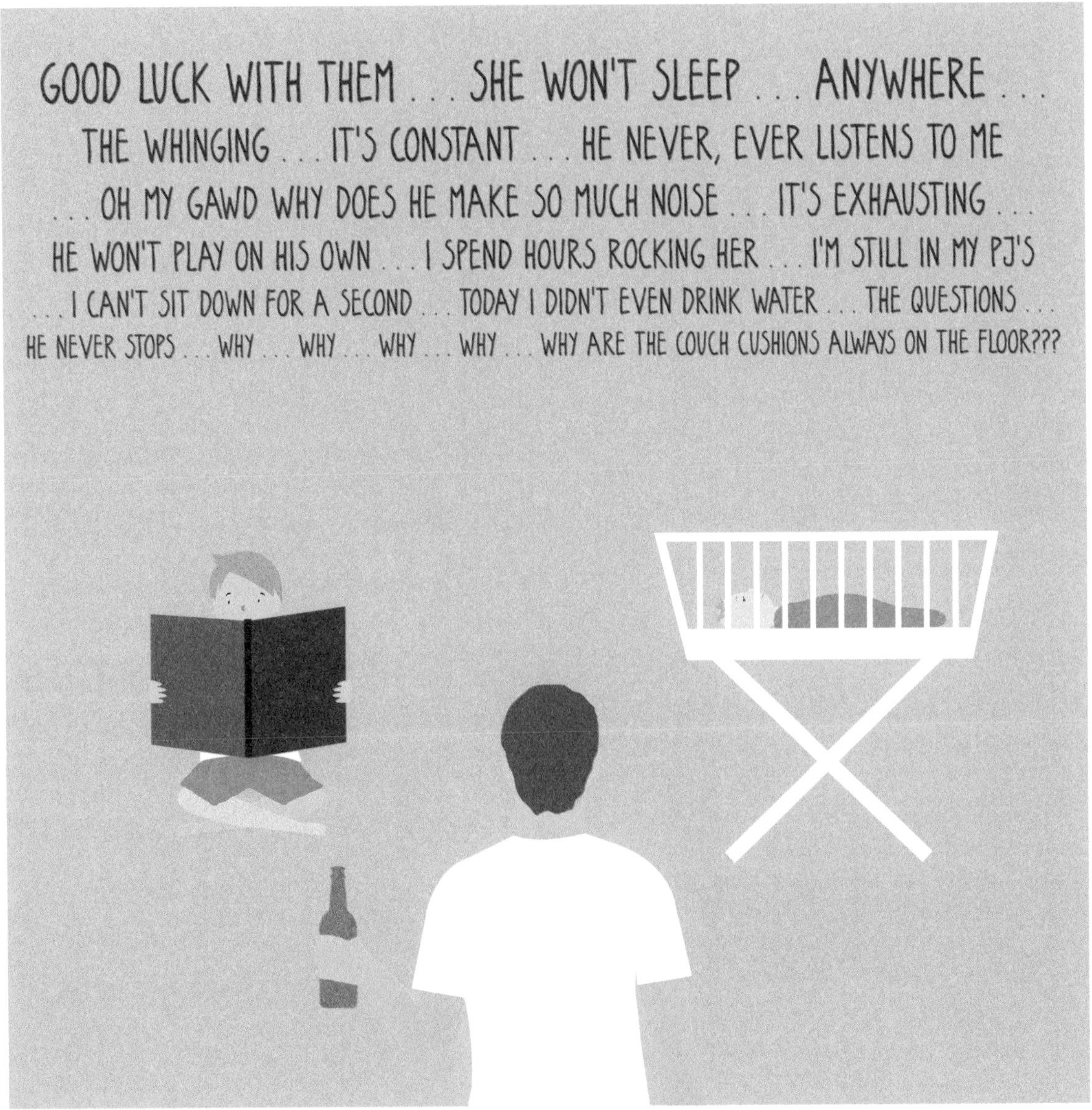
GOOD LUCK WITH THEM . . . SHE WON'T SLEEP . . . ANYWHERE . . .
THE WHINGING . . . IT'S CONSTANT . . . HE NEVER, EVER LISTENS TO ME
. . . OH MY GAWD WHY DOES HE MAKE SO MUCH NOISE . . . IT'S EXHAUSTING . . .
HE WON'T PLAY ON HIS OWN . . . I SPEND HOURS ROCKING HER . . . I'M STILL IN MY PJ'S
. . . I CAN'T SIT DOWN FOR A SECOND . . . TODAY I DIDN'T EVEN DRINK WATER . . . THE QUESTIONS . . .
HE NEVER STOPS . . . WHY . . . WHY . . . WHY . . . WHY . . . WHY ARE THE COUCH CUSHIONS ALWAYS ON THE FLOOR???

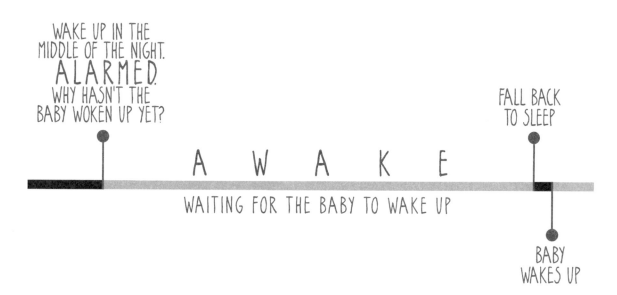

WAKE UP IN THE
MIDDLE OF THE NIGHT.
ALARMED.
WHY HASN'T THE
BABY WOKEN UP YET?

FALL BACK
TO SLEEP

A W A K E

WAITING FOR THE BABY TO WAKE UP

BABY
WAKES UP

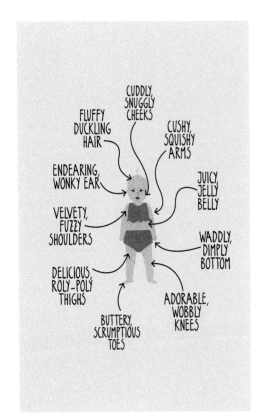

FLUFFY DUCKLING HAIR

CUDDLY, SNUGGLY CHEEKS

CUSHY, SQUISHY ARMS

ENDEARING, WONKY EAR

JUICY, JELLY BELLY

VELVETY, FUZZY SHOULDERS

WADDLY, DIMPLY BOTTOM

DELICIOUS, ROLY-POLY THIGHS

ADORABLE, WOBBLY KNEES

BUTTERY, SCRUMPTIOUS TOES

DEFLATED   TIRED   BLOATED   BROKEN

WEAK   MARKED   BUMPY

FAULTY   STRETCHED   IMPERFECT   BLEMISHED

FLAWED   FLABBY

My children don't see what I see. They see warmth and comfort. Arms so strong they can wrap them up and solve their problems. Eyes that adore them. Kisses that heal them. They see hands that hold them tight and can miraculously mend broken toys and bruised egos.

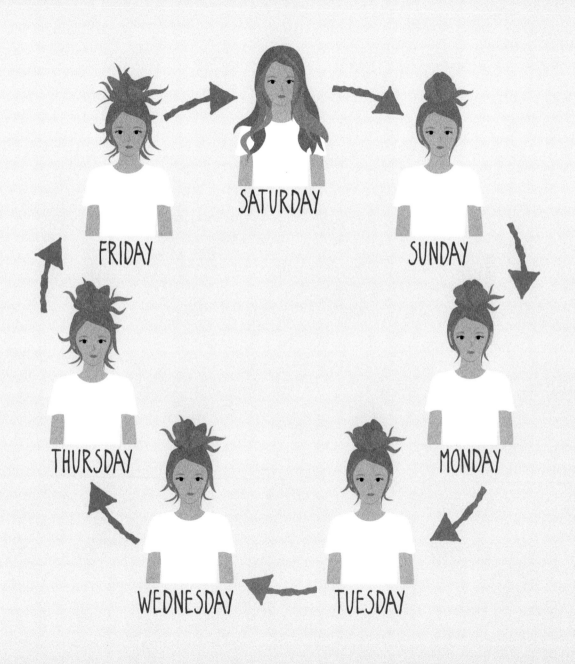

SATURDAY

SUNDAY

MONDAY

TUESDAY

WEDNESDAY

THURSDAY

FRIDAY

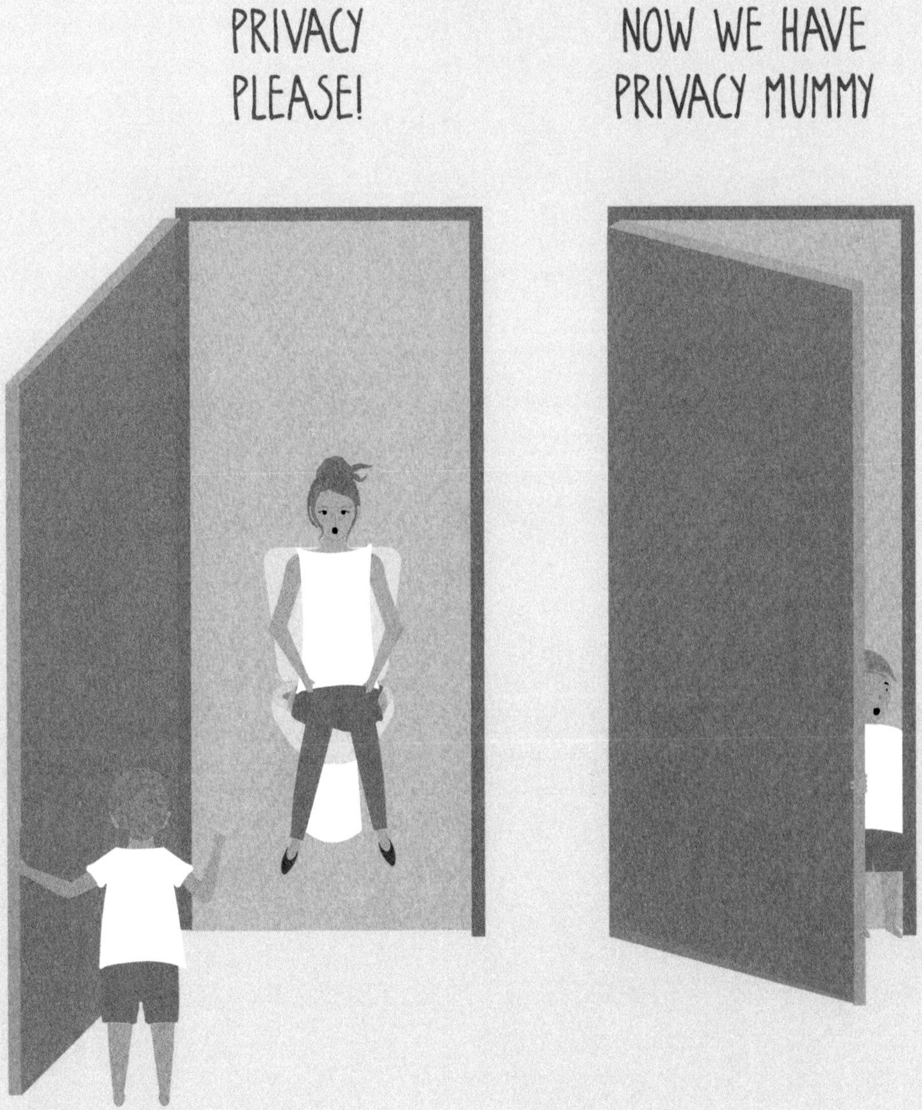
PRIVACY PLEASE!
NOW WE HAVE PRIVACY MUMMY

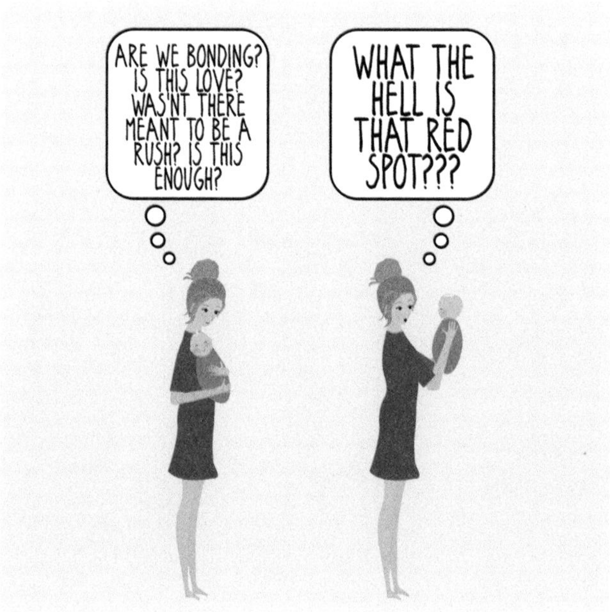
ARE WE BONDING? IS THIS LOVE? WAS'NT THERE MEANT TO BE A RUSH? IS THIS ENOUGH?
WHAT THE HELL IS THAT RED SPOT???

It can creep up on you, this maternal love thing. It was only minutes after my first was born and I distinctly remember thinking, "Well, I'm interested in you and you are rather cute, but I don't think we know each other well enough for it to be love."

There definitely was none of the magical rush you hear about. It probably took a few months till I could honestly say I loved him. I needed a smile. A giggle. Something other than the fact that his eyes followed me around the room when he was in the mood for food. The first time I felt genuinely concerned for him I knew that the love was something to be reckoned with. It might have been the time he rolled off the couch onto the wooden floor. Or the time he launched off my bed and into the wall. Or the time I dislocated his elbow. That's when I knew for sure that this was the real deal.

I just wish someone had warned me that just because your love is a slow burn rather than a hot spark, it doesn't mean it won't be the greatest love you ever know (which, incidentally, might also be some dating advice I pass on to my baby girl in twenty years).

TRAVELLING BEFORE KIDS

TRAVELLING WITH KIDS

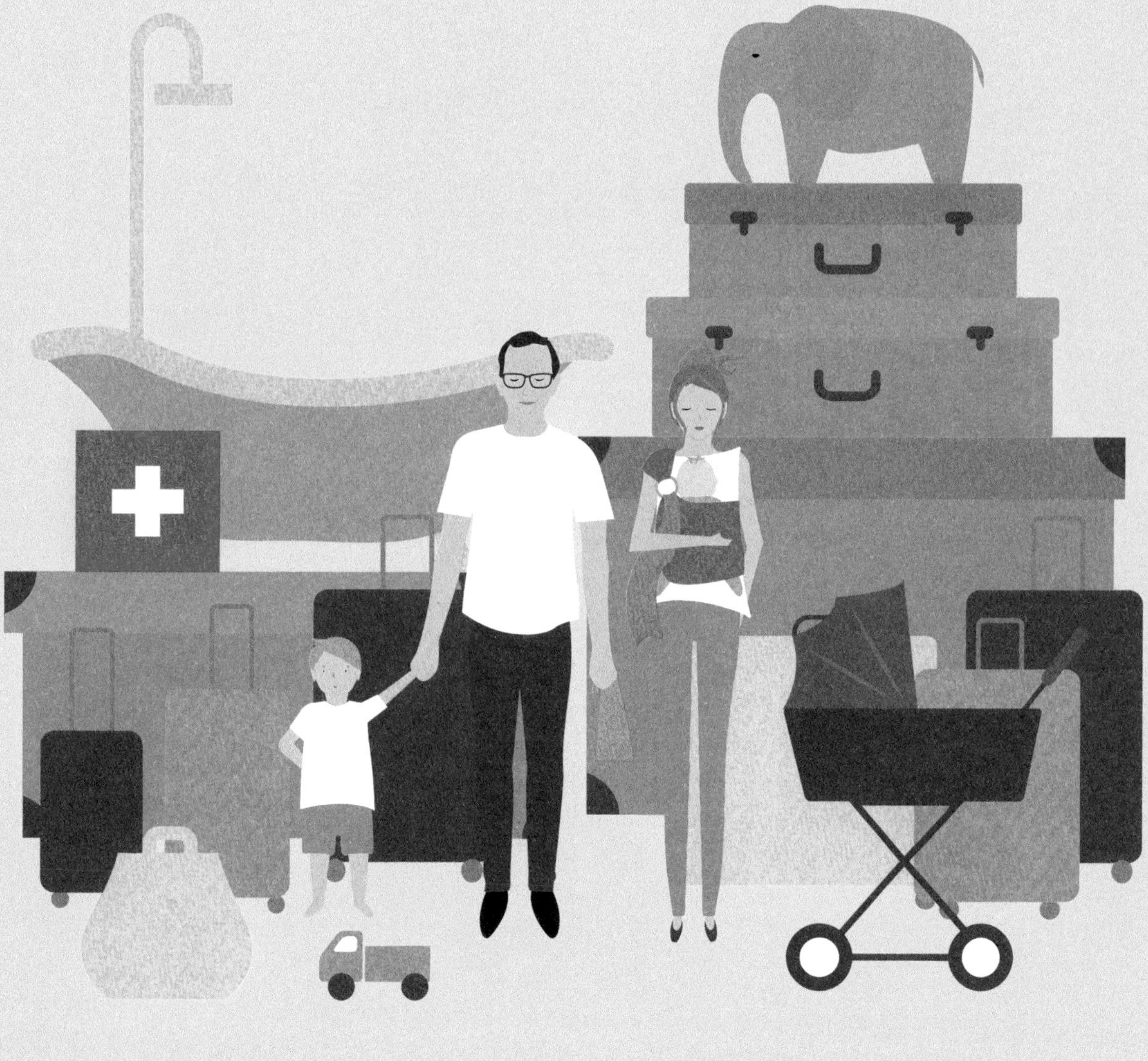

GIFTS FOR NEW PARENTS

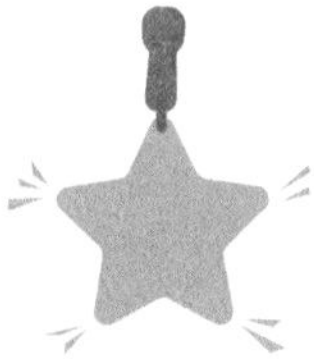

A CLIP-ON NIGHT-LIGHT
YOU'LL SPEND THE NEXT FEW YEARS ROAMING YOUR HOUSE AT NIGHT.

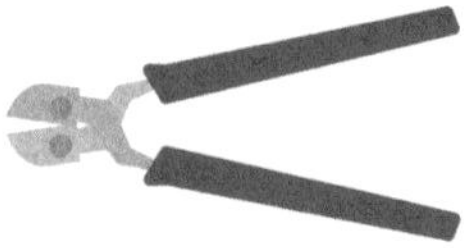

BOLT CUTTERS
YOU'LL UNDERSTAND THE FIRST TIME YOU TRY TO OPEN THE PACKAGING OF A KIDS' TOY

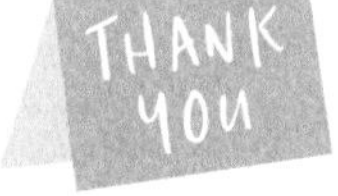
THANK YOU

A COMPLETED THANK-YOU CARD TO ME
ONE LESS THING FOR YOU TO WORRY ABOUT..

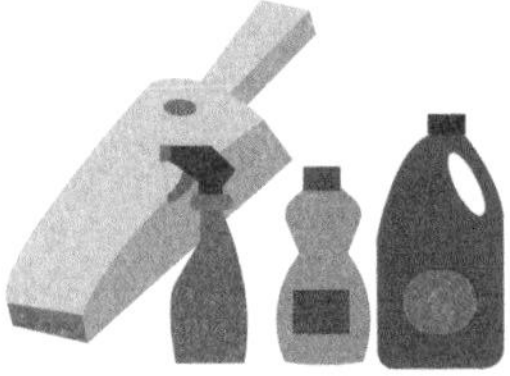

A MINI VACUUM CLEANER
STAIN REMOVER, CARPET CLEANER, SPRAY AND WIPE, BLEACH, DISINFECTANT (KIDS REALLY ARE FILTHY)

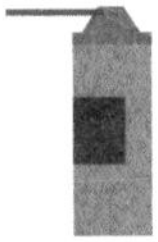

OIL FOR HINGES
YOU PROBABLY HAVEN'T NOTICED BUT EVERY DOOR IN YOUR HOUSE NOW SQUEAKS

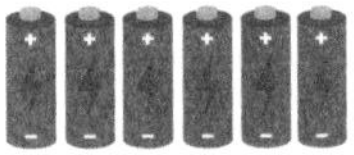

BATTERIES
YOU MAY HAVE EVERY INTENTION TO HAVE A HOUSE FULL OF WOODEN TOYS, BUT THE PLASTIC, SHOUTY ONES WILL FIND THEIR WAY IN.

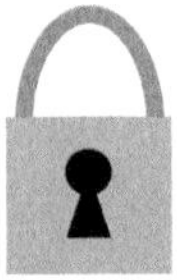

A LOCK FOR YOUR BATHROOM DOOR

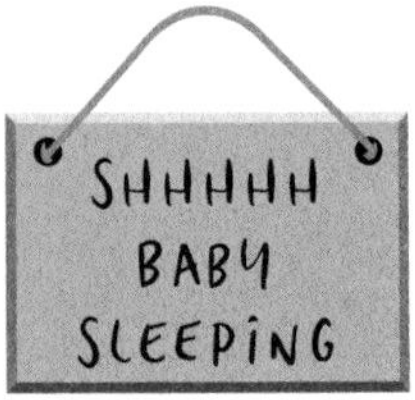
SHHHHH
BABY
SLEEPING

A SIGN FOR THE FRONT DOOR

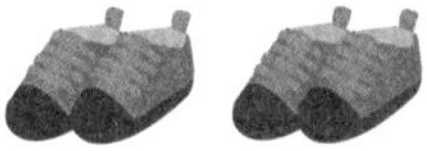

TWO PAIRS OF IDENTICAL FIRST SHOES.
YOU'LL INEVITABLY LOSE ONE OF THEIR FIRST ADORABLE BUT POINTLESS SHOES. YOU DON'T NEED THAT KIND OF EMOTIONAL TURMOIL.

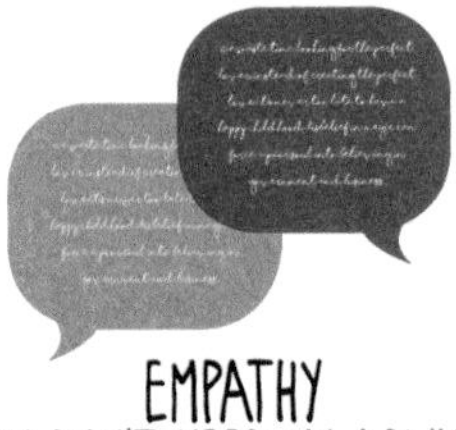

EMPATHY
YOU DON'T NEED MY ADVICE. BUT I WILL LET YOU COMPLAIN WHENEVER YOU WANT. I KNOW YOU STILL LOVE YOUR KIDS.

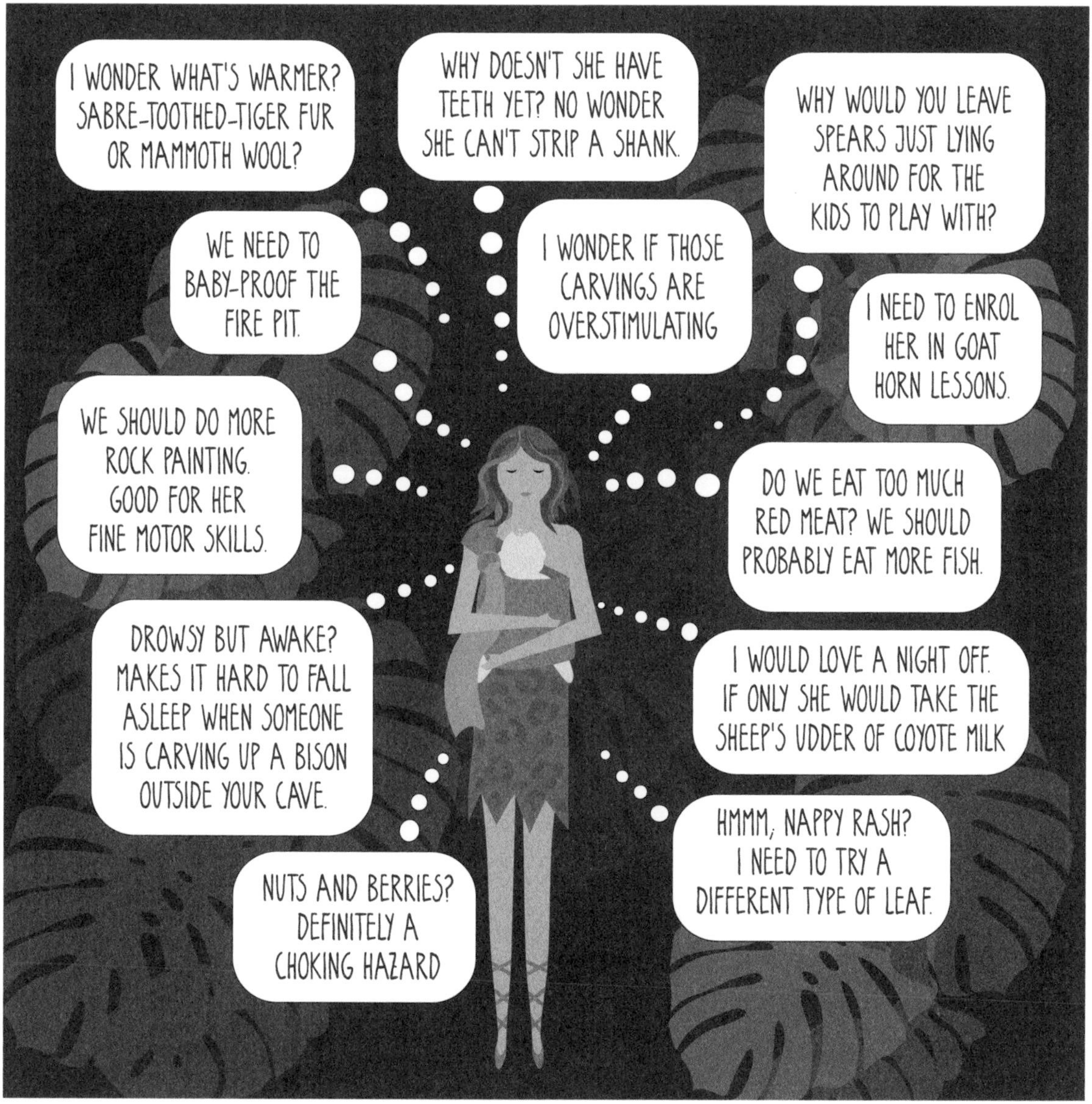
I WONDER WHAT'S WARMER? SABRE-TOOTHED-TIGER FUR OR MAMMOTH WOOL?
WHY DOESN'T SHE HAVE TEETH YET? NO WONDER SHE CAN'T STRIP A SHANK.
WHY WOULD YOU LEAVE SPEARS JUST LYING AROUND FOR THE KIDS TO PLAY WITH?
WE NEED TO BABY-PROOF THE FIRE PIT.
I WONDER IF THOSE CARVINGS ARE OVERSTIMULATING
I NEED TO ENROL HER IN GOAT HORN LESSONS.
WE SHOULD DO MORE ROCK PAINTING. GOOD FOR HER FINE MOTOR SKILLS.
DO WE EAT TOO MUCH RED MEAT? WE SHOULD PROBABLY EAT MORE FISH.
DROWSY BUT AWAKE? MAKES IT HARD TO FALL ASLEEP WHEN SOMEONE IS CARVING UP A BISON OUTSIDE YOUR CAVE.
I WOULD LOVE A NIGHT OFF. IF ONLY SHE WOULD TAKE THE SHEEP'S UDDER OF COYOTE MILK
HMMM, NAPPY RASH? I NEED TO TRY A DIFFERENT TYPE OF LEAF.
NUTS AND BERRIES? DEFINITELY A CHOKING HAZARD

. . . AND IN THAT MOMENT EVERYTHING WAS PERFECT . . .

can a baby smile too much?

How big is the space between a baby's two front teeth meant to be?
—Coco

My baby doesn't love me.
—Katya

How long is it appropriate to wear matching mother-daughter clothes?
—Kel

How often should a baby blink?
—Anna

When do babies get eyebrows?
—Jess

Crooked bum crack.
—Mara

Can a baby like a ceiling fan too much?
—Jamie

Can a toddler live on cheese alone?
—Shalom

Why does my baby's poop smell like movie-theatre popcorn?
—Ange

SIgns your baby is a genius.
—Kristin

Is my baby faking a cough?
—Sandia

When my daughter was born and we were doing skin to skin I noticed she had hair on her shoulders and back. I looked at my husband and said, "Zeke, google 'I have a furry baby.'" He said, "It's just pulling up puppies!!!" I quickly learned that it is very normal.
—Avery

Why do I find my second baby's smell intoxicating?
—Kelly

My baby smiles at shadows on the roof but doesn't sleep. Ever. Should I be concerned?
—Shalom

Why does my baby make goat noises?
—Stephanie

When does baby acne just become regular acne?
—Alison

I stubbed my toe and yelled out and my baby didn't react. I googled "early detection of psychopathy in infants."
—Lucie

Is it normal for a baby girl to only like men?
—Caitlin

Baby girl is only soothed by Queen's "Fat Bottomed Girls."
—Whitney

My baby smiles at shadows but doesn't sleep. Is this okay?
—Kylie

Will my toddler ever grow hair?
—Megan

Is my baby as bored as me?
—Saskia

How much earwax is too much earwax in a baby?
—Meredith

Can a baby get shaken baby syndrome from burping?
—Christy

Will my baby's brain develop if he hardly day sleeps?
—Sarah

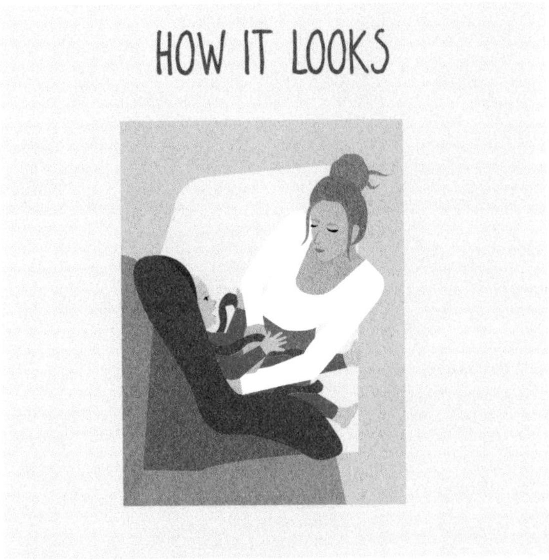
HOW IT LOOKS

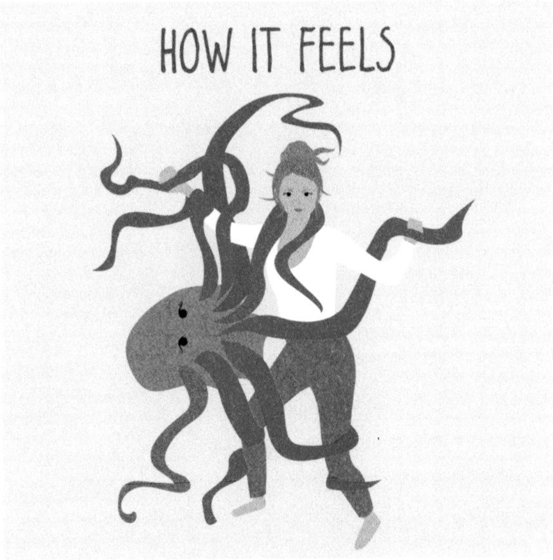
HOW IT FEELS

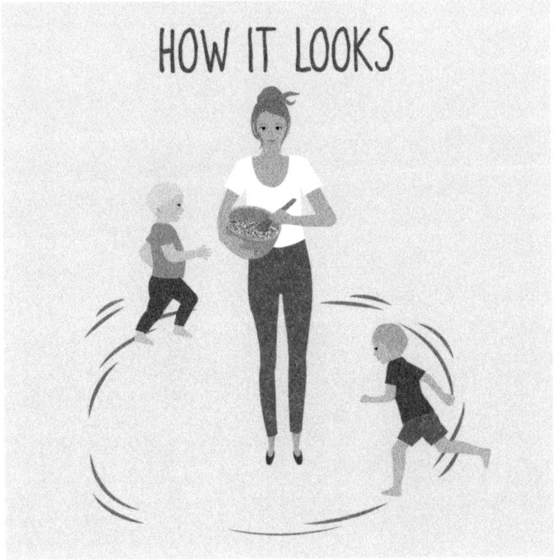
HOW IT LOOKS

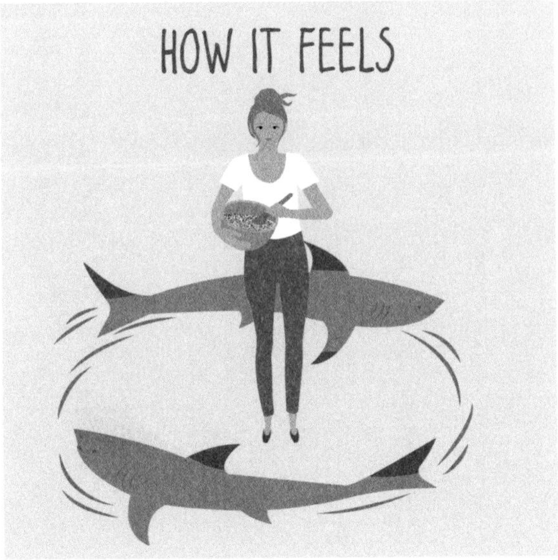
HOW IT FEELS

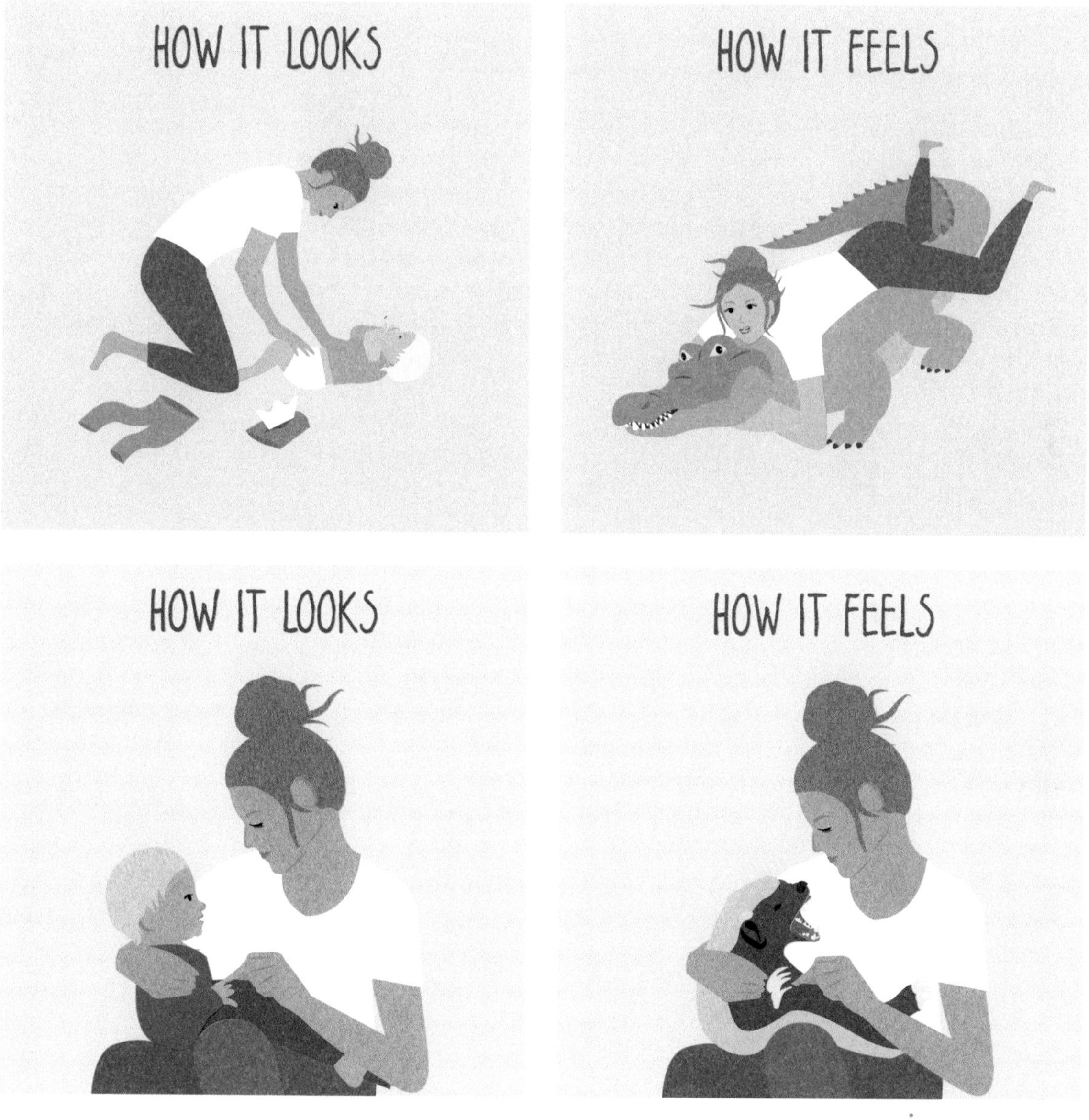
HOW IT LOOKS
HOW IT FEELS
HOW IT LOOKS
HOW IT FEELS

SECRET SUPERPOWERS

It's a game that expectant parents like to play—"Will they get my nose? My height? Hopefully they don't get my weird toes." And then they're born and we realise no matter whose traits they inherited, they are perfect. After all, most things are cute on a newborn.

Then we start to ponder their personalities. Will they inherit my character flaws? We start seeing glimmers of a developing disposition. For me, it made me acutely aware of my own perceived flaws.

I had hoped my children wouldn't inherit my shyness in a world that seems to favour the outgoing and the confident. But as my son's toddler bravado wore off, I did see a shyness emerge. A little boy who even at five would ask to be carried into a room, his face firmly planted in my neck. And suddenly I realised that a person who is shy can hide behind their slightly awkward demeanour and observe the world. He's a good listener—he doesn't miss a trick. Modesty is attractive, and shyness makes someone unthreatening and approachable. It's not such a bad thing.

I've also felt burdened by self-doubt. People will often point out that it's a form of impostor syndrome. The questioning voice on my shoulder refutes this; after all, wouldn't that imply that I'm better than I think I am? It turns out even my imposter syndrome has imposter syndrome. One of the great things about self-doubt is that it keeps your ego in check. It motivates you to prove yourself. And it forces you outside your comfort zone.

I've caught myself wishing my son wasn't as sensitive as I am. But sensitivity is far from a sign of weakness. The ability to think critically and analytically and pursue meaning is the backbone of creativity and invention. And sensitive souls are instinctively caring and nurturing.

As for that fiery temper, well, he definitely got that from somewhere. While passion in the hands of a five-year-old can seem irrational and explosive, it also means he loves deeply and is fiercely protective. I look forward to a future when his fire and moodiness gives way to passion that will inspire and influence action.

And just like how they make my physical imperfections look cute, my children somehow make my character flaws seem more appealing. As always, they inspire me. It's time to harness my own secret superpowers.

SHYNESS   FIERINESS   SELF-DOUBT   SENSITIVITY

THERE IS NO IN-BETWEEN

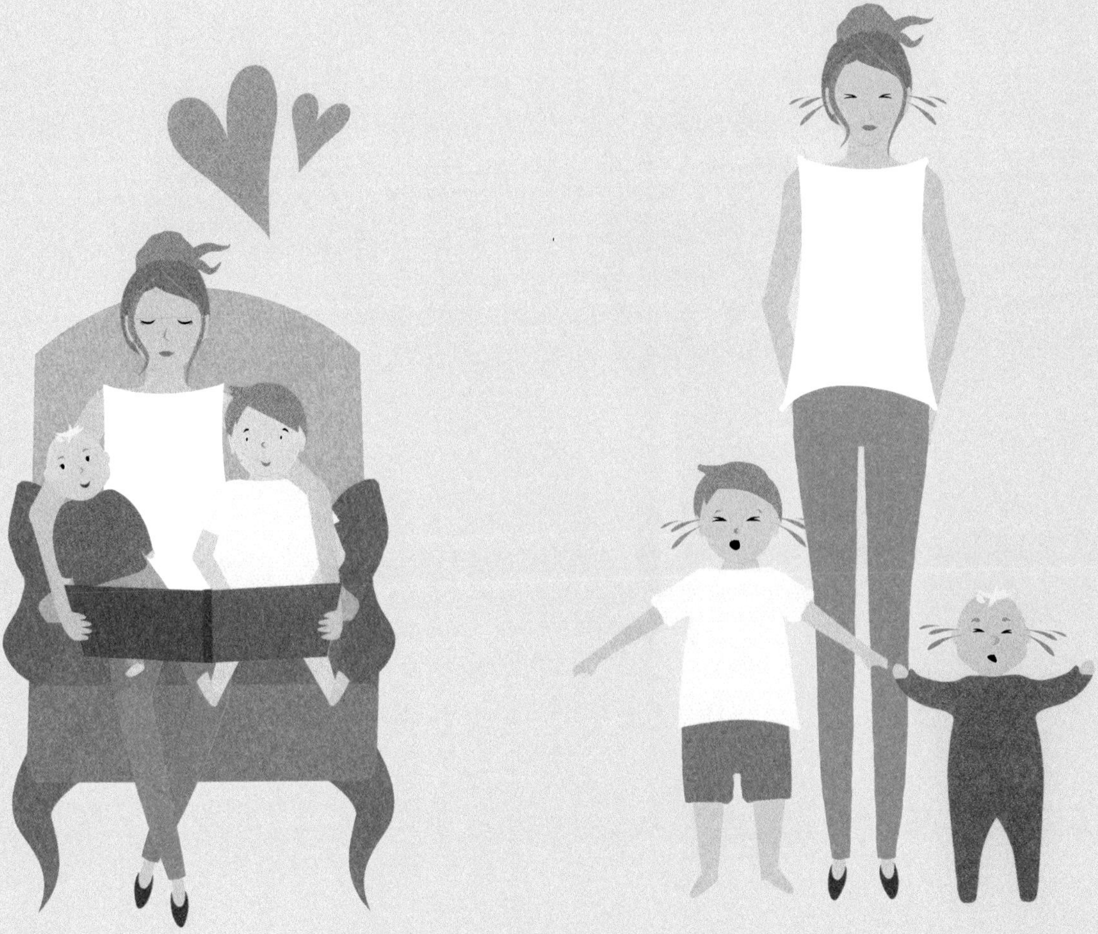

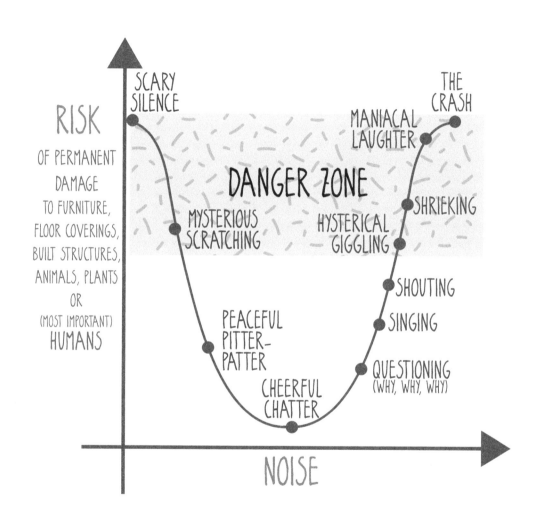

RISK

OF PERMANENT
DAMAGE
TO FURNITURE,
FLOOR COVERINGS,
BUILT STRUCTURES,
ANIMALS, PLANTS
OR
(MOST IMPORTANT)
HUMANS

SCARY
SILENCE

THE
CRASH

MANIACAL
LAUGHTER

DANGER ZONE

MYSTERIOUS
SCRATCHING

HYSTERICAL
GIGGLING

SHRIEKING

SHOUTING

SINGING

PEACEFUL
PITTER-
PATTER

QUESTIONING
(WHY, WHY, WHY)

CHEERFUL
CHATTER

NOISE

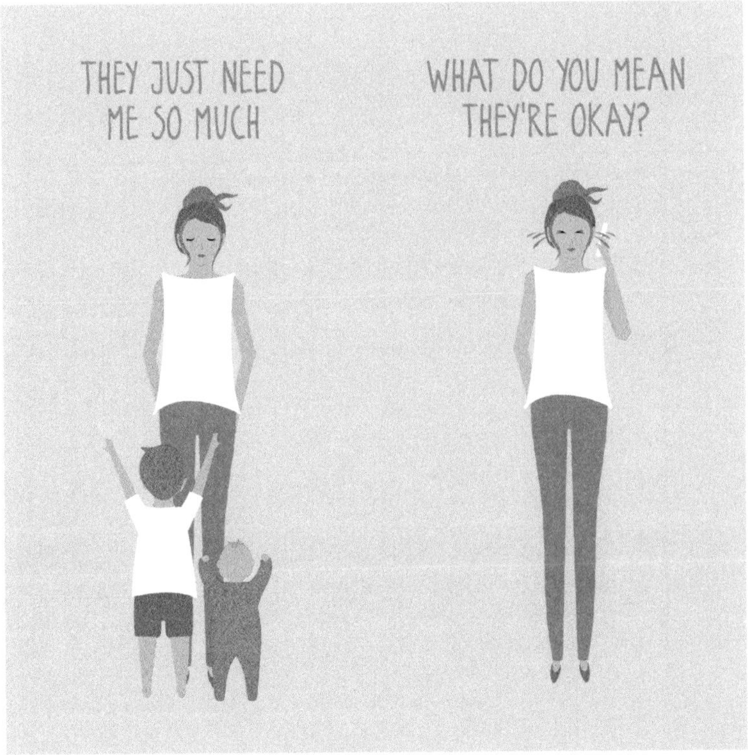
THEY JUST NEED ME SO MUCH
WHAT DO YOU MEAN THEY'RE OKAY?

NEEDING SPACE TO DO THINGS BY MYSELF, FOR MYSELF.

INTENSELY MISSING THEM THE SECOND WE'RE APART.

THE DESIRE TO GO AND NUZZLE THEM WHILE THEY SLEEP.

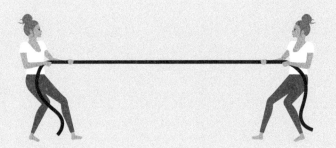

THE FEAR THIS WILL WAKE THEM UP.

THE URGE TO HOVER AND PROTECT THEM FROM ANY HARM.

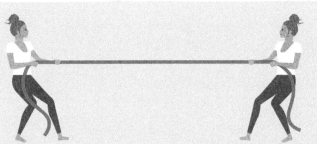

THE KNOWLEDGE THEY NEED TO LEARN BY TAKING RISKS.

LONGING TO BE PAST THE DIFFICULT PHASE YOU'RE CURRENTLY IN.

WANTING TO FREEZE THEM IN THIS MOMENT, EXACTLY AS THEY ARE.

When you are wishing
you were somewhere else,
it's worth remembering
there will come a time
when you will wish you were
exactly where you are right now.

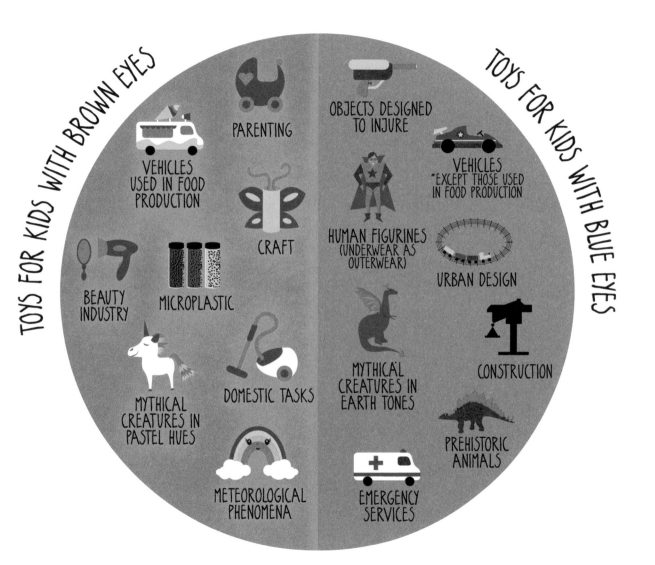

TOYS FOR KIDS WITH BROWN EYES

TOYS FOR KIDS WITH BLUE EYES

PARENTING

VEHICLES USED IN FOOD PRODUCTION

CRAFT

BEAUTY INDUSTRY

MICROPLASTIC

MYTHICAL CREATURES IN PASTEL HUES

DOMESTIC TASKS

METEOROLOGICAL PHENOMENA

OBJECTS DESIGNED TO INJURE

VEHICLES *EXCEPT THOSE USED IN FOOD PRODUCTION

HUMAN FIGURINES (UNDERWEAR AS OUTERWEAR)

URBAN DESIGN

MYTHICAL CREATURES IN EARTH TONES

CONSTRUCTION

EMERGENCY SERVICES

PREHISTORIC ANIMALS

ANATOMY OF A TODDLER'S DINNER

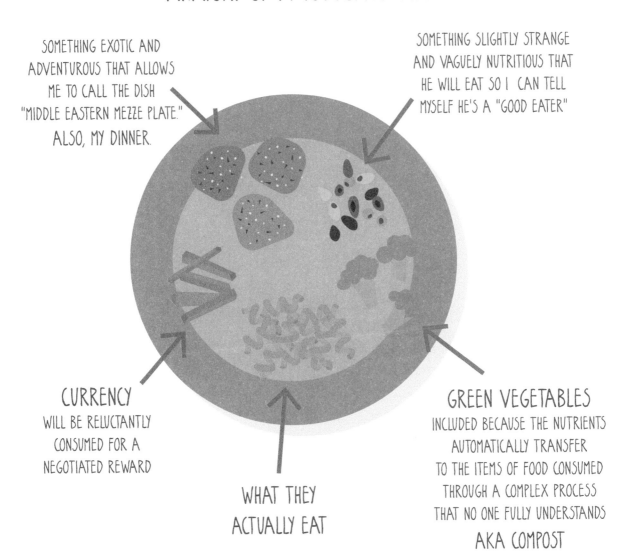

SOMETHING EXOTIC AND ADVENTUROUS THAT ALLOWS ME TO CALL THE DISH "MIDDLE EASTERN MEZZE PLATE." ALSO, MY DINNER.

SOMETHING SLIGHTLY STRANGE AND VAGUELY NUTRITIOUS THAT HE WILL EAT SO I CAN TELL MYSELF HE'S A "GOOD EATER"

CURRENCY
WILL BE RELUCTANTLY CONSUMED FOR A NEGOTIATED REWARD

WHAT THEY ACTUALLY EAT

GREEN VEGETABLES
INCLUDED BECAUSE THE NUTRIENTS AUTOMATICALLY TRANSFER TO THE ITEMS OF FOOD CONSUMED THROUGH A COMPLEX PROCESS THAT NO ONE FULLY UNDERSTANDS
AKA COMPOST

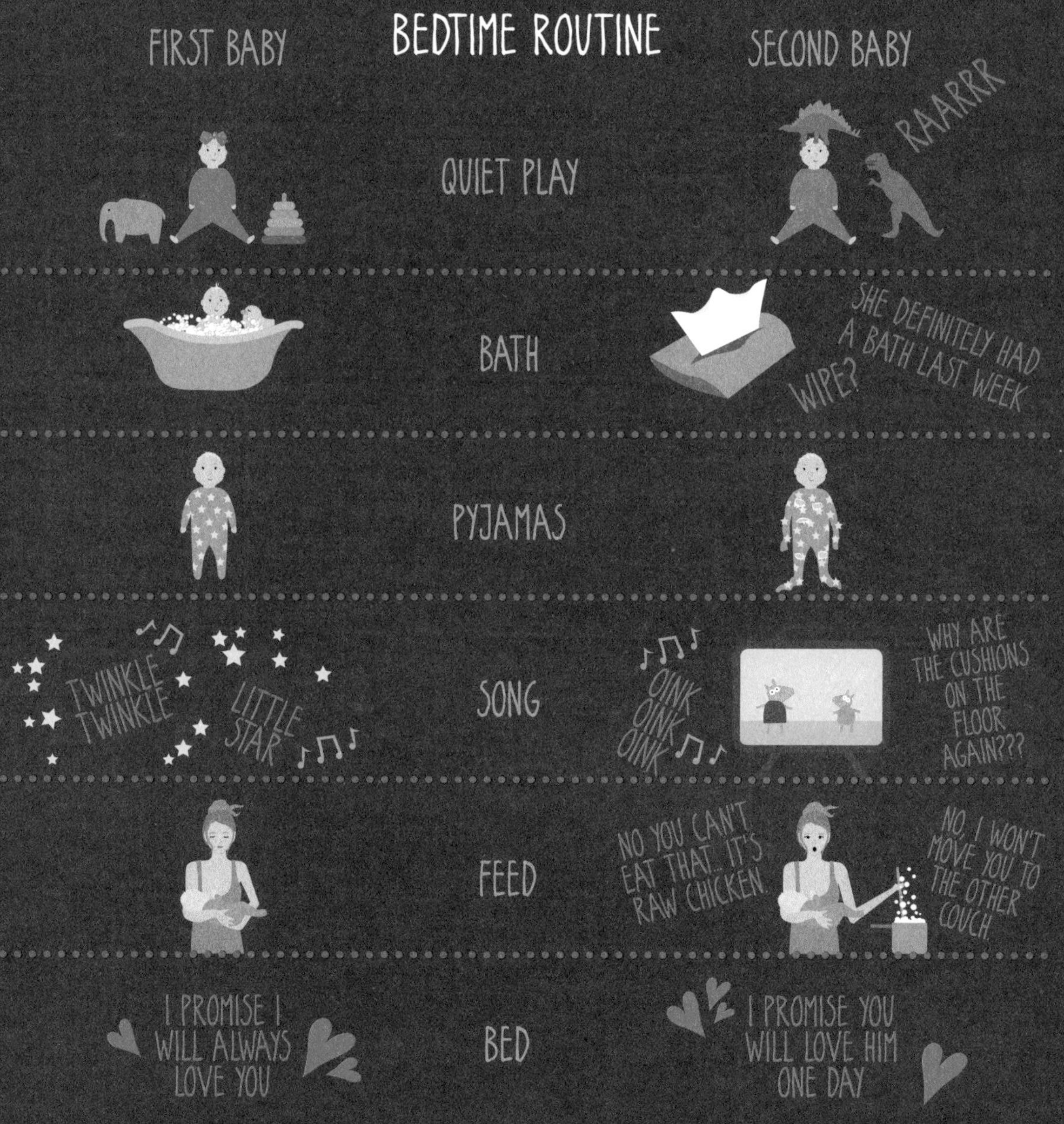
BEDTIME ROUTINE
FIRST BABY
SECOND BABY
QUIET PLAY
RAARRR
BATH
SHE DEFINITELY HAD A BATH LAST WEEK
WIPE?
PYJAMAS
SONG
TWINKLE TWINKLE
LITTLE STAR
OINK OINK OINK
WHY ARE THE CUSHIONS ON THE FLOOR AGAIN???
FEED
NO YOU CAN'T EAT THAT. IT'S RAW CHICKEN.
NO, I WON'T MOVE YOU TO THE OTHER COUCH.
BED
I PROMISE I WILL ALWAYS LOVE YOU
I PROMISE YOU WILL LOVE HIM ONE DAY

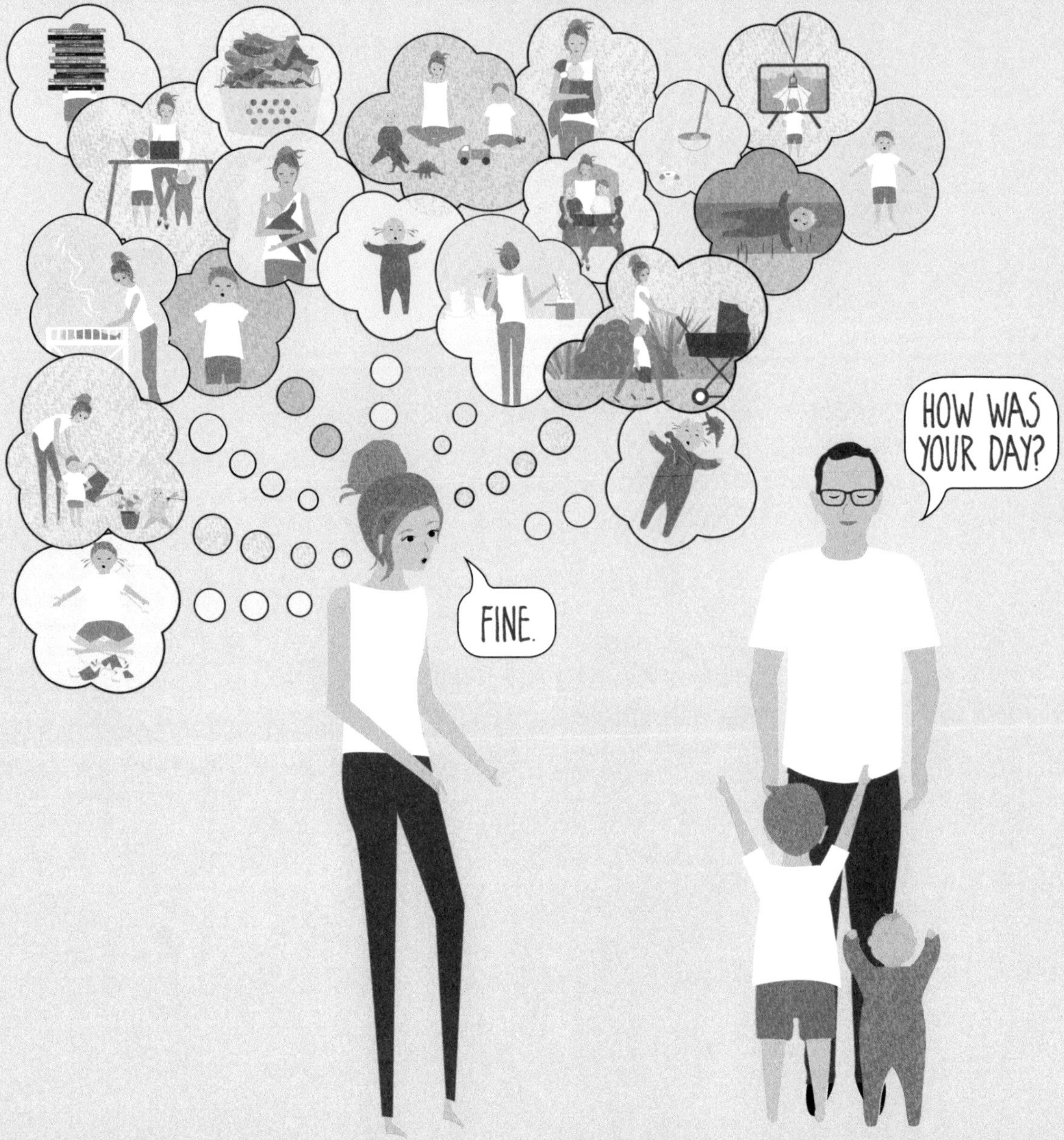
HOW WAS YOUR DAY?
FINE.

I know I'm lucky. I know they're perfect. We created two magical, beautiful and enchanting little humans and I love them with all my heart. I love them with parts of my heart I didn't know existed.

And it's not all tears and tantrums and nappy explosions and aching tiredness. Sometimes it's uncontrollable laughter. Sometimes it's cuddles and kisses and "I sooooo love you." Sometimes I'm overwhelmed by their eyelashes and fingers and noses and toes and I just have to squeeze and inhale them.

But sometimes I just really, really wish I got to be the one to walk in the door at 7:30 p.m. Calm. Unfazed by the mess. Slightly amused by the chaos. In control of my emotions. The hero who gets to take the helm and steer the ship.

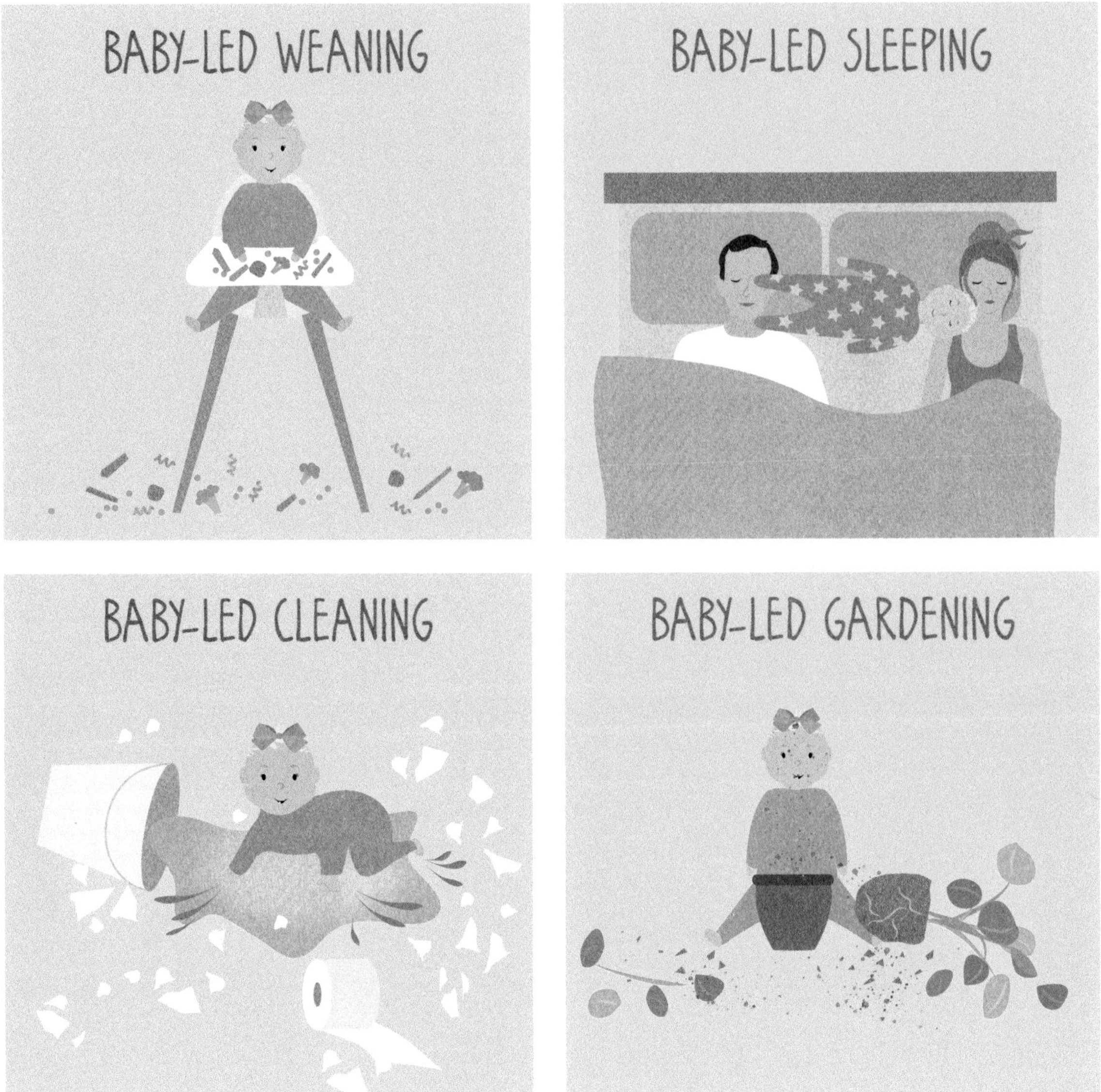
BABY-LED WEANING
BABY-LED SLEEPING
BABY-LED CLEANING
BABY-LED GARDENING

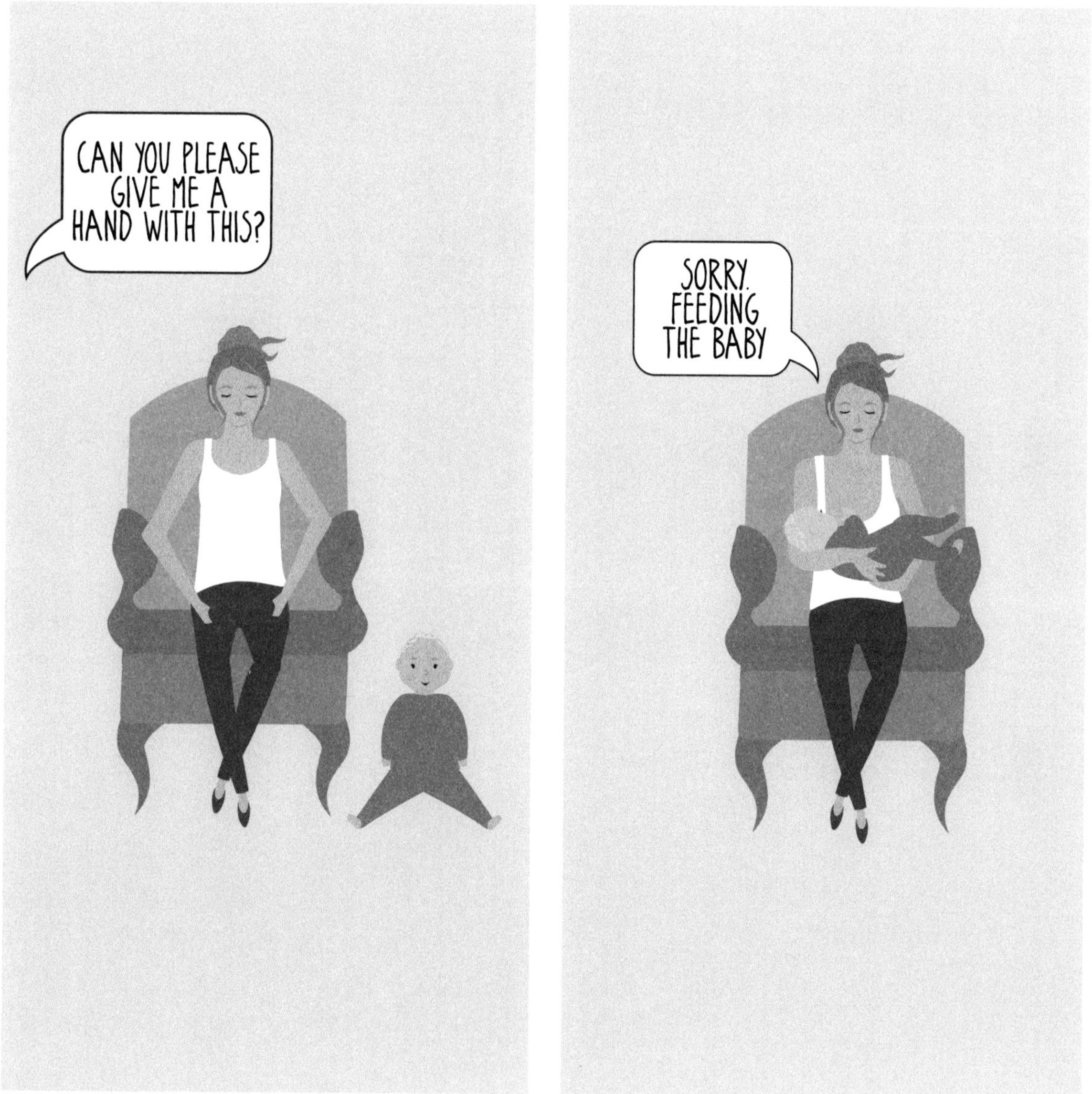
CAN YOU PLEASE GIVE ME A HAND WITH THIS?
SORRY. FEEDING THE BABY

I'M ALL OVER THIS . . . SELF-ACCEPTANCE . . . SETTING A GREAT EXAMPLE FOR MY DAUGHTER . . . NOT PASSING ON MY INSECURITIES . . . OUR BODIES ARE AMAZING!
WHY THE HELL WOULD YOU TAKE A PHOTO OF ME FROM THAT ANGLE???

HOW TO GET CHILDREN TO EAT VEGETABLES

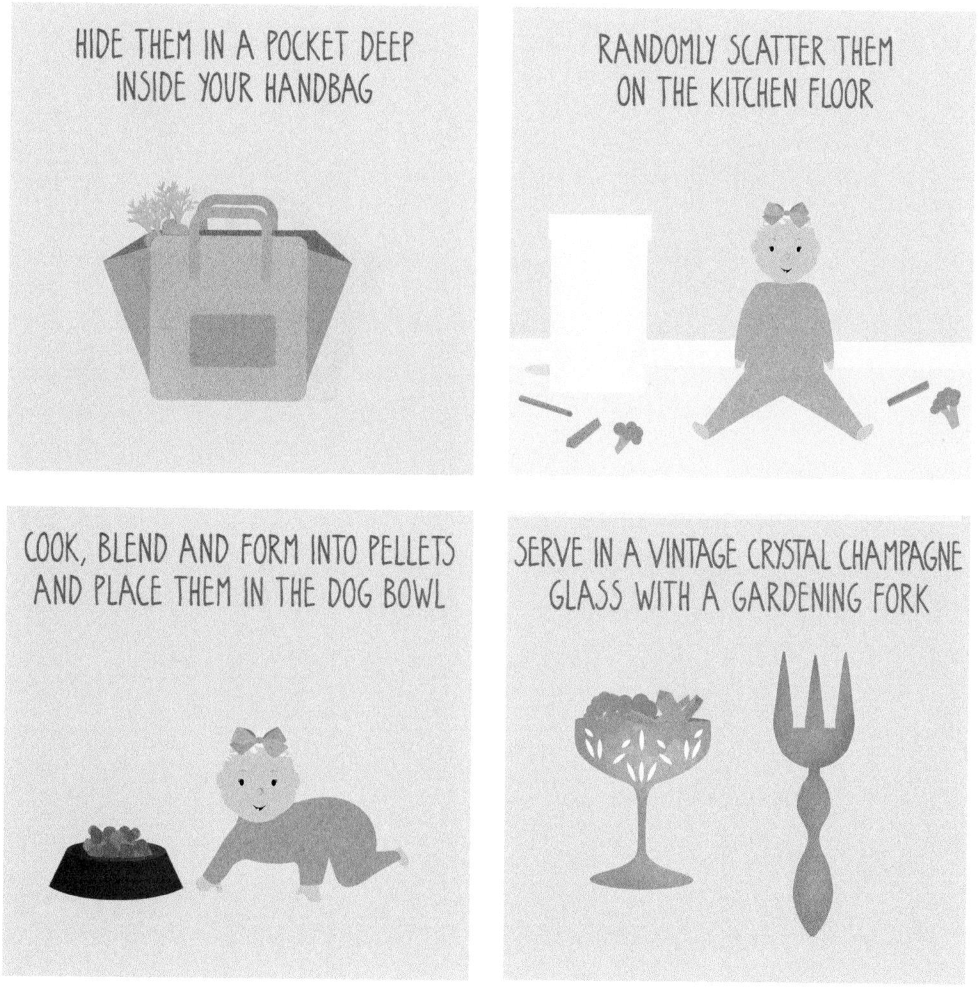
HIDE THEM IN A POCKET DEEP INSIDE YOUR HANDBAG
RANDOMLY SCATTER THEM ON THE KITCHEN FLOOR
COOK, BLEND AND FORM INTO PELLETS AND PLACE THEM IN THE DOG BOWL
SERVE IN A VINTAGE CRYSTAL CHAMPAGNE GLASS WITH A GARDENING FORK

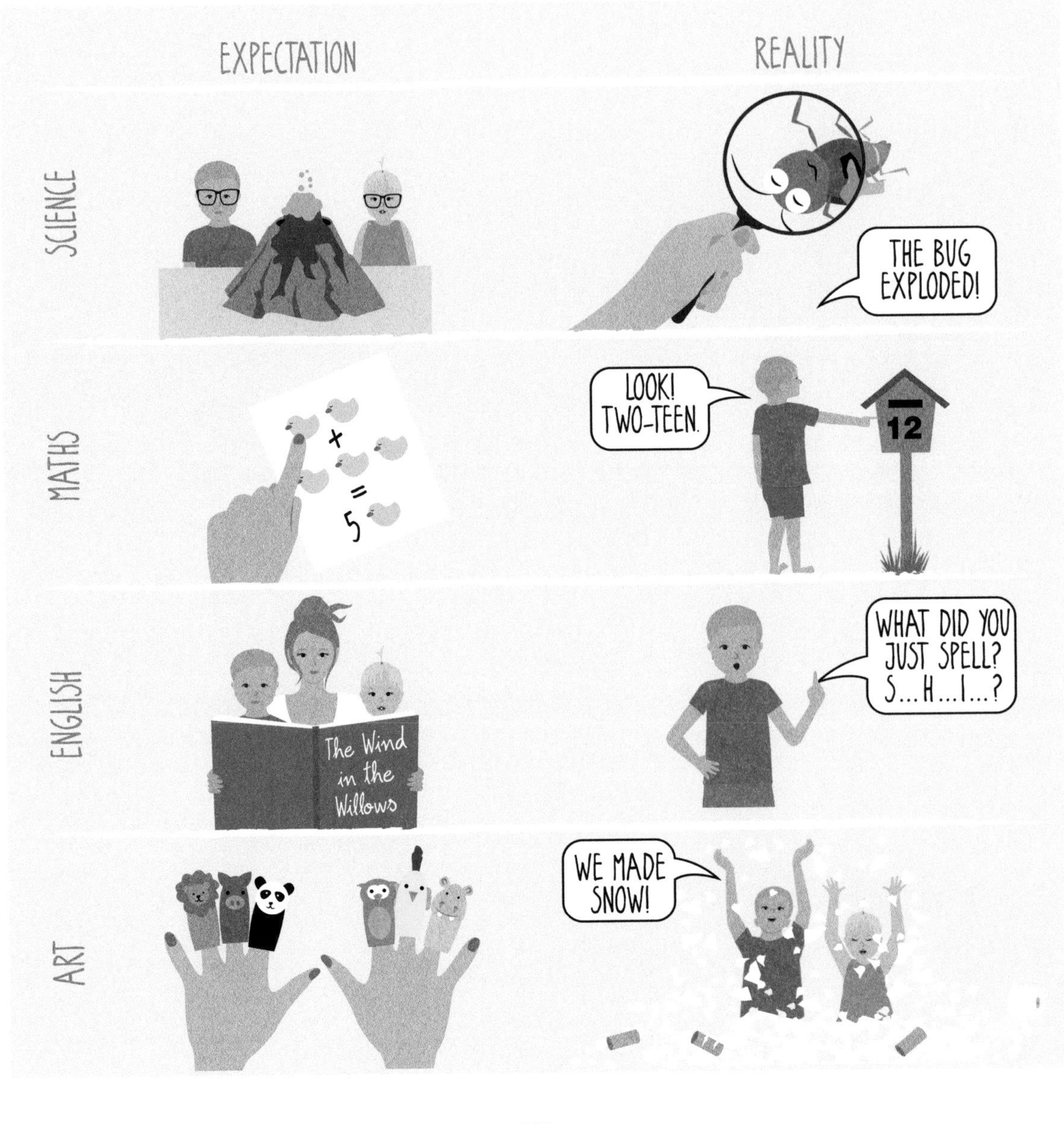
EXPECTATION
REALITY
SCIENCE
THE BUG EXPLODED!
MATHS
+
=
5
LOOK! TWO-TEEN.
12
ENGLISH
The Wind in the Willows
WHAT DID YOU JUST SPELL? S...H...I...?
ART
WE MADE SNOW!

EDUCATIONAL ACTIVITIES

The greatest parent you will ever be is the one you are right before you have your first child.

You've read the books. You've observed your friends. You've (dare I say it) judged strangers in shopping centres. And just like everything else you've ever worked for, with the right preparation, how hard can it be?

But then the baby arrives, and you realise nothing quite prepared you for the relentless neediness of this little person. Somehow you stay afloat, taking each day as it comes. At some point it becomes less about survival, and suddenly you realise you are responsible for educating and stimulating this ever-inquisitive little mind.

I always imagined that my enthusiasm for my landscape architecture career would be diverted into educational activities; with a Pinterest board full of crafts for toddlers and scientific experiments for preschoolers. But there was one thing I didn't count on: the slightly uncomfortable realisation that I actually find a lot of that stuff dead boring.

There are endless classes for little kids, and of course these activities have their place. I do, however, strongly object to the idea they are somehow essential for children's development. When I called a swim school to enquire about starting lessons for my thirteen-month-old, they incredulously told me, "Oh no, she's much too old to start now. She will be too far behind everyone." We hadn't even taken down the bunting from her first birthday party and already she was being told she was behind her peers. She doesn't need that kind of pressure, and I definitely don't need that degree of guilt.

Somehow, I had fallen into the trap that there was only one way to be a "good parent," and that was to provide endless educational activities at home and a week full of organised classes. But trying to achieve this wasn't making me a good parent. It was making me feel tired, guilt-ridden and inadequate.

I've realised I'm at my best when I involve them in things I have a genuine interest in. We garden together, pulling weeds and planting seeds. We wander the streets looking for architecturally interesting letter boxes and clever drainage details. We build train tracks, and I talk about the merits of locating higher-density housing near public transport. My children have the rest of their lives for formal education and extracurricular activities. But for now, I'm going to do my best to spark their passion for some of my own interests. And give them enough space to discover their own.

TRICKY DAY SURVIVAL GUIDE

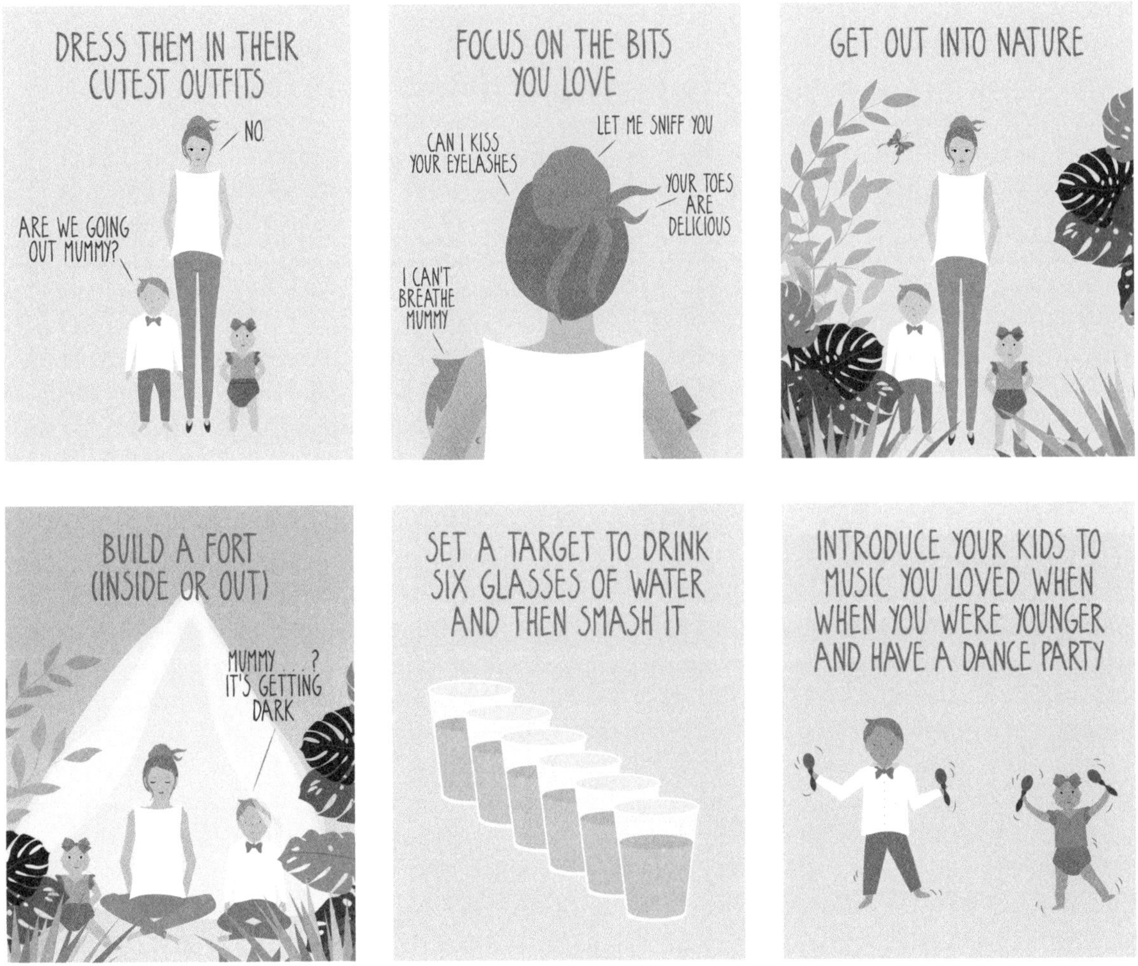
DRESS THEM IN THEIR CUTEST OUTFITS
ARE WE GOING OUT MUMMY?
NO.
FOCUS ON THE BITS YOU LOVE
CAN I KISS YOUR EYELASHES
LET ME SNIFF YOU
YOUR TOES ARE DELICIOUS
I CAN'T BREATHE MUMMY
GET OUT INTO NATURE
BUILD A FORT (INSIDE OR OUT)
MUMMY . . . ? IT'S GETTING DARK
SET A TARGET TO DRINK SIX GLASSES OF WATER AND THEN SMASH IT
INTRODUCE YOUR KIDS TO MUSIC YOU LOVED WHEN WHEN YOU WERE YOUNGER AND HAVE A DANCE PARTY

WRITE A LIST OF VERY SIMPLE TASKS TO ACHIEVE AND THEN TICK THEM OFF WITH GIANT TICKS

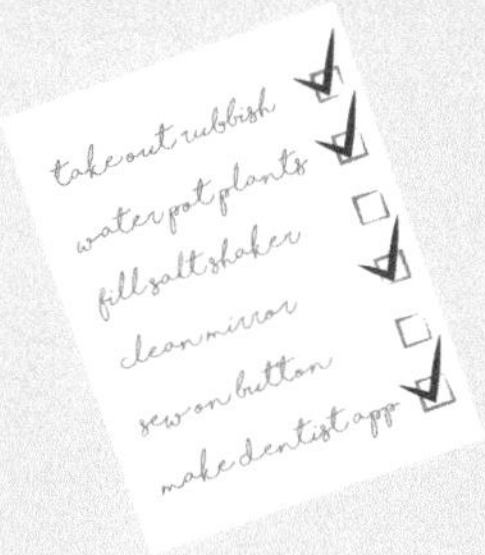
take out rubbish
water pot plants
fill salt shaker
clean mirror
sew on button
make dentist app

CUT UP SOME VEGETABLES AND SERVE THEM ON A REALLY FANCY PLATE. EAT THEM SOMEWHERE YOU DON'T NORMALLY ALLOW EATING.

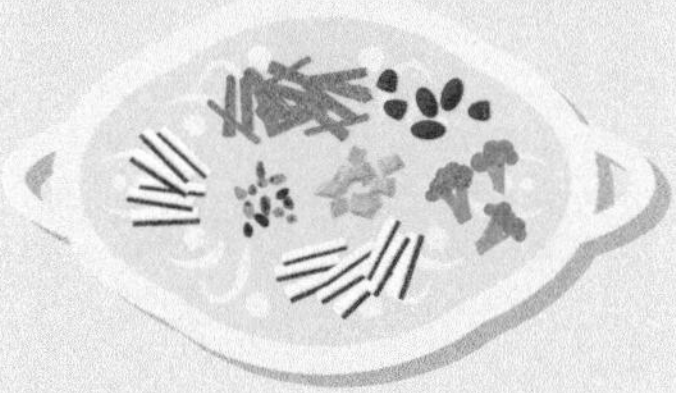

TEACH YOUR KIDS SOMETHING NEW AND MIND-BLOWING (EVEN IF YOU HAVE TO GOOGLE IT FIRST)

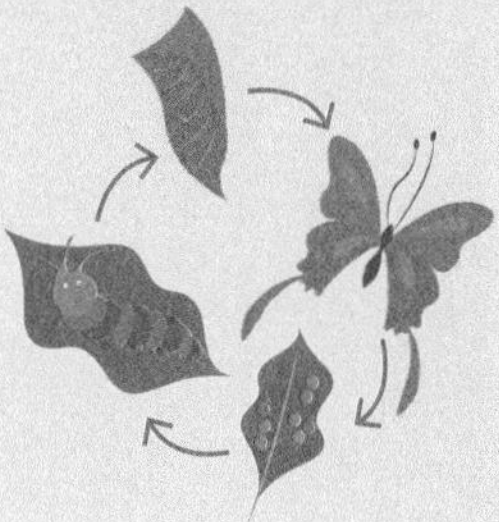

GET IN THE WATER—OCEAN, POOL, SPRINKLERS, HOSE OR EVEN JUST A BATH

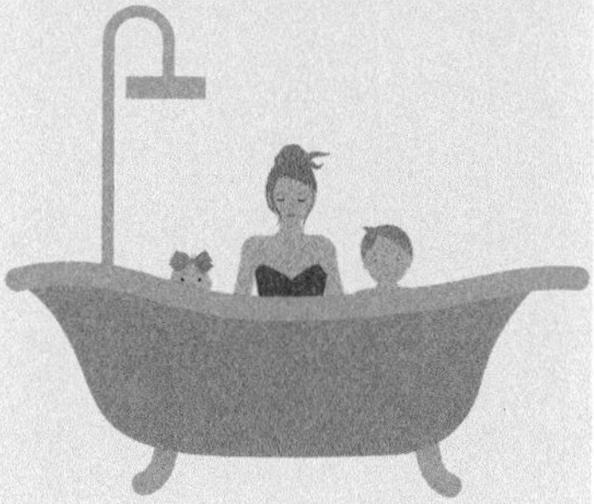

TIDY UP ONE DRAWER, ONE SHELF OR ONE CORNER OF A ROOM SO YOU FEEL IN CONTROL OF SOMETHING

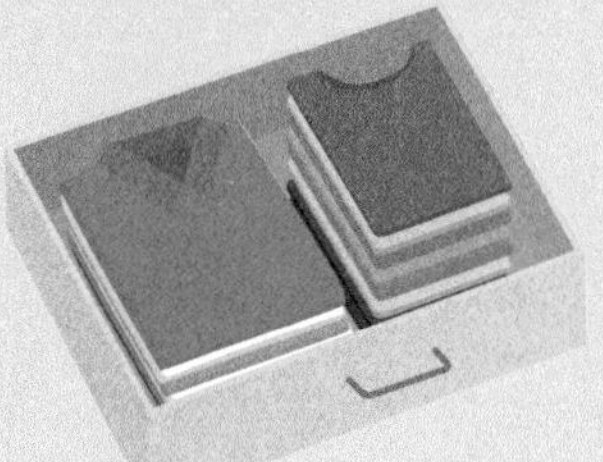

REMEMBER THAT TOMORROW IS A NEW DAY (AND IT'S NOT TOO FAR AWAY!)

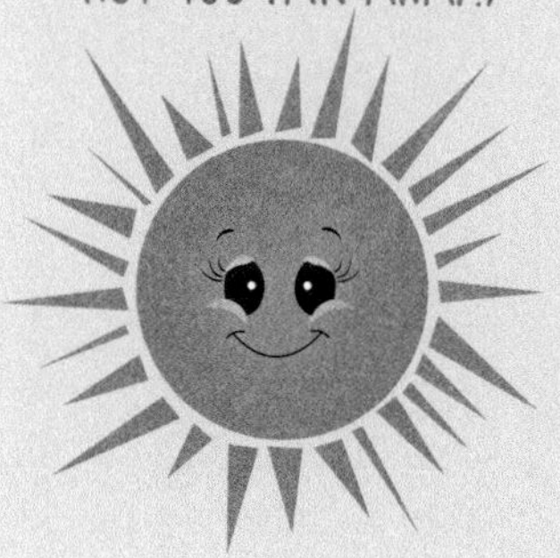

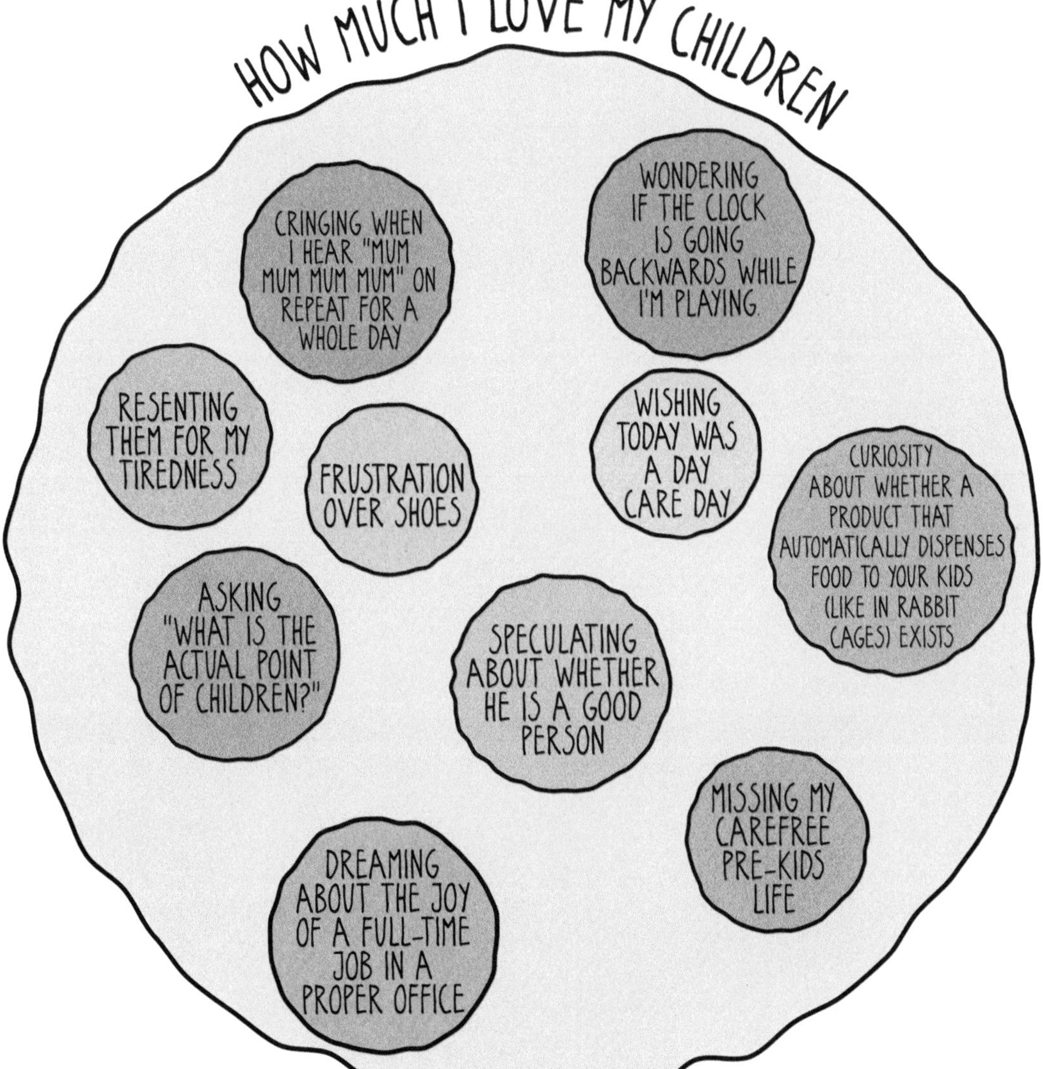
HOW MUCH I LOVE MY CHILDREN
CRINGING WHEN I HEAR "MUM MUM MUM MUM" ON REPEAT FOR A WHOLE DAY
WONDERING IF THE CLOCK IS GOING BACKWARDS WHILE I'M PLAYING.
RESENTING THEM FOR MY TIREDNESS
FRUSTRATION OVER SHOES
WISHING TODAY WAS A DAY CARE DAY
CURIOSITY ABOUT WHETHER A PRODUCT THAT AUTOMATICALLY DISPENSES FOOD TO YOUR KIDS (LIKE IN RABBIT CAGES) EXISTS
ASKING "WHAT IS THE ACTUAL POINT OF CHILDREN?"
SPECULATING ABOUT WHETHER HE IS A GOOD PERSON
MISSING MY CAREFREE PRE-KIDS LIFE
DREAMING ABOUT THE JOY OF A FULL-TIME JOB IN A PROPER OFFICE

PARENT LIKE YOUR NEIGHBOURS ARE LISTENING

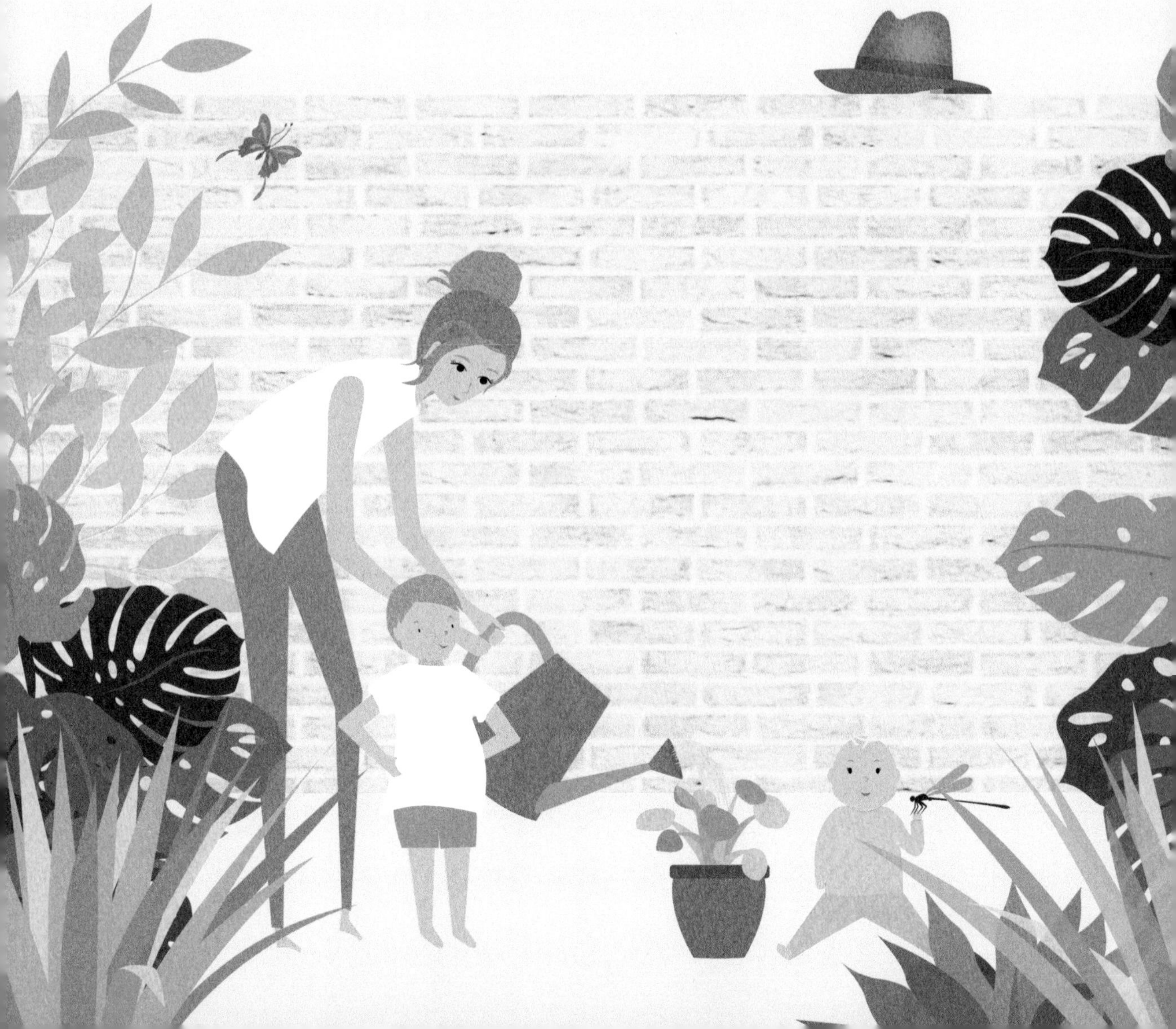

We were having one of those days. You know the ones—when my children's neediness seems to feed my impatience, or perhaps it's the other way around. I send my husband multiple texts about how hard it all is and instantly regret each one, feeling guilty for complaining. The house seems smaller than normal. The children seem louder. Things spiral out of control, and like dominoes we all fall into a pit of frustrated tears.

In a moment of clarity, I took the chaos outside into our garden and heard our neighbour sneeze. It was the sneeze that saved my day.

I became very aware of someone listening to my parenting skills. I suddenly had a lot of parenting skills. I was calm, patient, interested, engaged. I took the time to point out all the different plants in our garden, as they repeated the names back to me. We poked around together in the worm farm. We watered the plants and giggled hysterically when my son soaked us with the hose. I was the mum I always imagined I would be. And, consequently, my kids were absolute angels.

It's a strategy I often employ now, when the wheels start to fall off our afternoon: imagining a sneezing, judgey neighbour listening in.

The moment that I pretended to be a good mum, I became a good mum. And it was never really about the harsh judgement from a stranger, but that was enough to remind me that despite how I felt, I did know what I was doing. And I had the power to turn it into a much better day.

PROUD PARENTING MOMENTS

FOLLOWING COMPLEX STORIES

YOU MISSED A PAGE

LEARNING TO SPELL

Z...O...O... YOU JUST SPELLED ZOO! ARE WE GOING TO THE ZOO?

WIPING THEIR OWN BUM

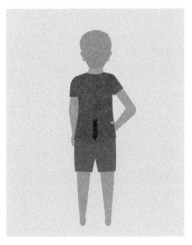

PUTTING SHOES ON

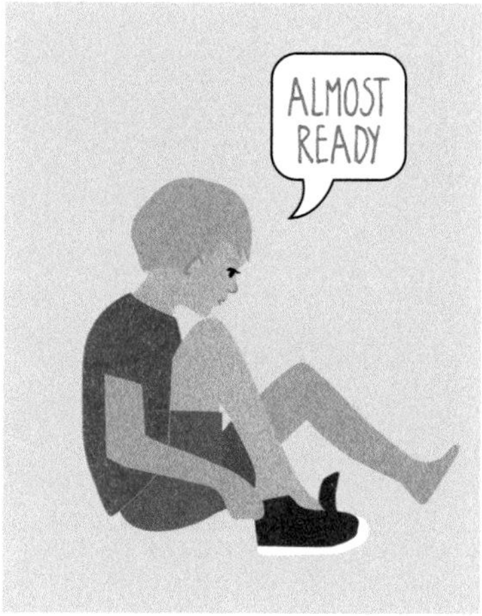
ALMOST READY

POURING THEIR OWN DRINK

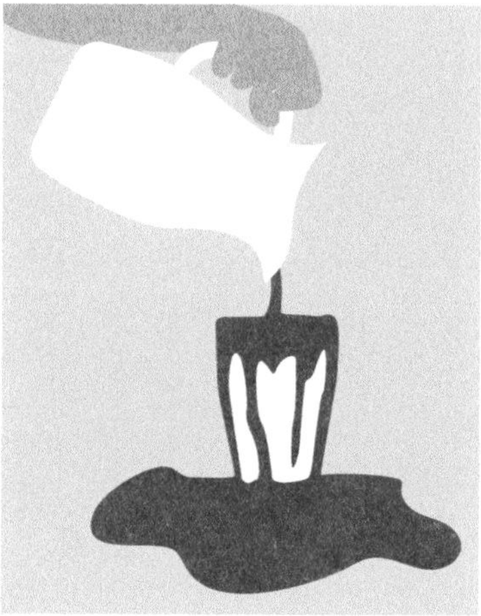

RECALLING VIVID DETAILS

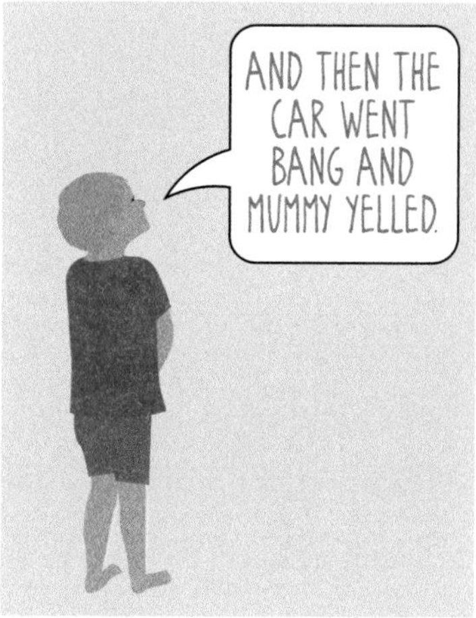
AND THEN THE CAR WENT BANG AND MUMMY YELLED.

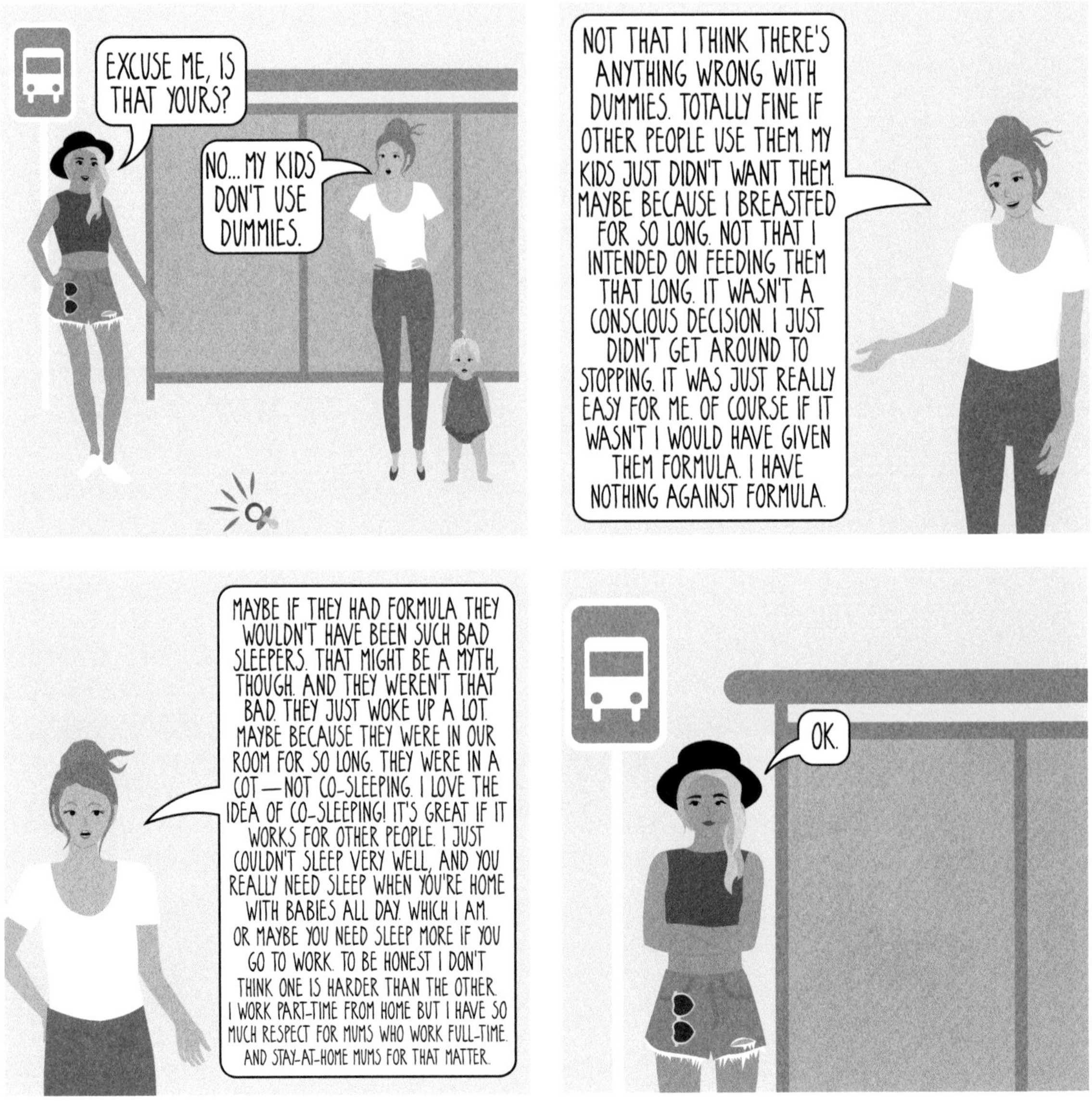
EXCUSE ME, IS THAT YOURS?
NO... MY KIDS DON'T USE DUMMIES.
NOT THAT I THINK THERE'S ANYTHING WRONG WITH DUMMIES. TOTALLY FINE IF OTHER PEOPLE USE THEM. MY KIDS JUST DIDN'T WANT THEM. MAYBE BECAUSE I BREASTFED FOR SO LONG. NOT THAT I INTENDED ON FEEDING THEM THAT LONG. IT WASN'T A CONSCIOUS DECISION. I JUST DIDN'T GET AROUND TO STOPPING. IT WAS JUST REALLY EASY FOR ME. OF COURSE IF IT WASN'T I WOULD HAVE GIVEN THEM FORMULA. I HAVE NOTHING AGAINST FORMULA.
MAYBE IF THEY HAD FORMULA THEY WOULDN'T HAVE BEEN SUCH BAD SLEEPERS. THAT MIGHT BE A MYTH, THOUGH. AND THEY WEREN'T THAT BAD. THEY JUST WOKE UP A LOT. MAYBE BECAUSE THEY WERE IN OUR ROOM FOR SO LONG. THEY WERE IN A COT—NOT CO-SLEEPING. I LOVE THE IDEA OF CO-SLEEPING! IT'S GREAT IF IT WORKS FOR OTHER PEOPLE. I JUST COULDN'T SLEEP VERY WELL, AND YOU REALLY NEED SLEEP WHEN YOU'RE HOME WITH BABIES ALL DAY. WHICH I AM. OR MAYBE YOU NEED SLEEP MORE IF YOU GO TO WORK. TO BE HONEST I DON'T THINK ONE IS HARDER THAN THE OTHER. I WORK PART-TIME FROM HOME BUT I HAVE SO MUCH RESPECT FOR MUMS WHO WORK FULL-TIME. AND STAY-AT-HOME MUMS FOR THAT MATTER.
OK.

I'm not quite the perfect parent I imagined I would be; there is somewhat less patience and craft and somewhat more hot chips and TV than I envisaged. But I'm reasonably confident in my choices—so why on earth do I feel the need to justify my decisions to anyone else? Why am I so afraid of being judged?

Motherhood finds us pitted against one another: how we birth, how we feed, whether we work, childcare and how we choose to educate. There's an assumption that if you fall onto one side, you're against the other. Suddenly I'm not only afraid of being criticised for my decisions, I'm also concerned that other people will think I'm criticising theirs.

I hear myself praising my children, congratulating them for trying their hardest no matter the outcome. I tell them not to worry what other people think of them.̇ But If I'm not confident in my own decisions, how can I expect my children to approach new challenges with courage? Maybe it's time I took some of my own advice, saved the strangers from my defensive, rambling monologues and backed myself.

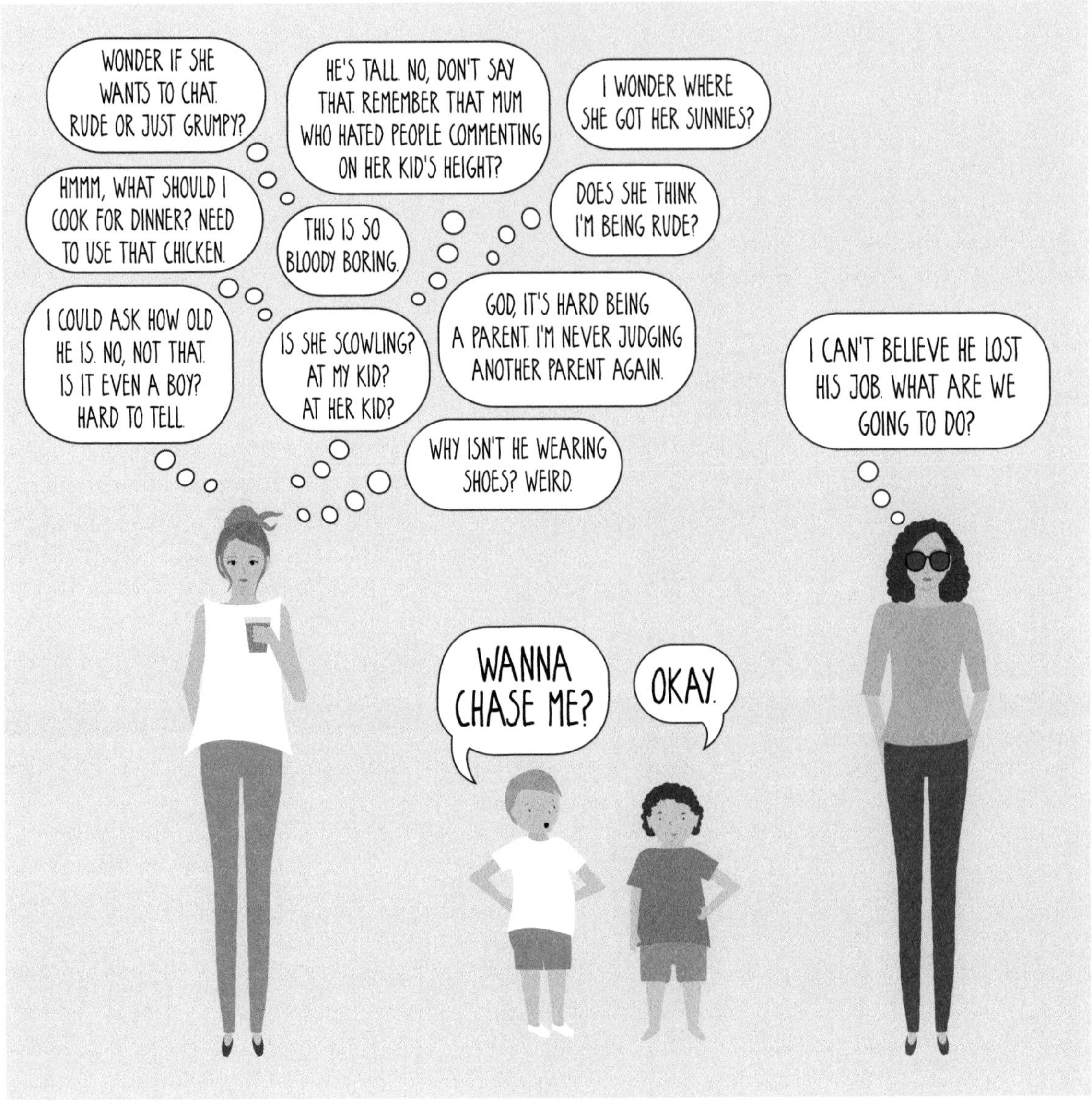
WONDER IF SHE WANTS TO CHAT. RUDE OR JUST GRUMPY?
HMMM, WHAT SHOULD I COOK FOR DINNER? NEED TO USE THAT CHICKEN.
I COULD ASK HOW OLD HE IS. NO, NOT THAT. IS IT EVEN A BOY? HARD TO TELL.
HE'S TALL. NO, DON'T SAY THAT. REMEMBER THAT MUM WHO HATED PEOPLE COMMENTING ON HER KID'S HEIGHT?
THIS IS SO BLOODY BORING.
IS SHE SCOWLING? AT MY KID? AT HER KID?
I WONDER WHERE SHE GOT HER SUNNIES?
DOES SHE THINK I'M BEING RUDE?
GOD, IT'S HARD BEING A PARENT. I'M NEVER JUDGING ANOTHER PARENT AGAIN.
WHY ISN'T HE WEARING SHOES? WEIRD.
I CAN'T BELIEVE HE LOST HIS JOB. WHAT ARE WE GOING TO DO?
WANNA CHASE ME?
OKAY.

LET'S GO ON A PICNIC
DELIGHTFUL
SCORCHY
BLUSTERY
DID YOU FORGET MY NAP?
I WISH I WORE SHORTS
I WISH I WORE JEANS
PESKY FLIES
MY LEGS ARE BROKEN
STUPIDLY HEAVY & AWKWARD
SO MUCH STUFF (BUT STRANGELY NOTHING WE ACTUALLY USED)
COMPLAINY
BITTEN
NUMB FROM SITTING ON THE GROUND
PEOPLE EVERYWHERE HAVING FUN
WHAT WAS THAT FOOD? WAS THAT A MEAL? WHY WAS THE CHEESE SLIMY? WHY IS EVERYTHING STICKY?
WARM + SPILLY
MYSTERIOUSLY SHOELESS
STALKY BIN CHICKEN
YAY, LET'S PACK UP THESE SCRAPS AND DIRTY DISHES AND CARRY THEM HOME.
ITCHY & POKEY GROUND
BITEY ANTS
PLACCY

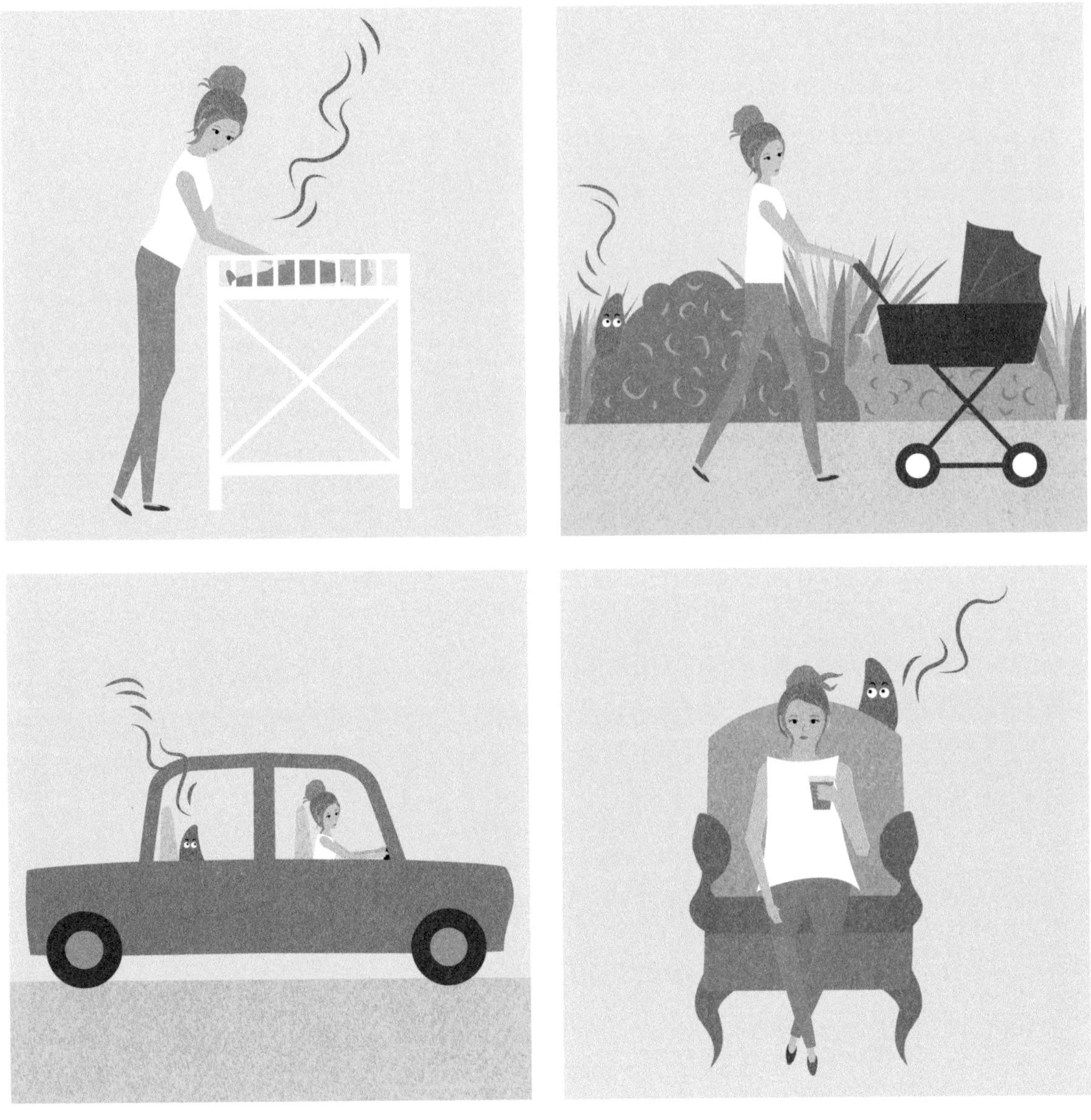

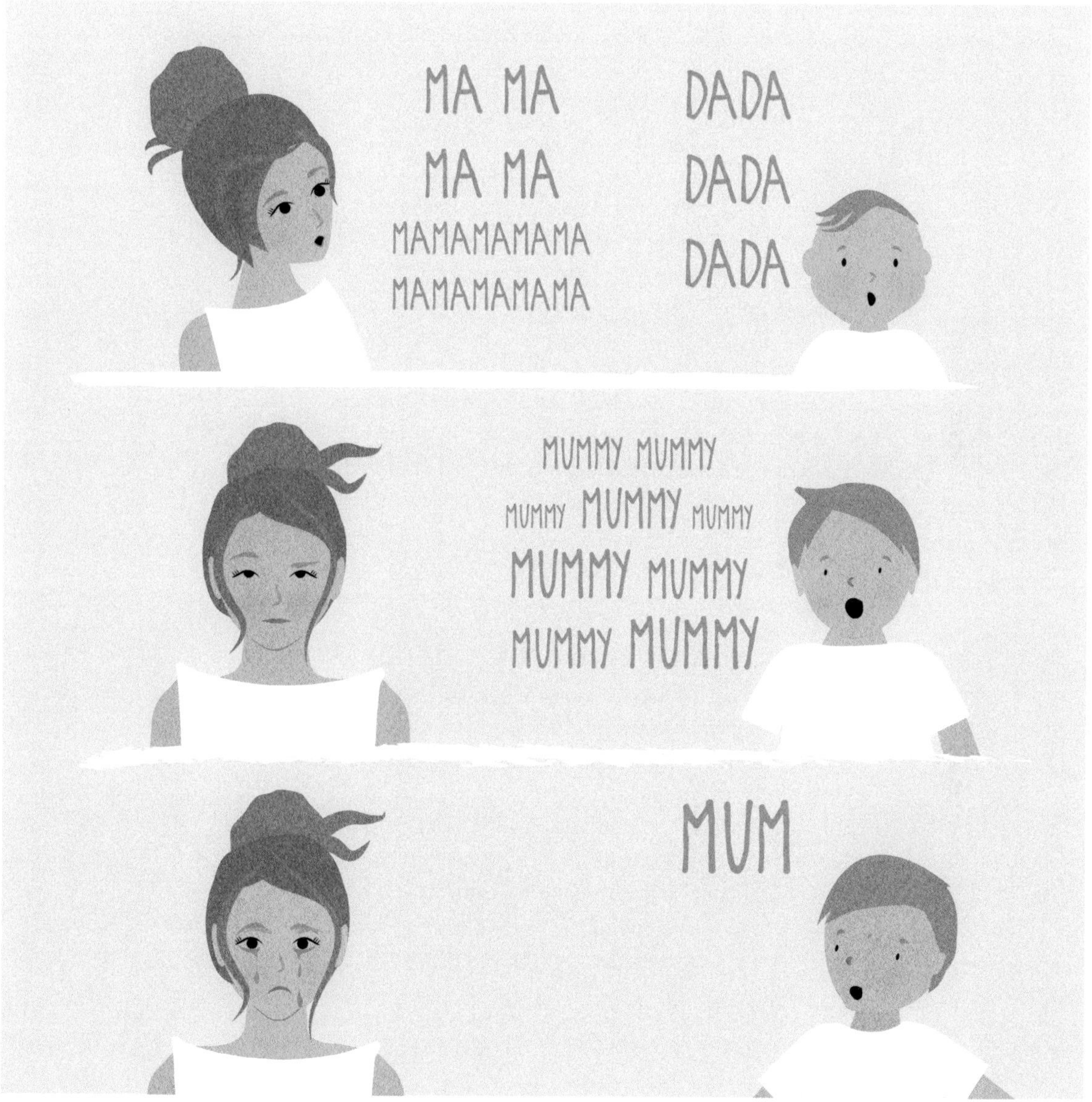
MA MA
MA MA
MAMAMAMAMA
MAMAMAMAMA
DADA
DADA
DADA
MUMMY MUMMY
MUMMY MUMMY MUMMY
MUMMY MUMMY
MUMMY MUMMY
MUM

Guilt. I'm sick of dragging it around with me. It's heavy. It weighs me down. I get all tangled up.

I pick it up in the most unlikely places. An observation from a stranger. A comment by a well-meaning friend. An article—oh, the articles. (Note to self: read fewer articles.)

Some days the burden is lighter. The things that previously plagued me seem silly and inconsequential. But other days (perhaps when I've been woken hourly overnight) my kids are doomed due to my poor parenting.

Part of me envies anyone who isn't shackled by the guilt. But maybe I need to accept that it's part of who I am as a parent. And what's more, it's actually part of who I am as good parent. The things I question are important to me. They acknowledge that I'm not a perfect parent (and that's okay). And more important, I really, really care.

It would be nice if it were a bit less cumbersome, but I'll keep on carrying it with me. The last thing I need is guilt about the guilt. I draw the line there.

MENTAL HEALTH IS...

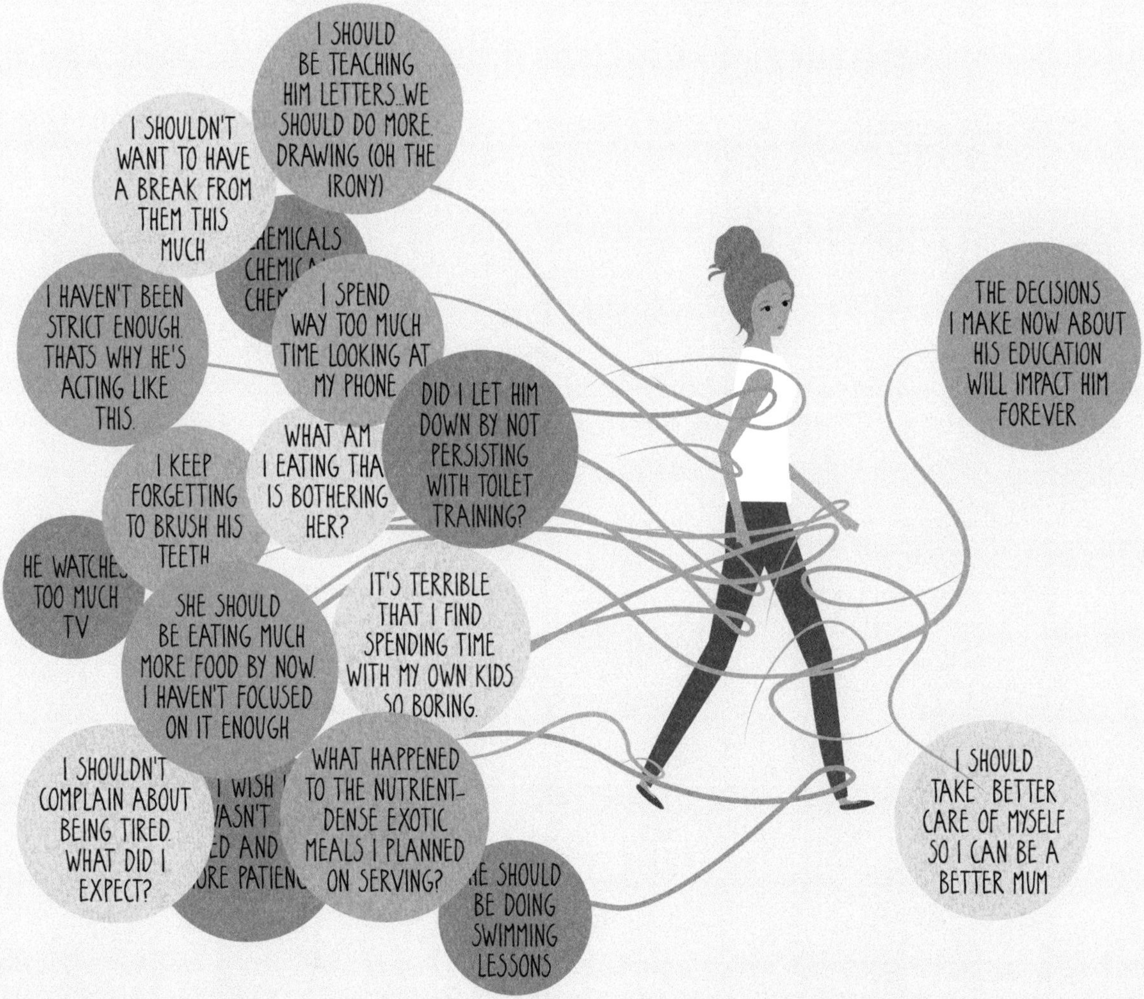
I SHOULD BE TEACHING HIM LETTERS...WE SHOULD DO MORE DRAWING (OH THE IRONY)
I SHOULDN'T WANT TO HAVE A BREAK FROM THEM THIS MUCH
I HAVEN'T BEEN STRICT ENOUGH. THATS WHY HE'S ACTING LIKE THIS.
I SPEND WAY TOO MUCH TIME LOOKING AT MY PHONE
DID I LET HIM DOWN BY NOT PERSISTING WITH TOILET TRAINING?
THE DECISIONS I MAKE NOW ABOUT HIS EDUCATION WILL IMPACT HIM FOREVER
I KEEP FORGETTING TO BRUSH HIS TEETH
TOO MUCH TV
SHE SHOULD BE EATING MUCH MORE FOOD BY NOW. I HAVEN'T FOCUSED ON IT ENOUGH
IT'S TERRIBLE THAT I FIND SPENDING TIME WITH MY OWN KIDS SO BORING.
I SHOULDN'T COMPLAIN ABOUT BEING TIRED. WHAT DID I EXPECT?
WHAT HAPPENED TO THE NUTRIENT-DENSE EXOTIC MEALS I PLANNED ON SERVING?
BE DOING SWIMMING LESSONS
I SHOULD TAKE BETTER CARE OF MYSELF SO I CAN BE A BETTER MUM

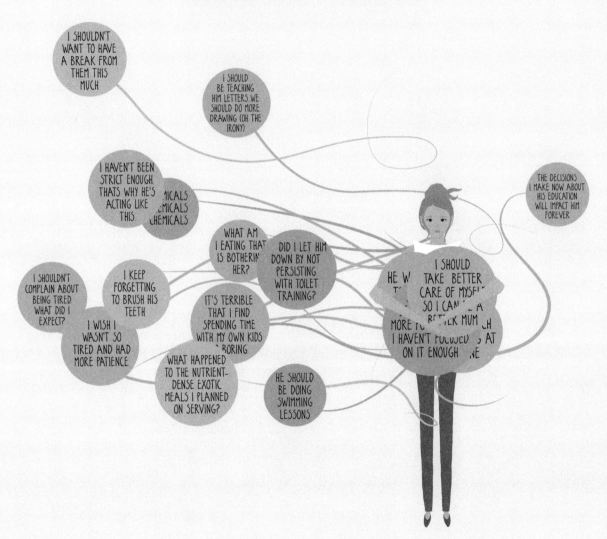

. . . AND KNOWING WHAT TO RELEASE.

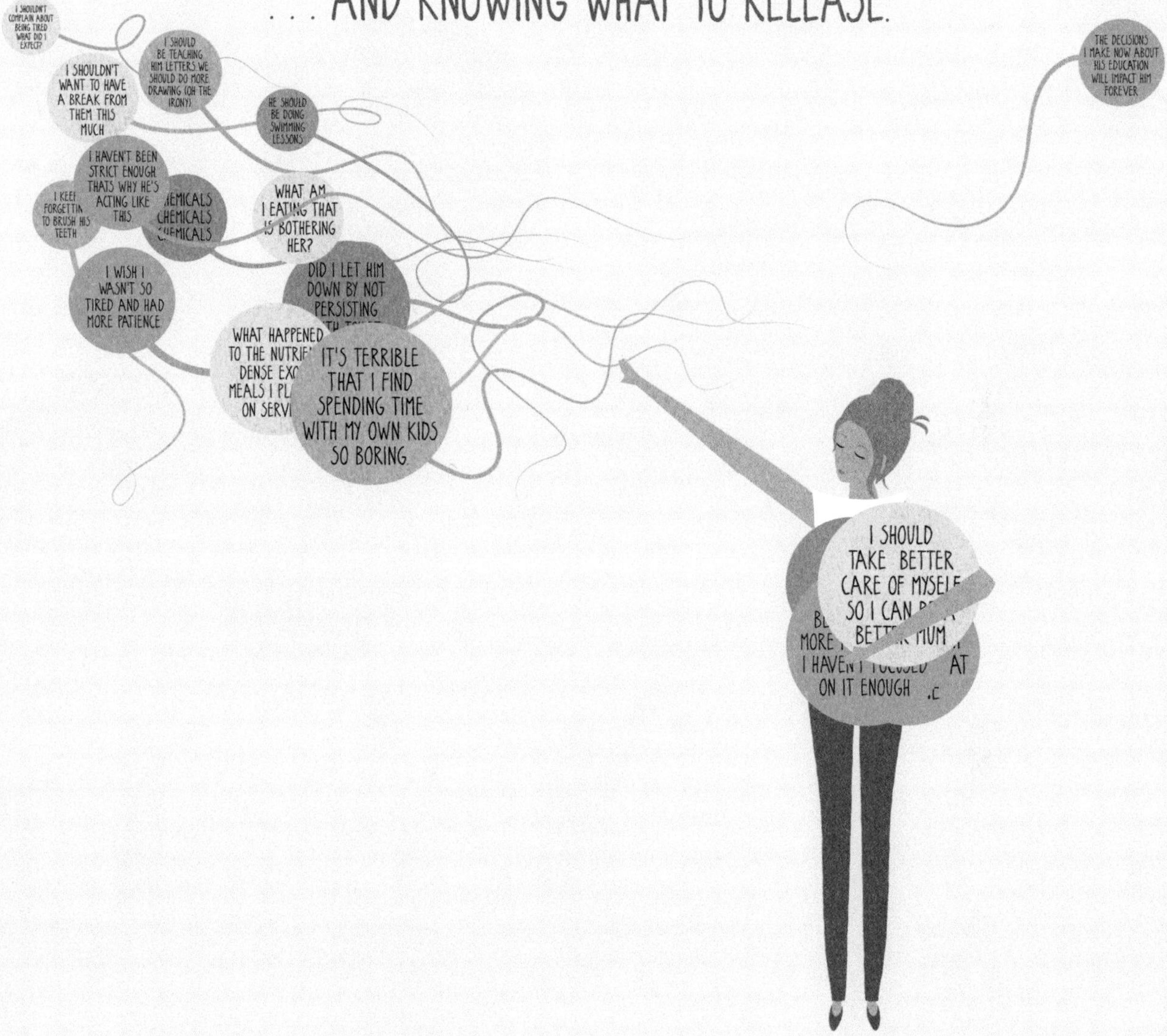

I SHOULDN'T COMPLAIN ABOUT BEING TIRED WHAT DID I EXPECT?
I SHOULD BE TEACHING HIM LETTERS WE SHOULD DO MORE DRAWING (OH THE IRONY)
I SHOULDN'T WANT TO HAVE A BREAK FROM THEM THIS MUCH
HE SHOULD BE DOING SWIMMING LESSONS
THE DECISIONS I MAKE NOW ABOUT HIS EDUCATION WILL IMPACT HIM FOREVER
I HAVEN'T BEEN STRICT ENOUGH THATS WHY HE'S ACTING LIKE THIS
WHAT AM I EATING THAT IS BOTHERING HER?
I WISH I WASN'T SO TIRED AND HAD MORE PATIENCE
IT'S TERRIBLE THAT I FIND SPENDING TIME WITH MY OWN KIDS SO BORING
I SHOULD TAKE BETTER CARE OF MYSELF
ON IT ENOUGH

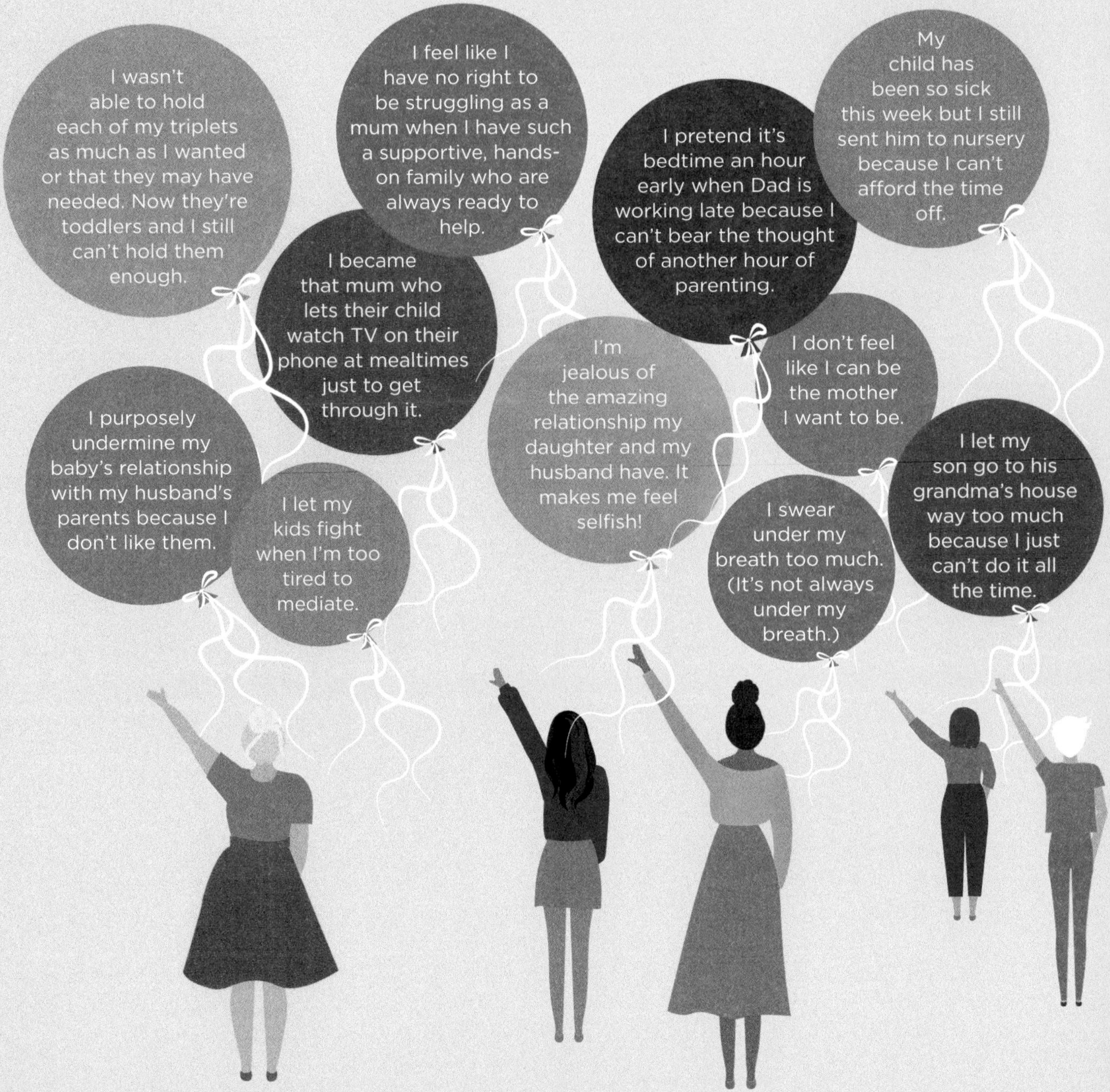
I wasn't able to hold each of my triplets as much as I wanted or that they may have needed. Now they're toddlers and I still can't hold them enough.
I feel like I have no right to be struggling as a mum when I have such a supportive, hands-on family who are always ready to help.
I pretend it's bedtime an hour early when Dad is working late because I can't bear the thought of another hour of parenting.
My child has been so sick this week but I still sent him to nursery because I can't afford the time off.
I became that mum who lets their child watch TV on their phone at mealtimes just to get through it.
I'm jealous of the amazing relationship my daughter and my husband have. It makes me feel selfish!
I don't feel like I can be the mother I want to be.
I purposely undermine my baby's relationship with my husband's parents because I don't like them.
I let my kids fight when I'm too tired to mediate.
I swear under my breath too much. (It's not always under my breath.)
I let my son go to his grandma's house way too much because I just can't do it all the time.

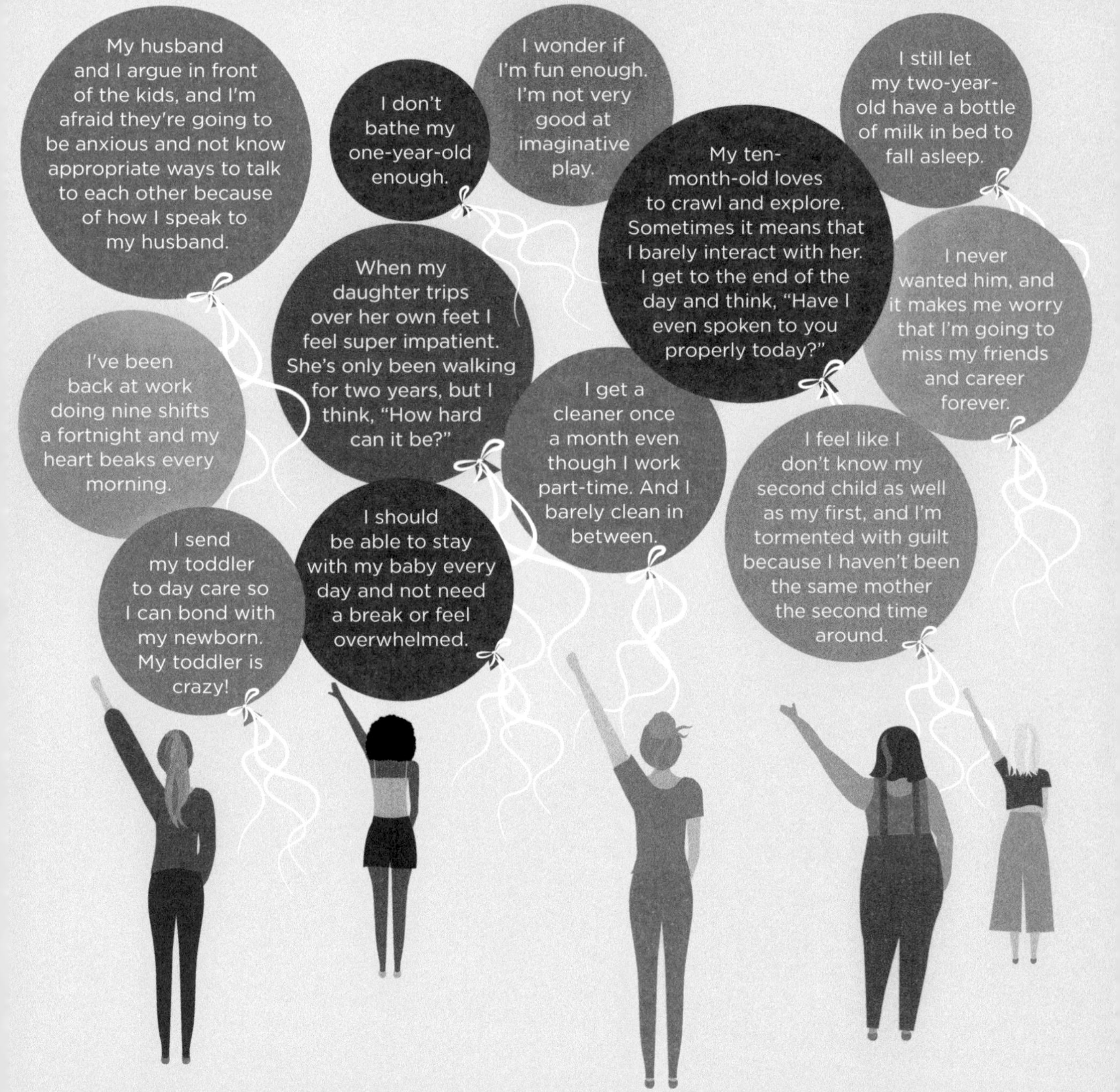
My husband and I argue in front of the kids, and I'm afraid they're going to be anxious and not know appropriate ways to talk to each other because of how I speak to my husband.
I don't bathe my one-year-old enough.
I wonder if I'm fun enough. I'm not very good at imaginative play.
I still let my two-year-old have a bottle of milk in bed to fall asleep.
My ten-month-old loves to crawl and explore. Sometimes it means that I barely interact with her. I get to the end of the day and think, "Have I even spoken to you properly today?"
When my daughter trips over her own feet I feel super impatient. She's only been walking for two years, but I think, "How hard can it be?"
I never wanted him, and it makes me worry that I'm going to miss my friends and career forever.
I've been back at work doing nine shifts a fortnight and my heart beaks every morning.
I get a cleaner once a month even though I work part-time. And I barely clean in between.
I feel like I don't know my second child as well as my first, and I'm tormented with guilt because I haven't been the same mother the second time around.
I should be able to stay with my baby every day and not need a break or feel overwhelmed.
I send my toddler to day care so I can bond with my newborn. My toddler is crazy!

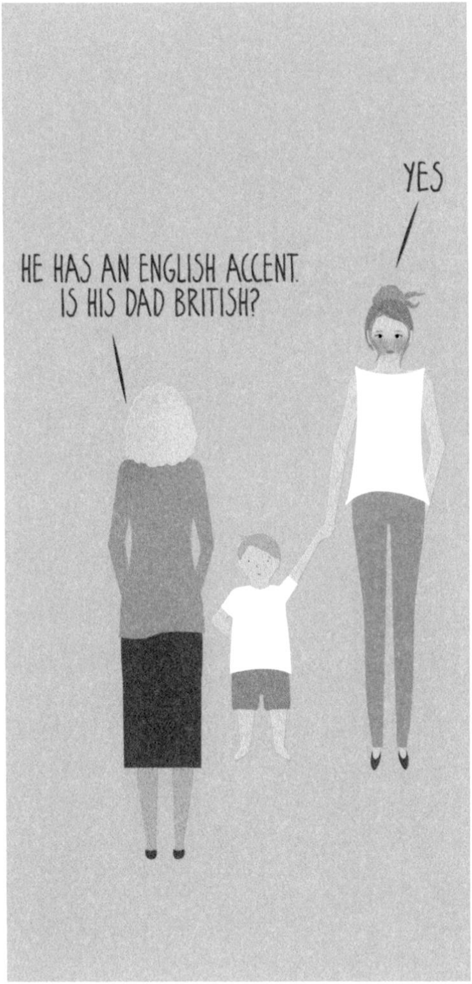
HE HAS AN ENGLISH ACCENT.
IS HIS DAD BRITISH?
YES
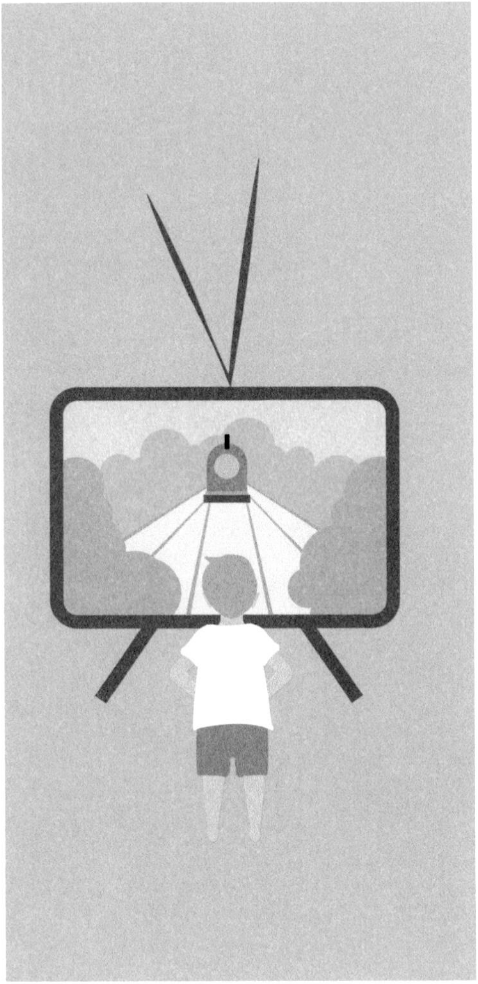

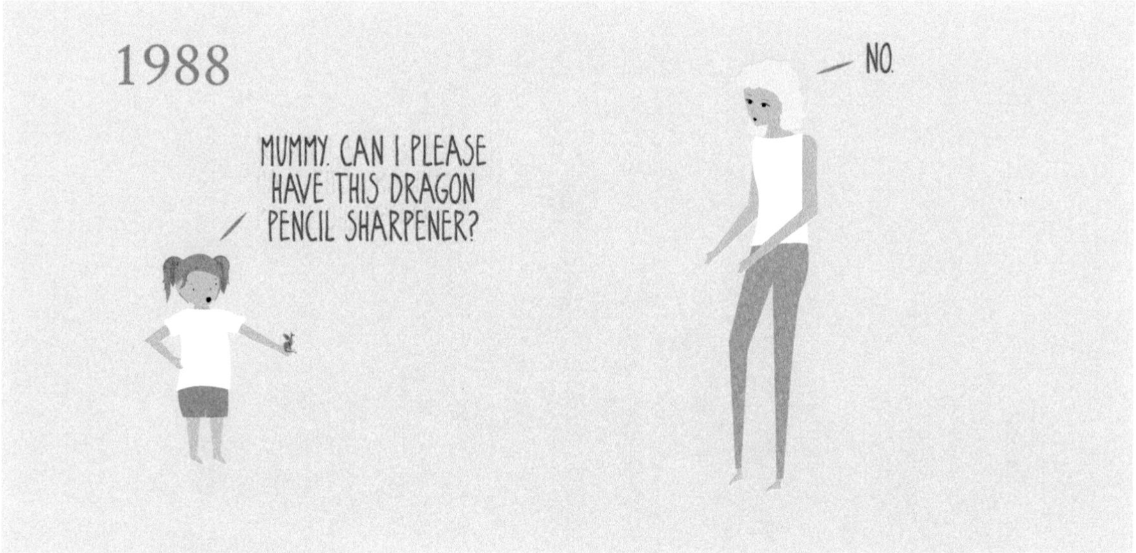
1988
MUMMY, CAN I PLEASE HAVE THIS DRAGON PENCIL SHARPENER?
NO.

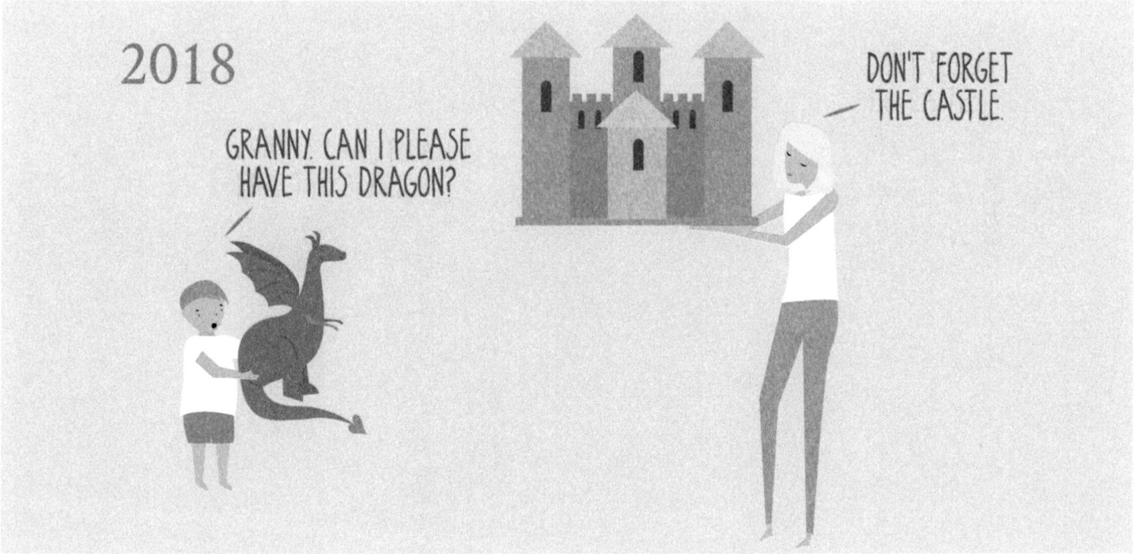
2018
GRANNY, CAN I PLEASE HAVE THIS DRAGON?
DON'T FORGET THE CASTLE.

BALANCE

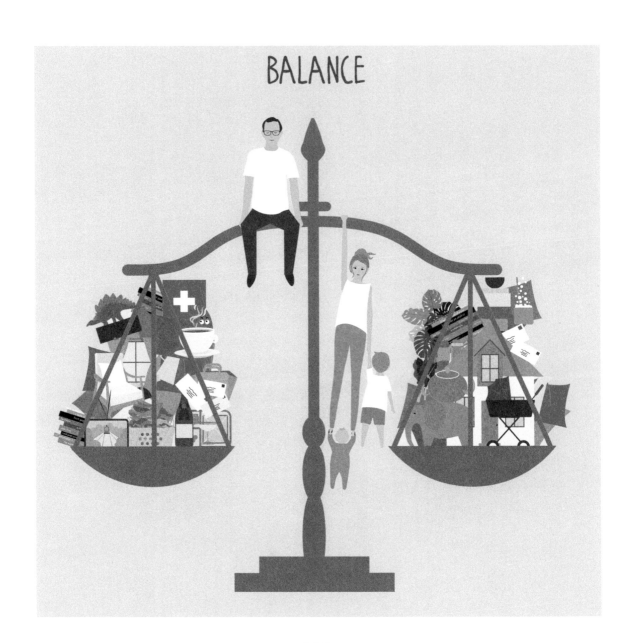

Balance. This is how I feel about it. The word makes me feel uncomfortable. I don't have it. I don't want it. I'm not sure if it even exists.

Balance implies you can easily compartmentalise your life into neat packages that sit politely on scales in perfect harmony. But you can't neatly compartmentalise your life. Have you met a three-year-old? They aren't easily boxed up. And there is nothing neat about running a business from home while trying to keep a family afloat.

And for the most part, I love that. It's messy. It's chaotic. It's very, very busy. Ideas come to me in the middle of the night. I never stop thinking about new drawings I want to do. I scribble down notes at the dining table while my children finish their dinner. I'm always discussing new project ideas with anyone who will listen. I want my children to watch their mother working hard at something she absolutely loves. Passion is contagious.

If I was striving for balance, I would no doubt feel like I was failing at every aspect of my life. And while occasionally I'm swept up in those feelings, the reality is, I'm not. I'm creating an awesomely intermingled jigsaw puzzle of "work" and "life" and I don't know where when one ends and the next begins. And that's exactly how I want it to be.

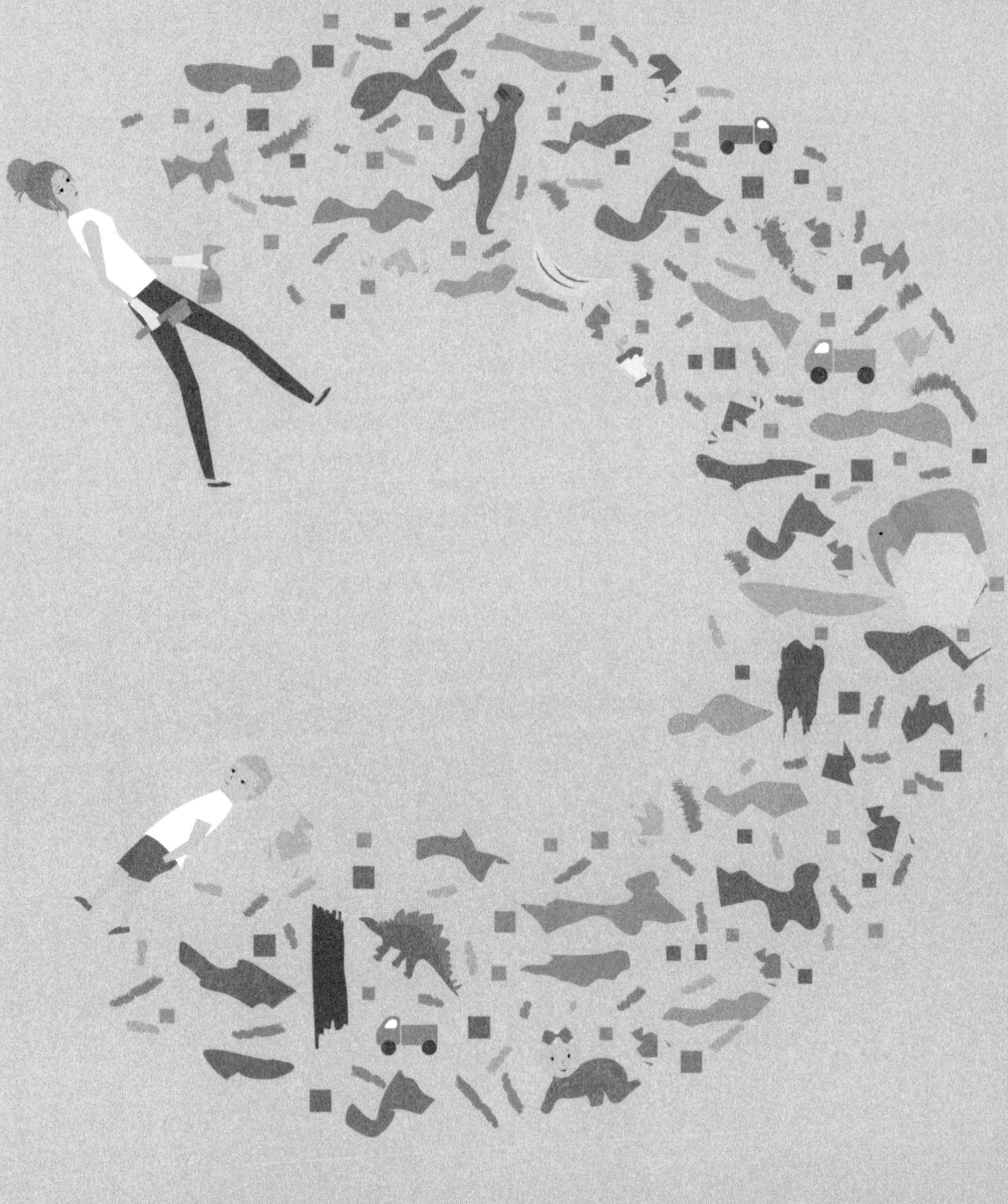

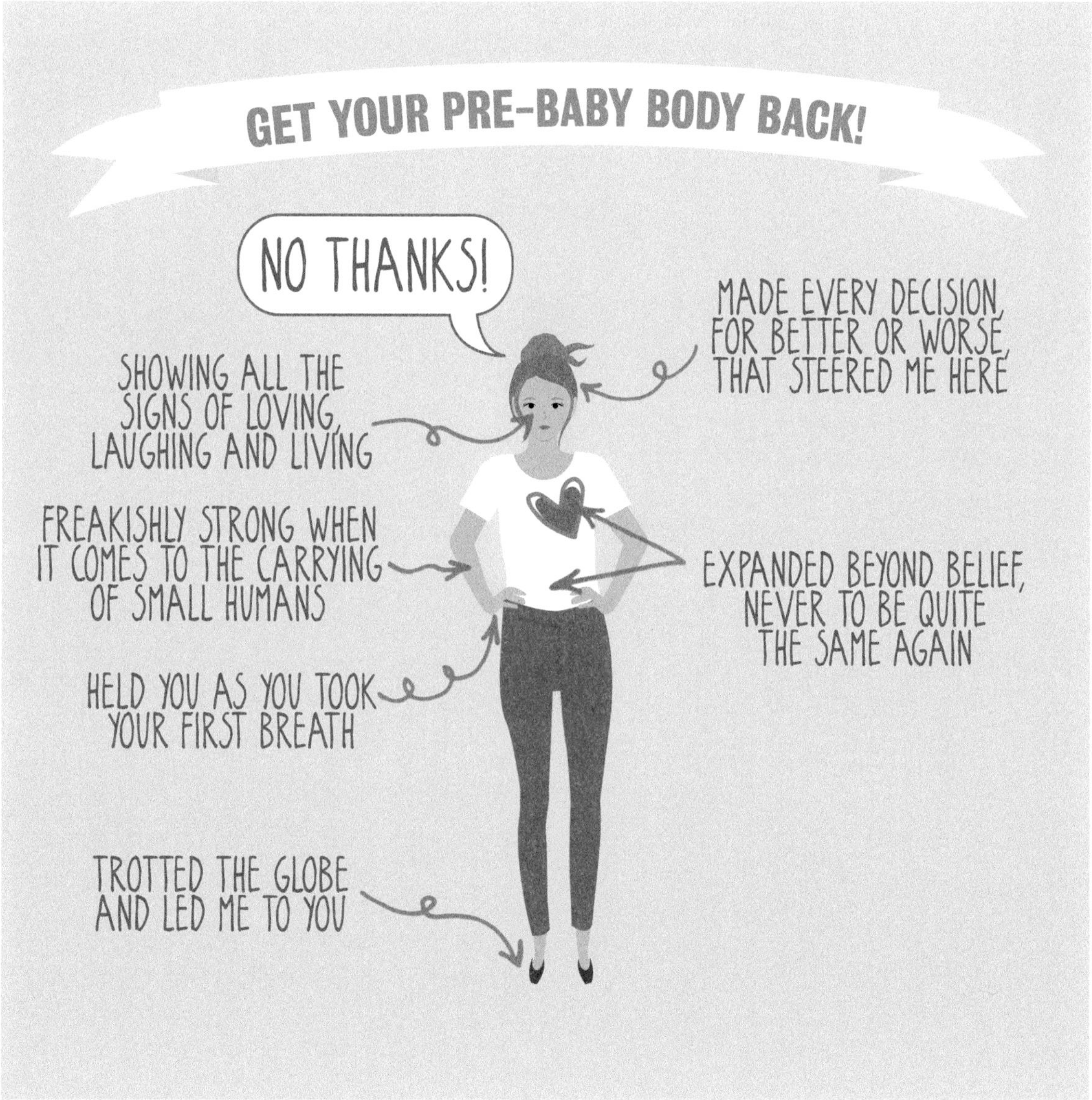
GET YOUR PRE-BABY BODY BACK!
NO THANKS!
SHOWING ALL THE SIGNS OF LOVING, LAUGHING AND LIVING
MADE EVERY DECISION, FOR BETTER OR WORSE, THAT STEERED ME HERE
FREAKISHLY STRONG WHEN IT COMES TO THE CARRYING OF SMALL HUMANS
EXPANDED BEYOND BELIEF, NEVER TO BE QUITE THE SAME AGAIN
HELD YOU AS YOU TOOK YOUR FIRST BREATH
TROTTED THE GLOBE AND LED ME TO YOU

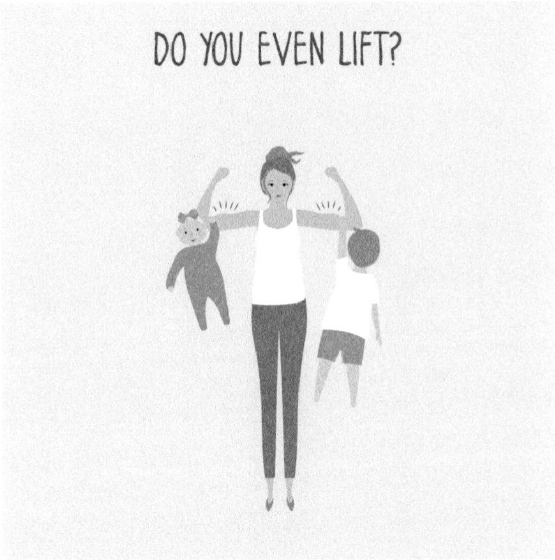
DO YOU EVEN LIFT?

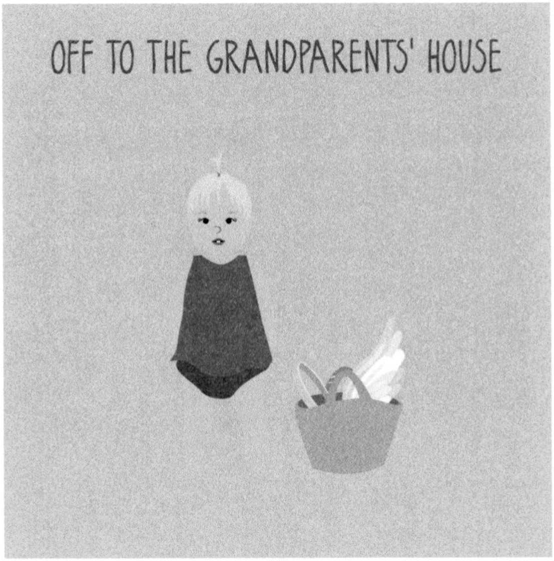
OFF TO THE GRANDPARENTS' HOUSE

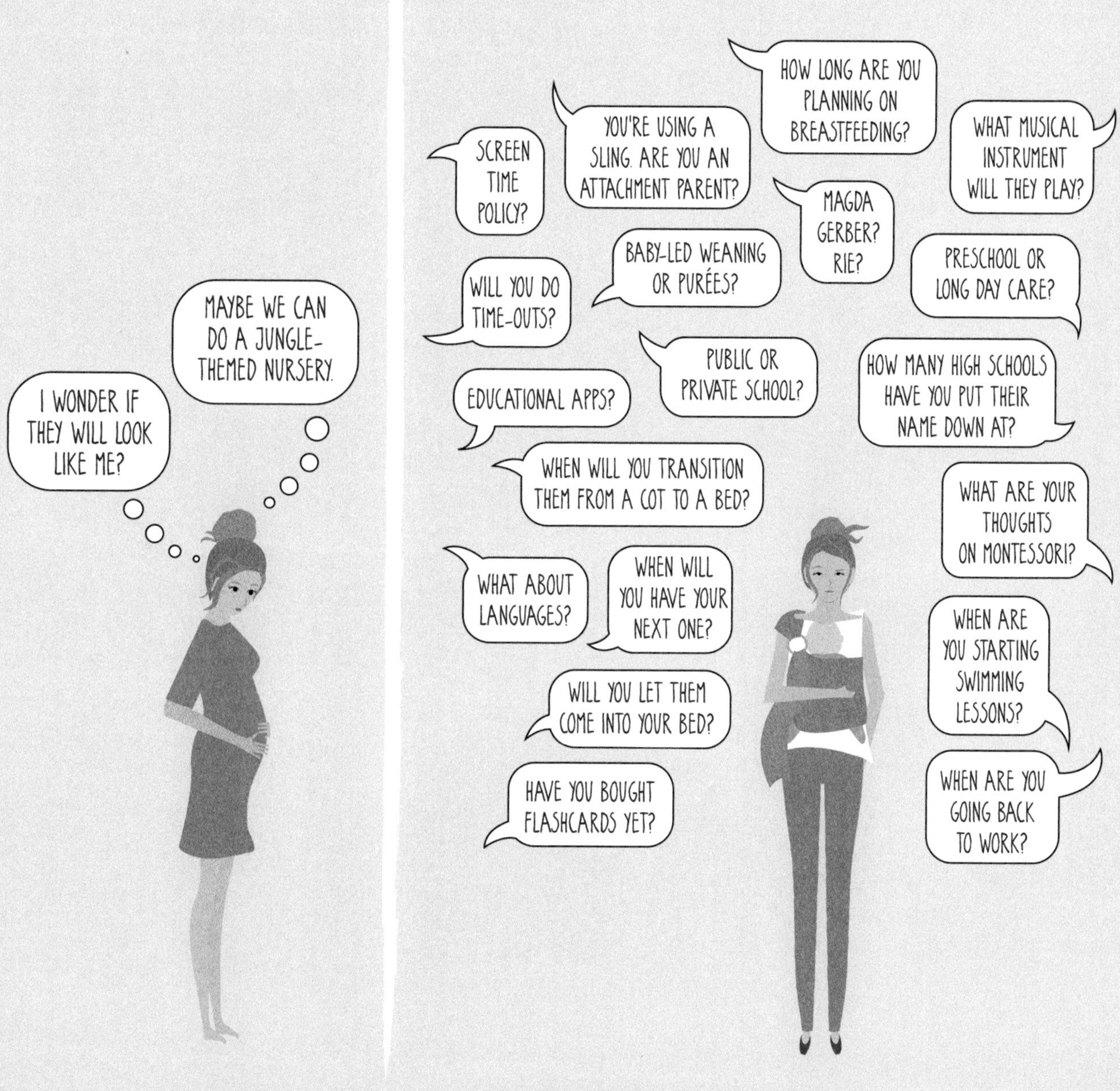
I WONDER IF THEY WILL LOOK LIKE ME?
MAYBE WE CAN DO A JUNGLE-THEMED NURSERY.
HOW LONG ARE YOU PLANNING ON BREASTFEEDING?
YOU'RE USING A SLING. ARE YOU AN ATTACHMENT PARENT?
WHAT MUSICAL INSTRUMENT WILL THEY PLAY?
SCREEN TIME POLICY?
MAGDA GERBER? RIE?
BABY-LED WEANING OR PURÉES?
PRESCHOOL OR LONG DAY CARE?
WILL YOU DO TIME-OUTS?
PUBLIC OR PRIVATE SCHOOL?
HOW MANY HIGH SCHOOLS HAVE YOU PUT THEIR NAME DOWN AT?
EDUCATIONAL APPS?
WHEN WILL YOU TRANSITION THEM FROM A COT TO A BED?
WHAT ARE YOUR THOUGHTS ON MONTESSORI?
WHAT ABOUT LANGUAGES?
WHEN WILL YOU HAVE YOUR NEXT ONE?
WHEN ARE YOU STARTING SWIMMING LESSONS?
WILL YOU LET THEM COME INTO YOUR BED?
HAVE YOU BOUGHT FLASHCARDS YET?
WHEN ARE YOU GOING BACK TO WORK?

THINGS I CAN DO WITH A BABY ON MY HIP

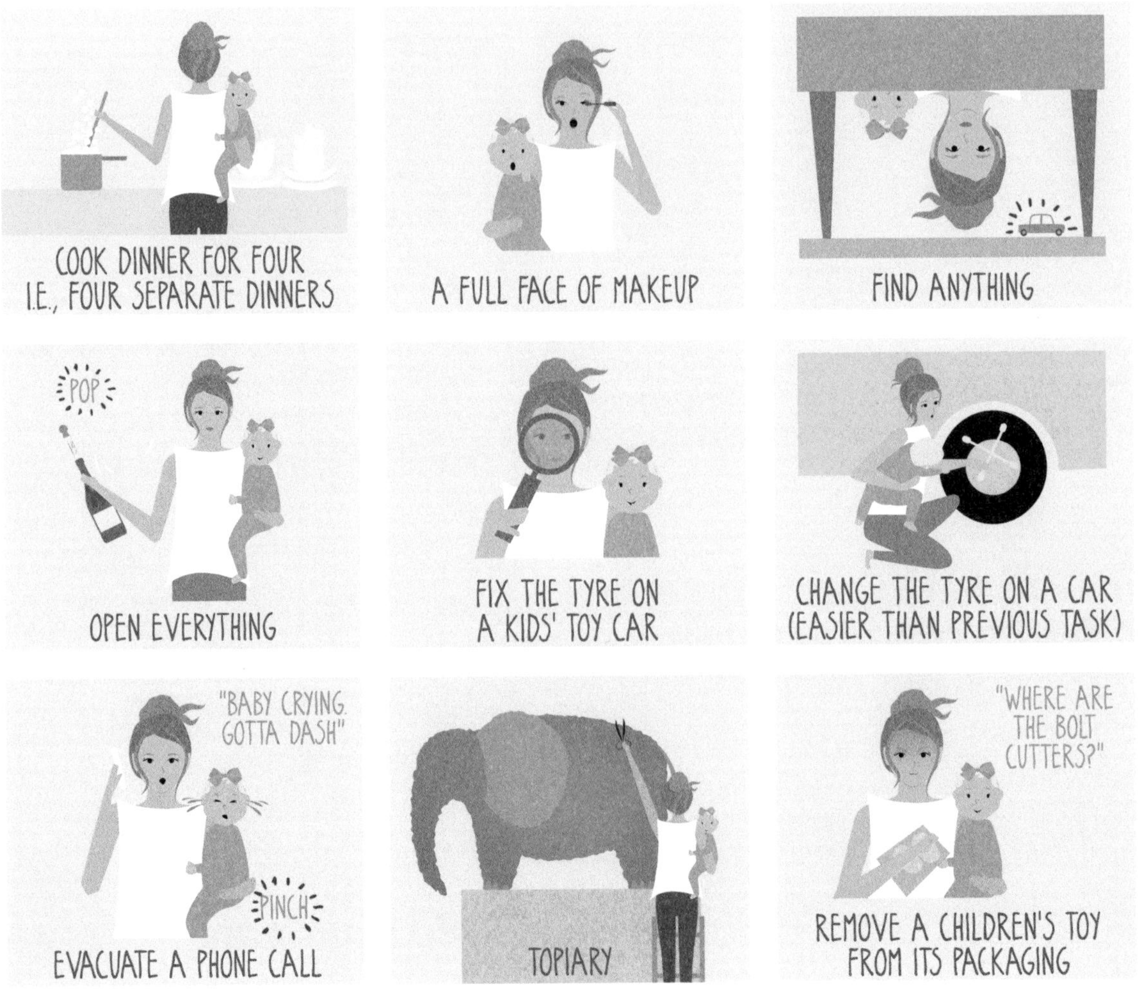
COOK DINNER FOR FOUR
I.E., FOUR SEPARATE DINNERS
A FULL FACE OF MAKEUP
FIND ANYTHING
POP
OPEN EVERYTHING
FIX THE TYRE ON
A KIDS' TOY CAR
CHANGE THE TYRE ON A CAR
(EASIER THAN PREVIOUS TASK)
"BABY CRYING.
GOTTA DASH"
PINCH
EVACUATE A PHONE CALL
TOPIARY
"WHERE ARE
THE BOLT
CUTTERS?"
REMOVE A CHILDREN'S TOY
FROM ITS PACKAGING

THOUGHTS I HAVE AT THE PLAYGROUND

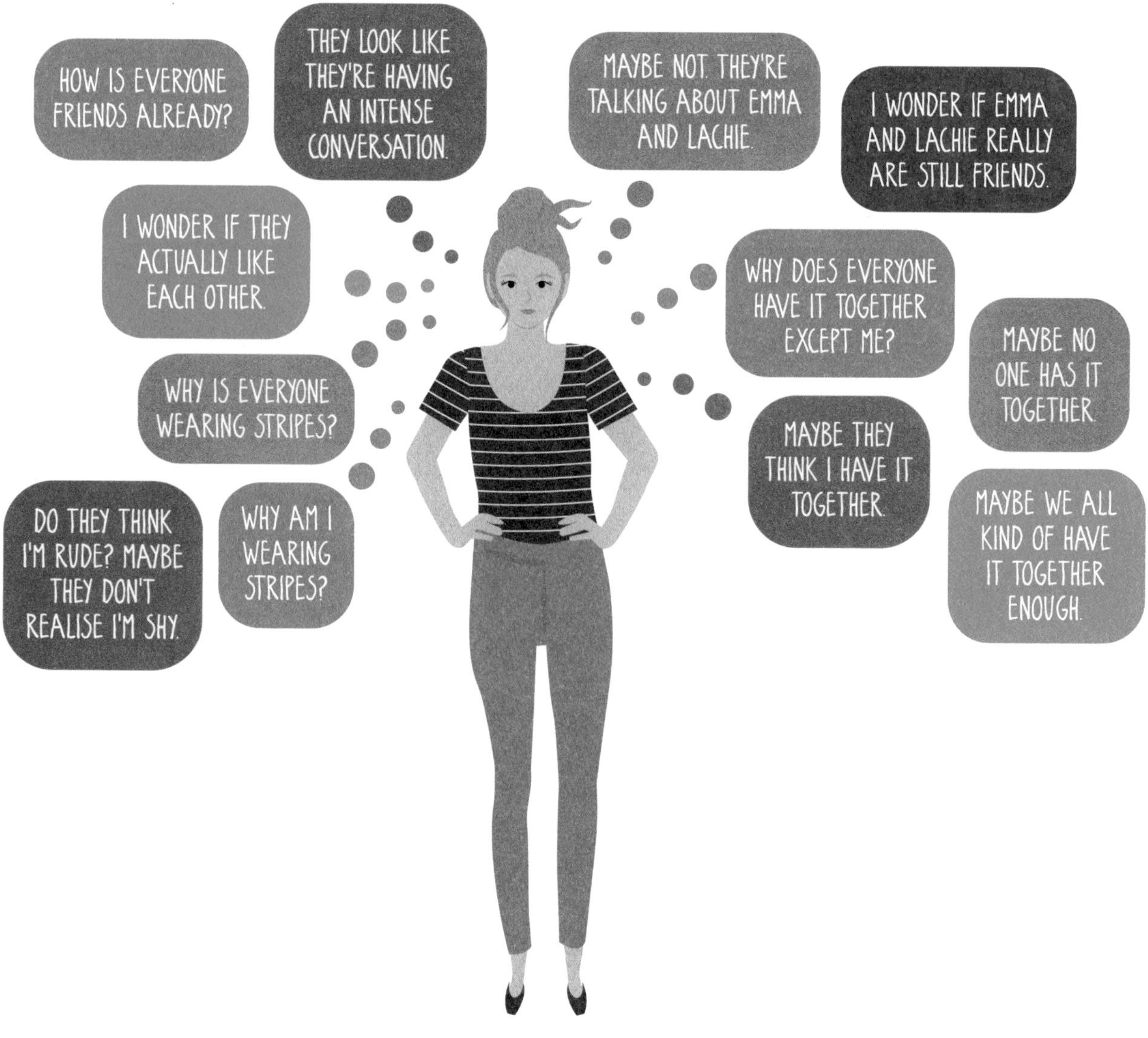
HOW IS EVERYONE FRIENDS ALREADY?
THEY LOOK LIKE THEY'RE HAVING AN INTENSE CONVERSATION.
MAYBE NOT. THEY'RE TALKING ABOUT EMMA AND LACHIE.
I WONDER IF EMMA AND LACHIE REALLY ARE STILL FRIENDS.
I WONDER IF THEY ACTUALLY LIKE EACH OTHER.
WHY DOES EVERYONE HAVE IT TOGETHER EXCEPT ME?
MAYBE NO ONE HAS IT TOGETHER.
WHY IS EVERYONE WEARING STRIPES?
MAYBE THEY THINK I HAVE IT TOGETHER.
MAYBE WE ALL KIND OF HAVE IT TOGETHER ENOUGH.
DO THEY THINK I'M RUDE? MAYBE THEY DON'T REALISE I'M SHY.
WHY AM I WEARING STRIPES?

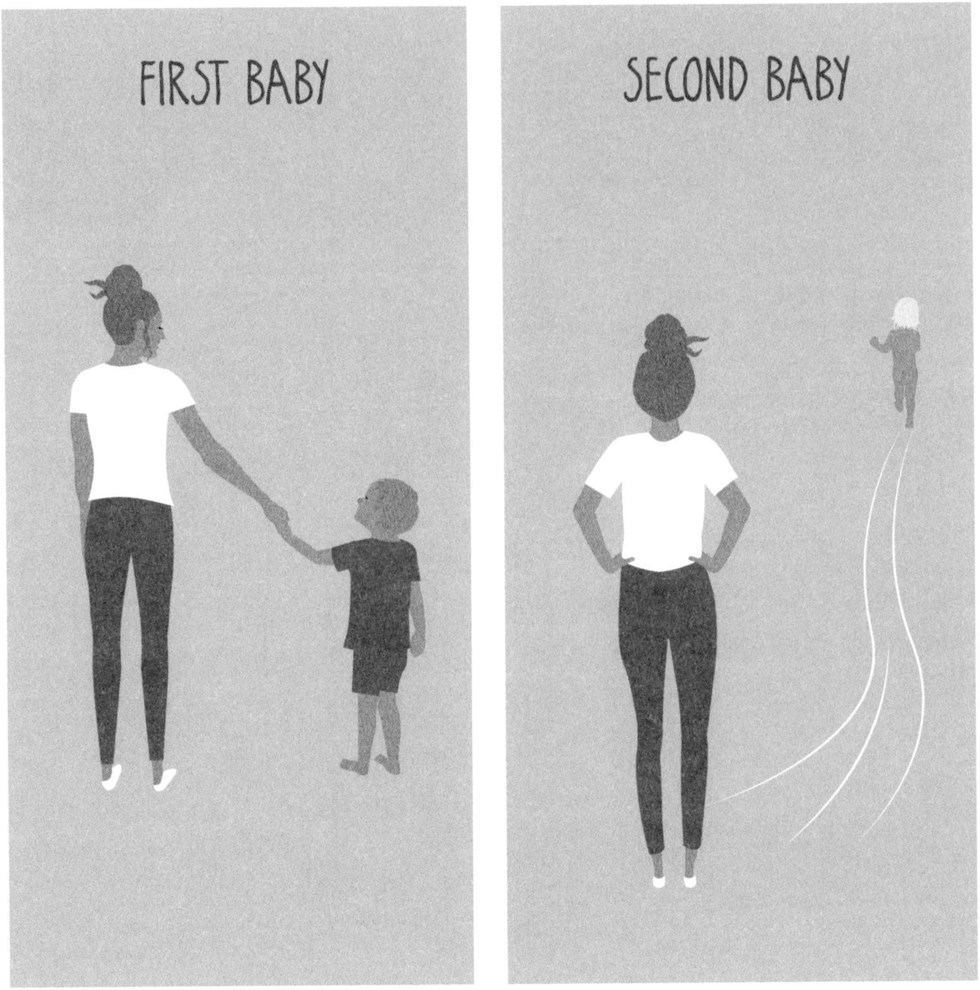
FIRST BABY
SECOND BABY

REFLECTING ON BIRTH ORDER

My two children neatly fall into the "first child" and "second child" stereotypes. My oldest is cautious, sensitive, conservative and a perfectionist. First children are statistically more likely to be leaders. His birth "required assistance," and requiring assistance would be a good way to describe everything he has done ever since. My second-born is daring and independent. She came into the world without much of a fuss, practically delivering herself, and has been busy trying to make everyone obsolete ever since. She is, apparently, more likely to be a criminal.

It's no great surprise that my children possess these traits given how differently they were parented in the first few years of their life. As a first-time mum I was a thorough researcher and strategic planner. I cooked organic food from scratch. I sprouted legumes, fermented cabbage and milked almonds. I have no doubt I was utterly insufferable to someone with less enthusiasm for the relative digestibility of various ancient grains. I was never intentionally righteous, but I was at home for long days with a baby I couldn't control, so I desperately tried to gain control of the things I could.

This enthusiasm well and truly evaporated when I was finding my feet as a mum of two. My daughter had her first glorious taste of hot chips long before she turned one. It may have been a dramatic fall off my high horse, but I was too sleep-deprived and busy to even notice.

Bedtime for baby number one was calm and ritualistic. Dressed in organic, merino pyjamas with tinkly, tinkly music playing in a dimly lit room, he was read to, sung to, cuddled, fed and finally placed in a cot where I waited with my hand resting on him until he was fast asleep. My daughter wore the same organic, merino pyjamas, two sizes too big for her and threadbare by this stage. I held her with one arm and breastfed her under a fluorescent light while coaxing her big brother into eating his dinner, then casually flung her into her cot before running back to make sure the house hadn't been disassembled in my absence.

Just as I love both my children for all their differences, I have a special place in my heart for the two extremes of motherhood I represented at those various stages. After all, the future of the world depends on sensitive, compassionate leaders and bold, brave rebels.

CREATIVE GAMES FOR LAZY DAYS

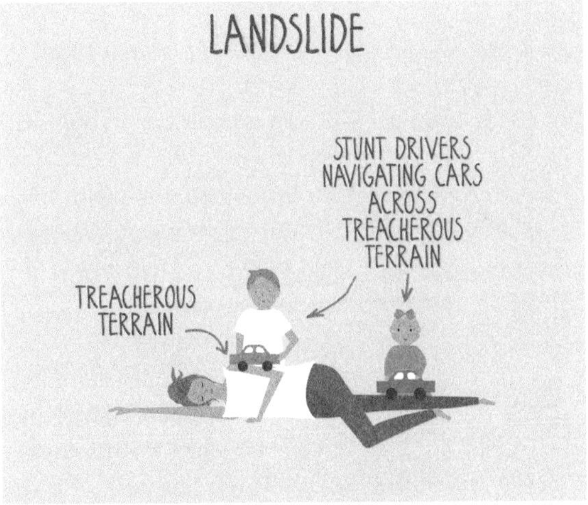
LANDSLIDE
STUNT DRIVERS NAVIGATING CARS ACROSS TREACHEROUS TERRAIN
TREACHEROUS TERRAIN

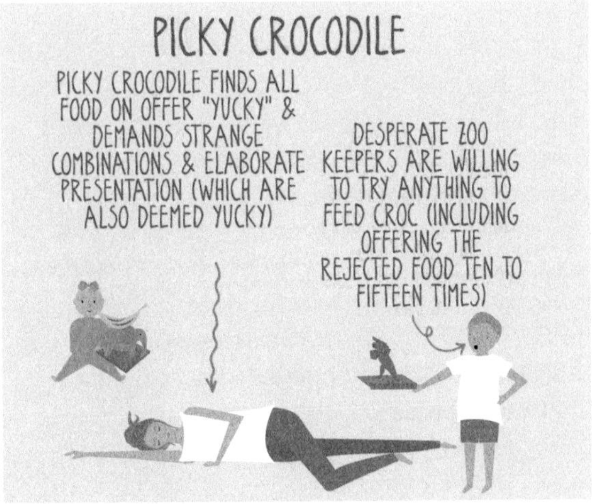
PICKY CROCODILE
PICKY CROCODILE FINDS ALL FOOD ON OFFER "YUCKY" & DEMANDS STRANGE COMBINATIONS & ELABORATE PRESENTATION (WHICH ARE ALSO DEEMED YUCKY)
DESPERATE ZOO KEEPERS ARE WILLING TO TRY ANYTHING TO FEED CROC (INCLUDING OFFERING THE REJECTED FOOD TEN TO FIFTEEN TIMES)

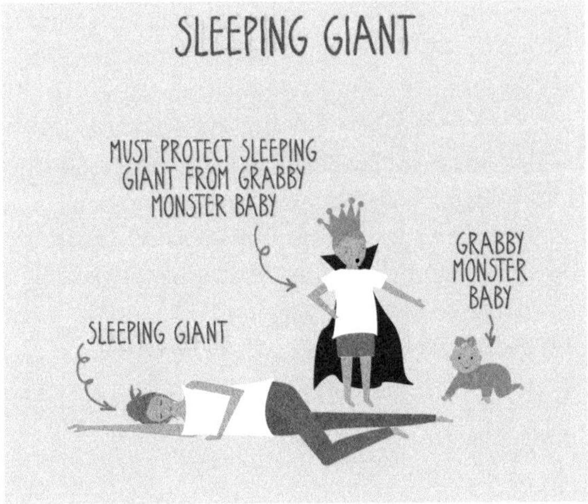
SLEEPING GIANT
MUST PROTECT SLEEPING GIANT FROM GRABBY MONSTER BABY
GRABBY MONSTER BABY
SLEEPING GIANT

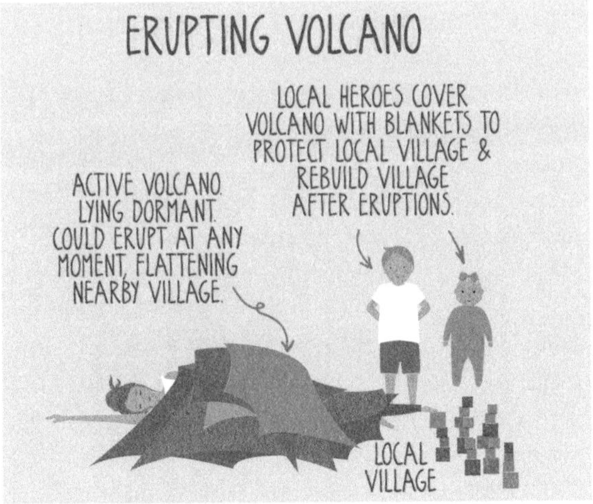
ERUPTING VOLCANO
LOCAL HEROES COVER VOLCANO WITH BLANKETS TO PROTECT LOCAL VILLAGE & REBUILD VILLAGE AFTER ERUPTIONS.
ACTIVE VOLCANO. LYING DORMANT. COULD ERUPT AT ANY MOMENT, FLATTENING NEARBY VILLAGE.
LOCAL VILLAGE

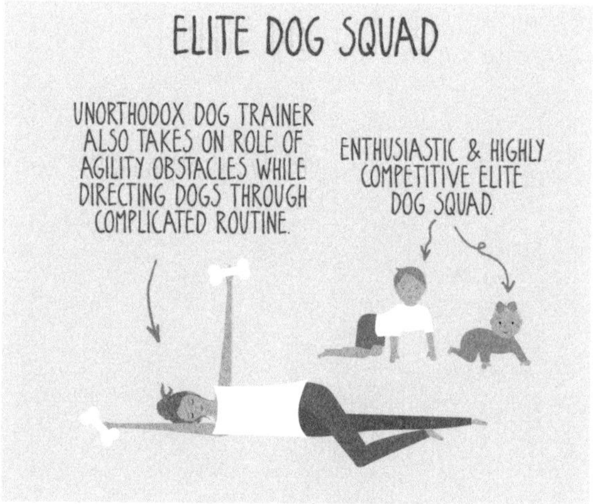
ELITE DOG SQUAD
UNORTHODOX DOG TRAINER ALSO TAKES ON ROLE OF AGILITY OBSTACLES WHILE DIRECTING DOGS THROUGH COMPLICATED ROUTINE.
ENTHUSIASTIC & HIGHLY COMPETITIVE ELITE DOG SQUAD.

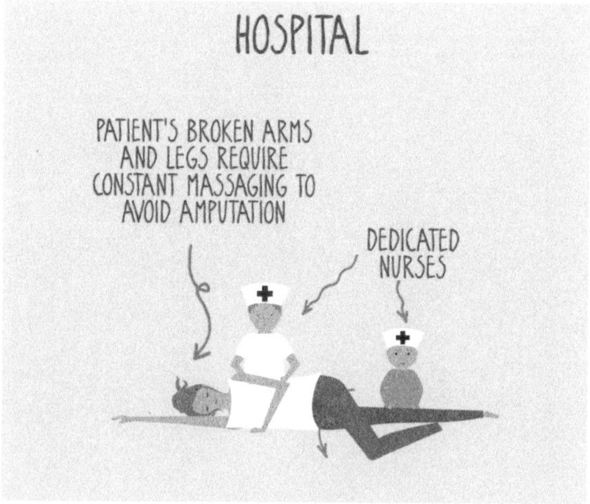
HOSPITAL
PATIENT'S BROKEN ARMS AND LEGS REQUIRE CONSTANT MASSAGING TO AVOID AMPUTATION
DEDICATED NURSES

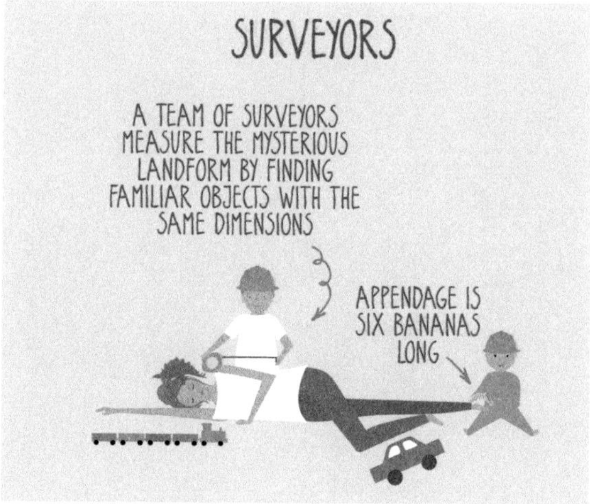
SURVEYORS
A TEAM OF SURVEYORS MEASURE THE MYSTERIOUS LANDFORM BY FINDING FAMILIAR OBJECTS WITH THE SAME DIMENSIONS
APPENDAGE IS SIX BANANAS LONG

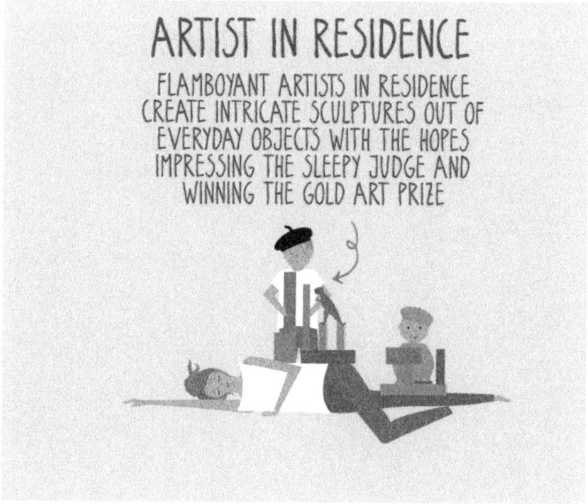
ARTIST IN RESIDENCE
FLAMBOYANT ARTISTS IN RESIDENCE CREATE INTRICATE SCULPTURES OUT OF EVERYDAY OBJECTS WITH THE HOPES IMPRESSING THE SLEEPY JUDGE AND WINNING THE GOLD ART PRIZE

MUMMY . . . CARRY THIS LEAF?

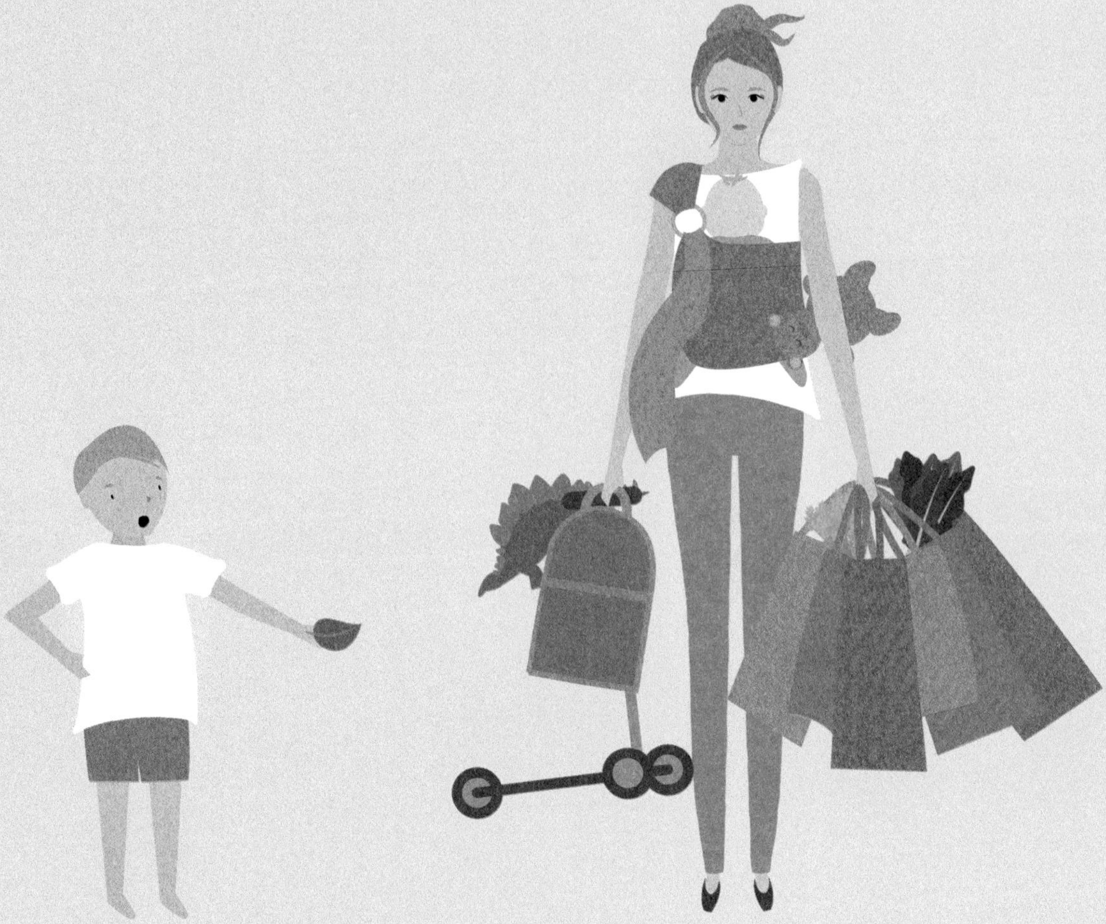

CHECKLIST FOR LEAVING THE HOUSE

- ● Keys
- ● Phone
- ● Wallet

YOU'RE GOOD TO GO.
MWAHAHAHAHAHA NOT SO FAST, MAMA. THOSE WERE THE DAYS.

- ● **HEAD COUNT:** Count the number of humans coming with you. Keep a note of this number. You will need to refer back to this later in the day.

- ● **SHOES:** Does everyone have a pair on? Yep, even you. Look down. Actually check.

- ● **SNACKS:** Yes, I know there will be a café there. Pack snacks. **Pack all the snacks.**

- ● **WATER BOTTLES:** The **approved** bottles (for god's sake, please don't take the **wrong** bottles!).

- ● **TOILET:** Has everyone who can use a toilet used one in the last ten minutes? Including you **(especially you!).**

- ● **NAPPIES:** For everyone else. Enough to last consecutive nappy explosions from the time you leave till the time you return home.

- ● **WIPES:** For nappy changes, snot wiping, food mess, drink spills, biohazardous waste cleanup and nuclear meltdown.

- ● **ALL-WEATHER GEAR:** Suitable apparel should you encounter: searing-hot sunshine, torrential rain, gale-force winds, hail, sleet, snow, cyclone, earthquake, meteor shower.

- ● **CHANGE OF CLOTHES:** For everyone, should their outfit get covered in food, drink, vomit, poo, blood, mud or paint or be shredded by a wild mongoose.

- ● **MISCELLANOUS:** Toys, books, pencils, stickers, scooters, sporting equipment, protective gear, fire extinguisher, hunting apparatus, canoe.

- ● **BAND-AIDS:** Whatever you do, do not forget the Band-Aids.

AND THAT'S IT!

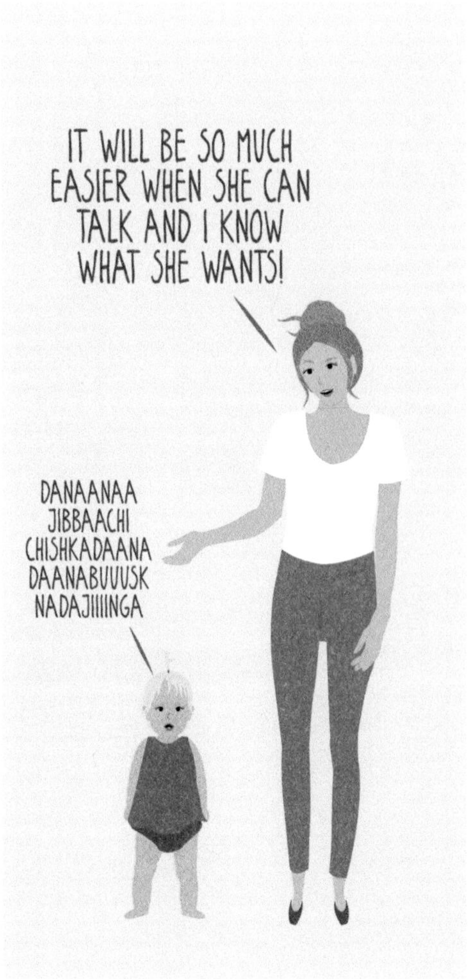
IT WILL BE SO MUCH EASIER WHEN SHE CAN TALK AND I KNOW WHAT SHE WANTS!
DANAANAA JIBBAACHI CHISHKADAANA DAANABUUUSK NADAJIIIINGA

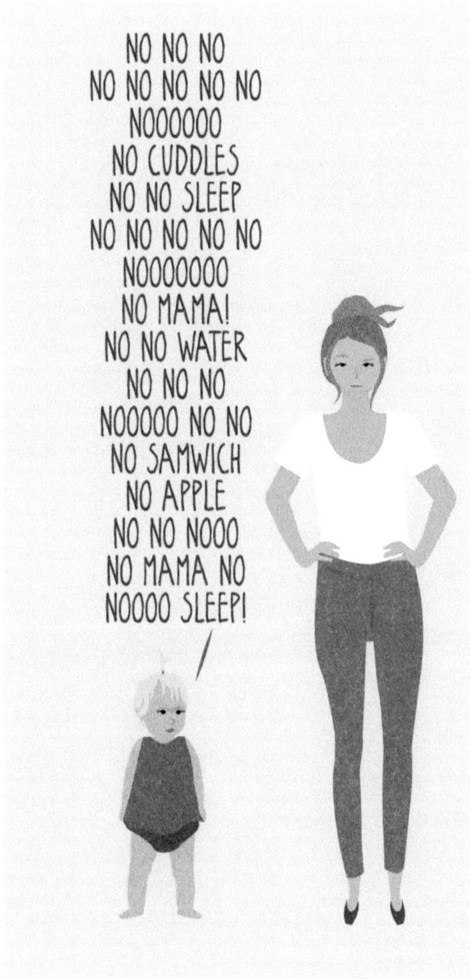
NO NO NO
NO NO NO NO NO
NOOOOOO
NO CUDDLES
NO NO SLEEP
NO NO NO NO NO
NOOOOOOO
NO MAMA!
NO NO WATER
NO NO NO
NOOOOO NO NO
NO SAMWICH
NO APPLE
NO NO NOOO
NO MAMA NO
NOOOO SLEEP!

HOW TO RAISE PLANET ALLIES

(WITHOUT TERRIFYING THEM)

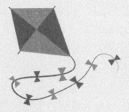

GET OUTSIDE.
WE NEED THEM TO LOVE WHAT WE WANT THEM TO DEFEND.

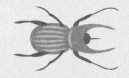

INVESTIGATE SOME OF OUR LESS CUTE CREATURES. SPARK THEIR CURIOSITY.

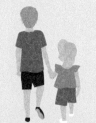

CHOOSE TO WALK SOMEWHERE INSTEAD OF DRIVING.

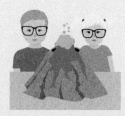

ENCOURAGE AN INTEREST IN SCIENCE SO THEY GROW UP TO ACCEPT AND RESPECT IT.

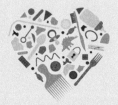

GO FOR A WALK ALONG THE BEACH OR IN THE BUSH AND PICK UP RUBBISH.

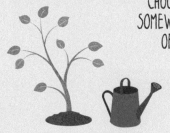

PLANT A TREE
TOGETHER FOR SOMEONE TO ENJOY IN TWENTY YEARS' TIME.

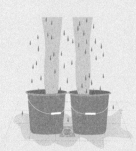

DEMONSTRATE WATER- AND ENERGY-SAVING BEHAVIOUR AS PART OF YOUR DAILY ROUTINE.

THIS IS OUR WORLD

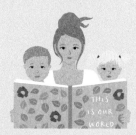

READ A BOOK WITH A MESSAGE OF COMPASSION, HOPE AND POSITIVE ACTION. BUY MULTIPLE COPIES AS GIFTS.

SARDINES

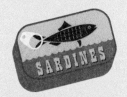

MAKE SOME SUSTAINABLE FOOD SWAPS AND BRIEFLY EXPLAIN WHY.

GARAGE SALE

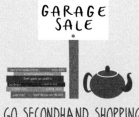

GO SECONDHAND SHOPPING TOGETHER.

THINGS THAT KEEP ME AWAKE AT NIGHT
(IN EQUAL MEASURE)

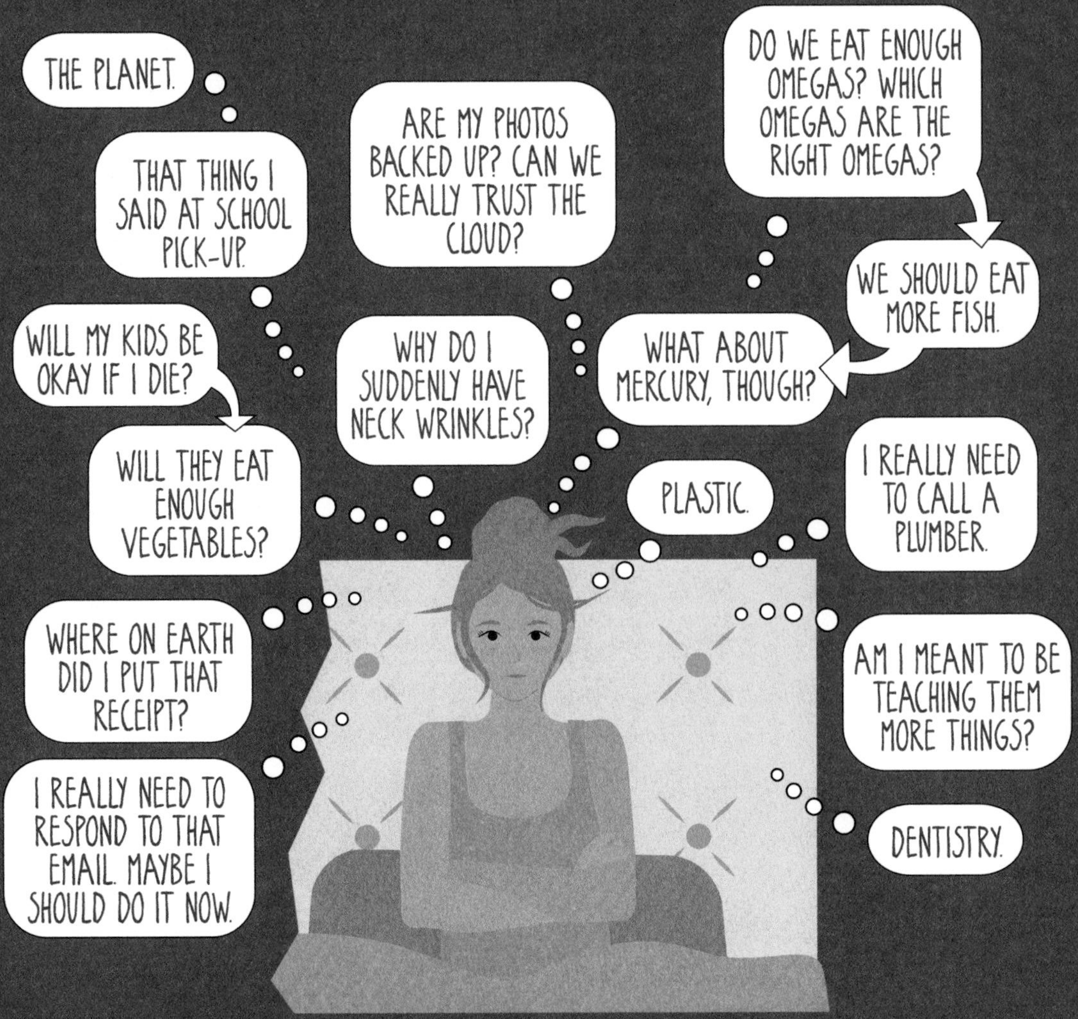

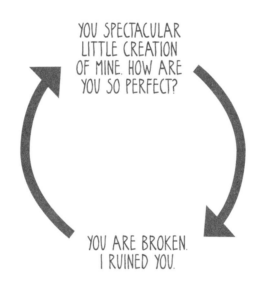

YOU SPECTACULAR
LITTLE CREATION
OF MINE. HOW ARE
YOU SO PERFECT?

YOU ARE BROKEN.
I RUINED YOU.

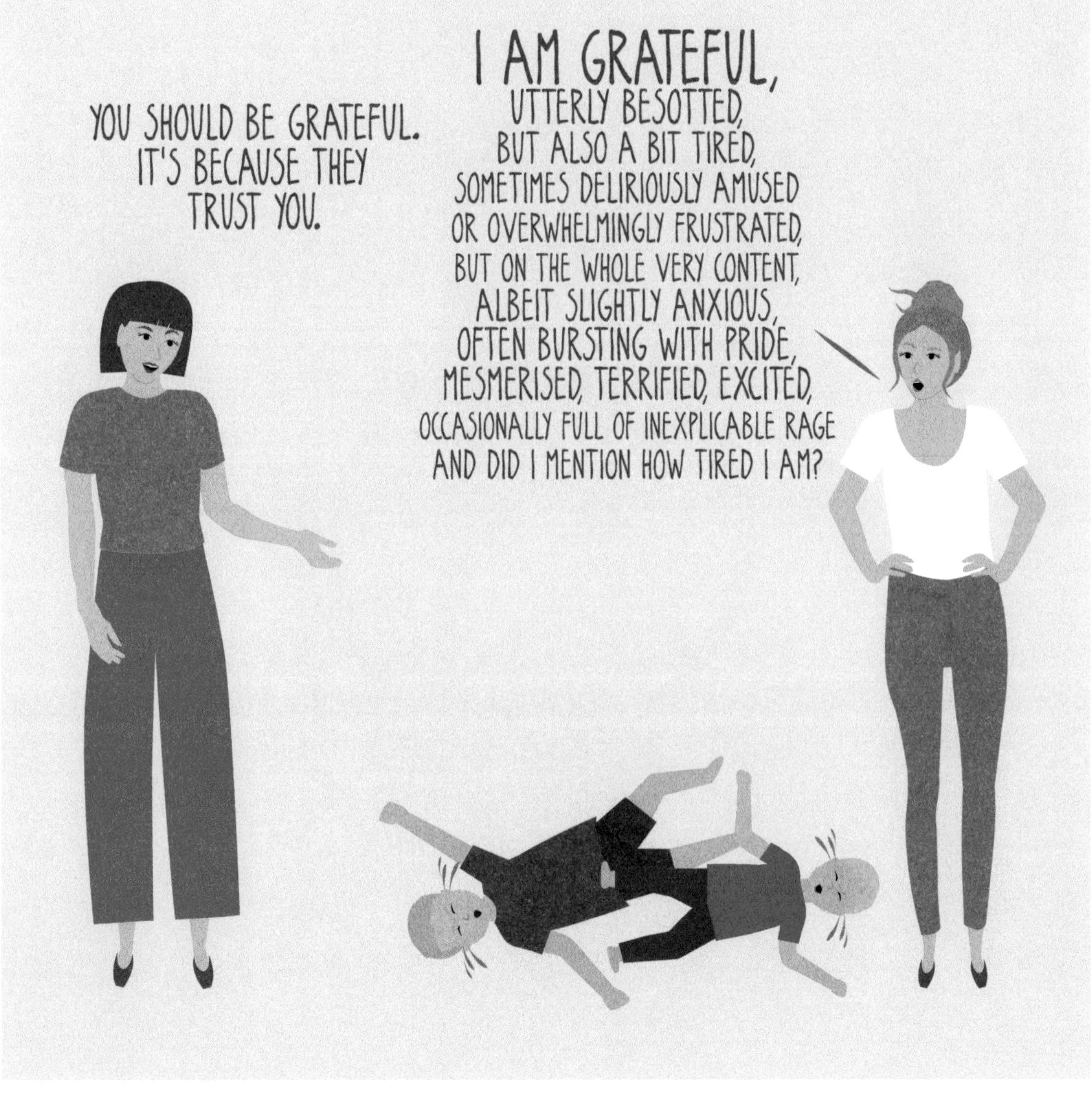
YOU SHOULD BE GRATEFUL. IT'S BECAUSE THEY TRUST YOU.
I AM GRATEFUL, UTTERLY BESOTTED, BUT ALSO A BIT TIRED, SOMETIMES DELIRIOUSLY AMUSED OR OVERWHELMINGLY FRUSTRATED, BUT ON THE WHOLE VERY CONTENT, ALBEIT SLIGHTLY ANXIOUS, OFTEN BURSTING WITH PRIDE, MESMERISED, TERRIFIED, EXCITED, OCCASIONALLY FULL OF INEXPLICABLE RAGE AND DID I MENTION HOW TIRED I AM?

1,095 HOURS OF ROCKING,
147 HOURS OF SHOOSHING,
125,680 STEPS TAKEN THROUGH HALLWAYS AT NIGHT,
1,463 HOURS OF FEEDING,
2,195 NURSERY RHYMES SUNG,
4,017 NAPPIES CHANGED,
3,285 TIMES BRUSHING THEIR TEETH,
17,524 TEARS WIPED AWAY,
3,832 OUTFIT NEGOTIATIONS,
416 PLAY DATES,
5,968 BOOKS READ,
7,386 BATTLES TO GET INTO THE BATH,
7,386 BATTLES TO GET OUT OF THE BATH,
2,810 HOURS SPENT PLAYING GAMES INCORRECTLY,
5,475 MEALS PREPARED,
6,125 HOURS OF WONDERING IF I AM GOOD ENOUGH,
152 HOURS TRYING TO LOCATE MISSING SHOES,
912 "IS THIS NORMAL?" GOOGLE SEARCHES,
1,706 HOURS COMFORTING IN SILENCE,
210,240 QUESTIONS ASKED AND ANSWERED,

AND IN THE BLINK OF AN EYE HE STARTED SCHOOL.

HOW I SEE ME

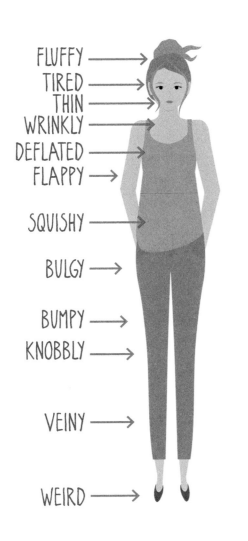

FLUFFY ⟶
TIRED ⟶
THIN ⟶
WRINKLY ⟶
DEFLATED ⟶
FLAPPY ⟶

SQUISHY ⟶

BULGY ⟶

BUMPY ⟶
KNOBBLY ⟶

VEINY ⟶

WEIRD ⟶

HOW THEY SEE ME

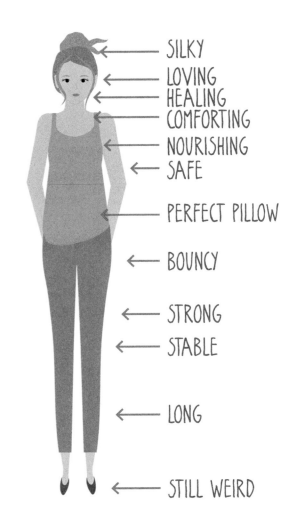

⟵ SILKY
⟵ LOVING
⟵ HEALING
⟵ COMFORTING
⟵ NOURISHING
⟵ SAFE

⟵ PERFECT PILLOW

⟵ BOUNCY

⟵ STRONG
⟵ STABLE

⟵ LONG

⟵ STILL WEIRD

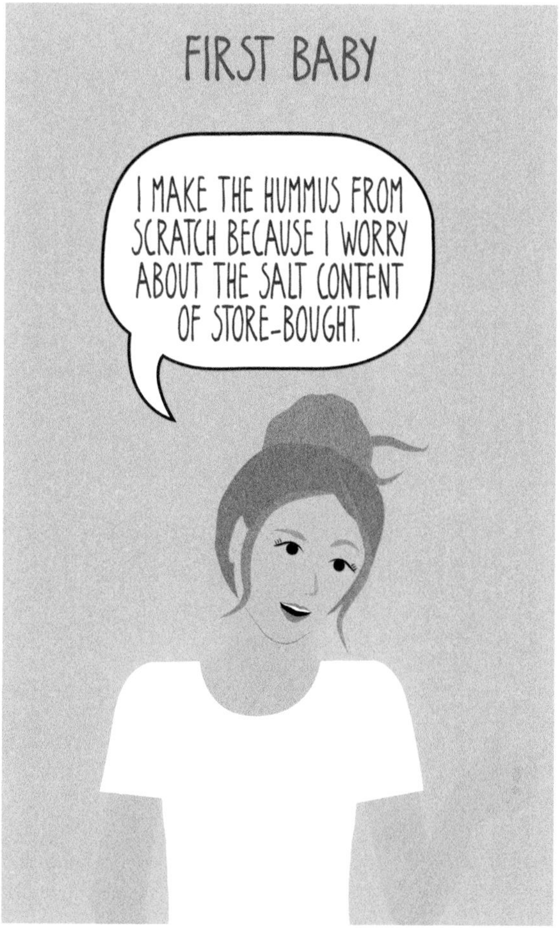
FIRST BABY
I MAKE THE HUMMUS FROM SCRATCH BECAUSE I WORRY ABOUT THE SALT CONTENT OF STORE-BOUGHT.

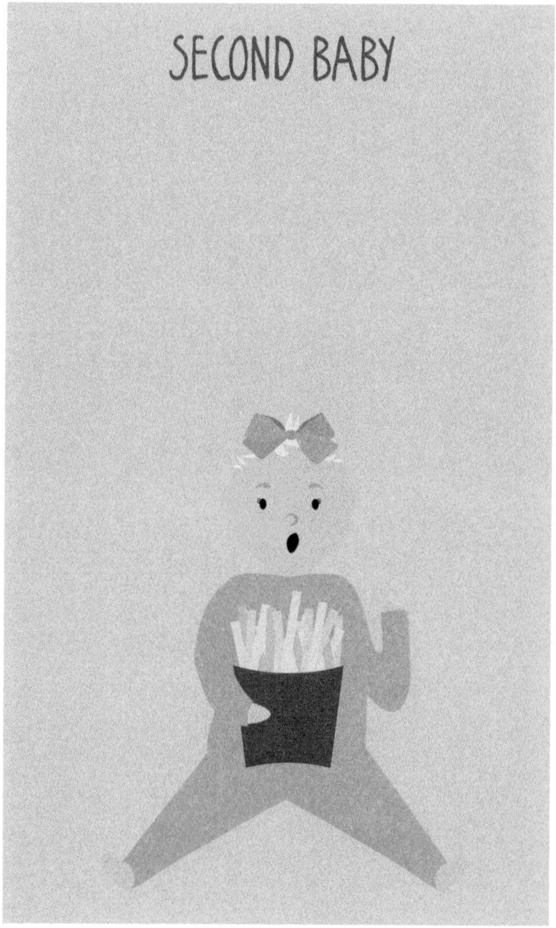
SECOND BABY

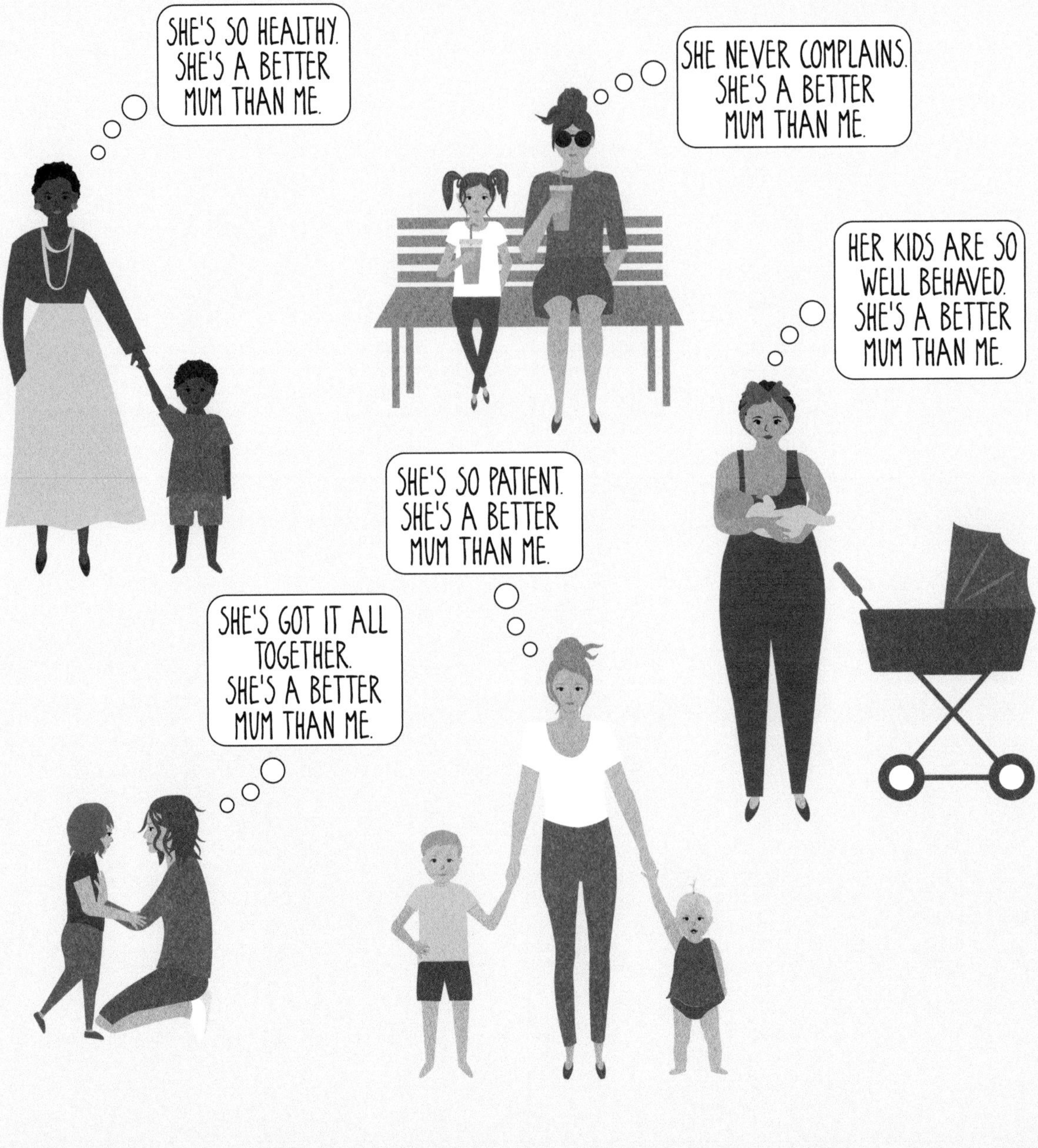
SHE'S SO HEALTHY. SHE'S A BETTER MUM THAN ME.
SHE NEVER COMPLAINS. SHE'S A BETTER MUM THAN ME.
HER KIDS ARE SO WELL BEHAVED. SHE'S A BETTER MUM THAN ME.
SHE'S SO PATIENT. SHE'S A BETTER MUM THAN ME.
SHE'S GOT IT ALL TOGETHER. SHE'S A BETTER MUM THAN ME.

BEDTIME ROUTINE FOR NEWBORNS MUMS

6:30 PM   Twinkle twinkle LITTLE . . . zzzzzz. Almost drop baby.

7:00 PM   Place baby in COT. Drowsy but . . . Who are you kidding? Fast asleep. Walk into the stark light to find HOUSE HAS BEEN RANSACKED BY WILD MONKEYS. Pour a glass of wine. Gather all stray objects and deposit into a basket. HIDE BASKET. Drink wine WATCHING . . . ACTUALLY, NO IDEA WHAT YOU ARE WATCHING.

9:45 PM   Climb into bed. Close eyes.

10:05 PM   Baby cries. How can it be time for a feed already? Resettle or feed? Google wine and breastfeeding. Read SIX articles telling you baby will get drunk. SEVENTH article FROM SCIENCY WEBSITE assures you everything will be okay. Feed.

10:30 PM   Close eyes for JUST a minute.

12:35 AM   Wake up hugging baby. Check baby is breathing. Realise baby is a pillow. Where the F__K is the baby? Find baby in the cot sleeping. Go back to bed. Close eyes.

1:05 AM   Baby cries. Feed baby. Scroll Facebook to stay awake. Article: plastic = evil. Add $165 worth of glass food containers to cart. Forget PayPal password.

1:45 AM   Put baby back in cot.

2:35 AM   Remember the name of the plant you've been trying to remember all week. Can't get name out of head. Text plant name to friend. Close eyes.

3:10 AM   Baby cries. Feed baby. Overcome by inexplicable rage about parking ticket you received three weeks ago. Especially since the council has such a SHOCKING street tree policy. Compose angry email to council about street tree policy.

4:45 AM   Baby cries. Is this a night feed or breakfast? Breakfast. BREAKFAST = coffee.

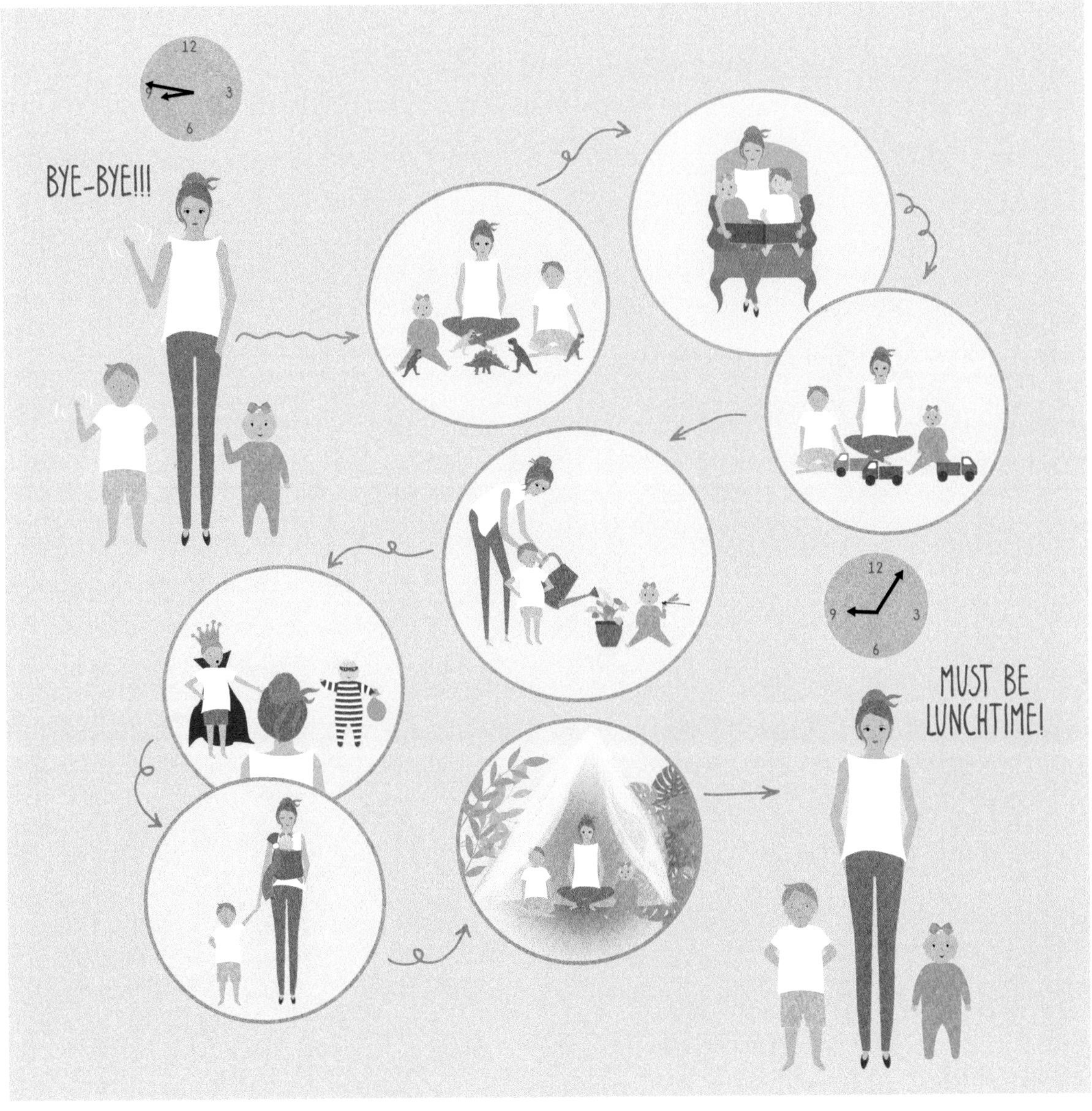
BYE-BYE!!!
MUST BE LUNCHTIME!

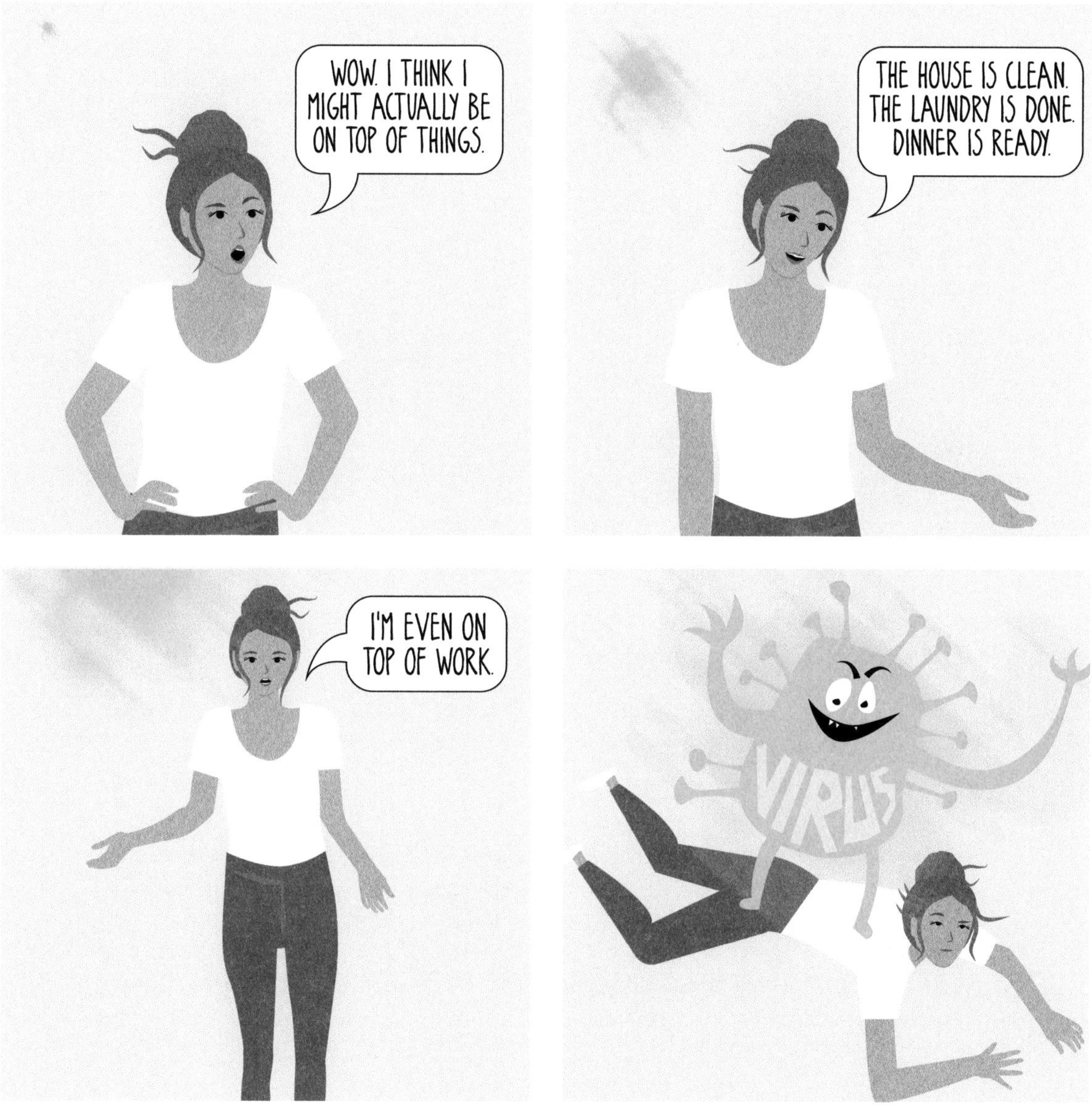
WOW. I THINK I MIGHT ACTUALLY BE ON TOP OF THINGS.
THE HOUSE IS CLEAN. THE LAUNDRY IS DONE. DINNER IS READY.
I'M EVEN ON TOP OF WORK.
VIRUS

WHAT I THINK HE WANTS

WHAT HE ACTUALLY WANTS

After a few years of ambitious, Pinterest-perfect parties, in the interest of my mental health, we decided to keep things low-key for our son's fourth birthday. I was nervous in the lead-up to the day, as he was dropping daily hints about his upcoming pirate birthday party. The day arrived, and we had his four doting grandparents over, fish and chips for dinner and a packet cake adorned by a pirate toy. As his tired head hit the pillow that night, he squeezed me and said, "That was the best party ever." Sometimes you need the wisdom of a four-year-old to give you some perspective on what is really worth celebrating.

EARTH-FRIENDLY GIFT WRAPPING

USE ANYTHING FROM
"THE DRAWER"

DECORATE THE MAILING
BOX WITH FOLIAGE

WRAP IT IN OLD CLOTHES
THAT CAN'T BE SALVAGED

WRAP IT IN
BANANA LEAVES

WRAP IT IN
BANANA SKINS

WRAP IT IN A LETTUCE LEAF
(LOW-CARB OPTION)

WRAP YOUR MIND
AROUND THE POWER
OF KINDNESS

WRAP YOUR ARMS
AROUND THE
PEOPLE YOU LOVE

WRAP YOUR HEART
AROUND WHAT
REALLY MATTERS

THINGS WE DON'T SAY TO DADS

HE'S GOT HIS HANDS FULL

HOW DO YOU JUGGLE WORKING AND PARENTING?

IF YOU'RE HERE, WHO'S LOOKING AFTER THE KIDS?

JUST BE GRATEFUL

There is an ever-present double standard rooted firmly in traditional gender roles, and it's to the detriment of everyone. The "useless dad" cliché—dressing the kids in inappropriate clothing and bumbling through nappy changes—is only somewhat accurate, because the majority of mothers have had much more on-the-job training. Dads out in public with their children get showered with praise for being good dads. This perpetuates the stereotype that it's out of the ordinary for men to care for their children.

The solution doesn't lie in withholding praise from dads. They probably are doing a good job after all. But if we truly want to lessen the burden on working mothers, we need to treat them the same way we treat working fathers. Smiling admiringly, looking them in the eye and telling them they are doing a great job would be a good place to start.

MICRO ACTS OF KINDNESS

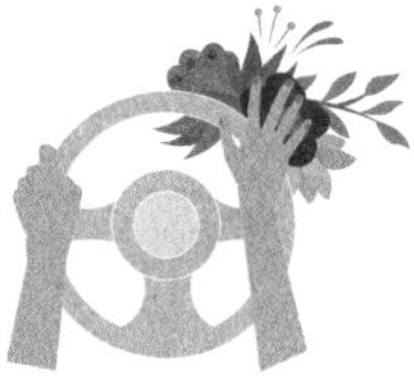

THE WAVE
THAT WAS ALMOST AN ANGRY HONK, ACKNOWLEDGING OUR HUMANITY.

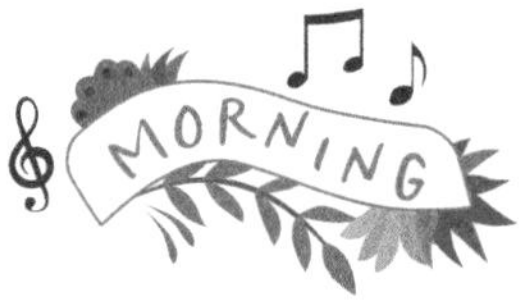
MORNING

THE JOYFUL GREETING
ON A GLOOMY DAY THAT SHIFTS AN EQUALLY GLOOMY MOOD.

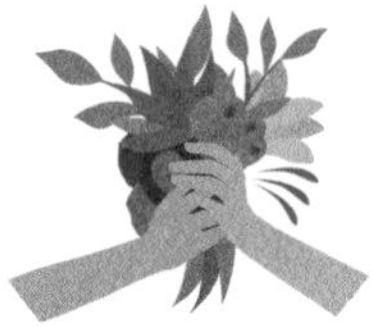

THE REASSURING SMILE
THAT CONVEYS PRAISE IN A CHALLENGING SITUATION.

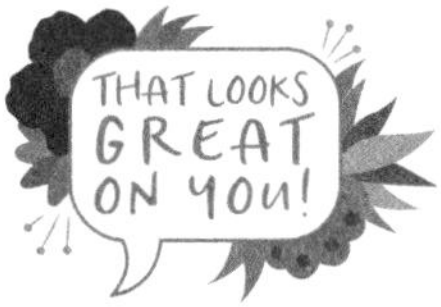
THAT LOOKS GREAT ON YOU!

THE SPONTANEOUS COMPLIMENT
THAT COULD HAVE LINGERED AS A PASSING THOUGHT.

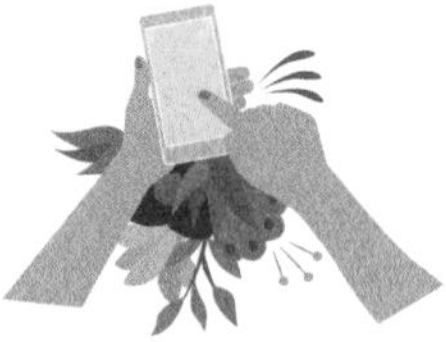

THE SCROLL
PAST SOMETHING CONTROVERSIAL, ARMED WITH THE WISDOM THAT MANY ARGUMENTS ARE FUTILE.

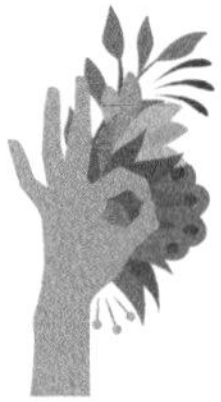

THE APPROVING NOD
THAT REPLACES THE JUDGEMENTAL GLARE THAT WAS ANTICIPATED.

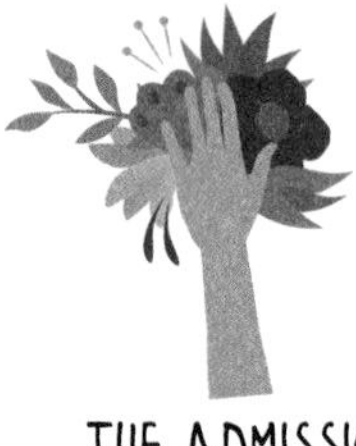

THE ADMISSION
OF A PRIOR MISHAP THAT BRINGS COMFORT WITH ITS FAMILIARITY.

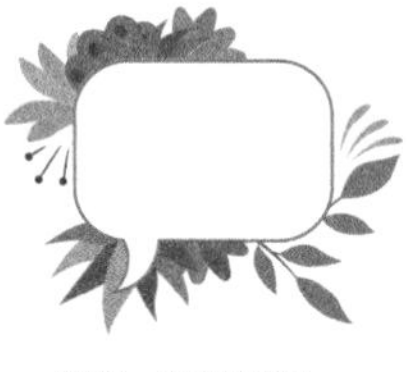

THE SILENCE
THAT COULD HAVE BEEN A CRITICISM OF SOMEONE WHO IS DOING THEIR BEST.

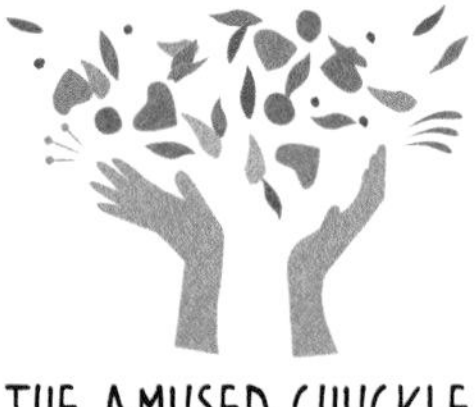

THE AMUSED CHUCKLE
THAT RECOGNISES A SHARED DELIGHT IN SOMETHING ABSURD AND JOYFUL.

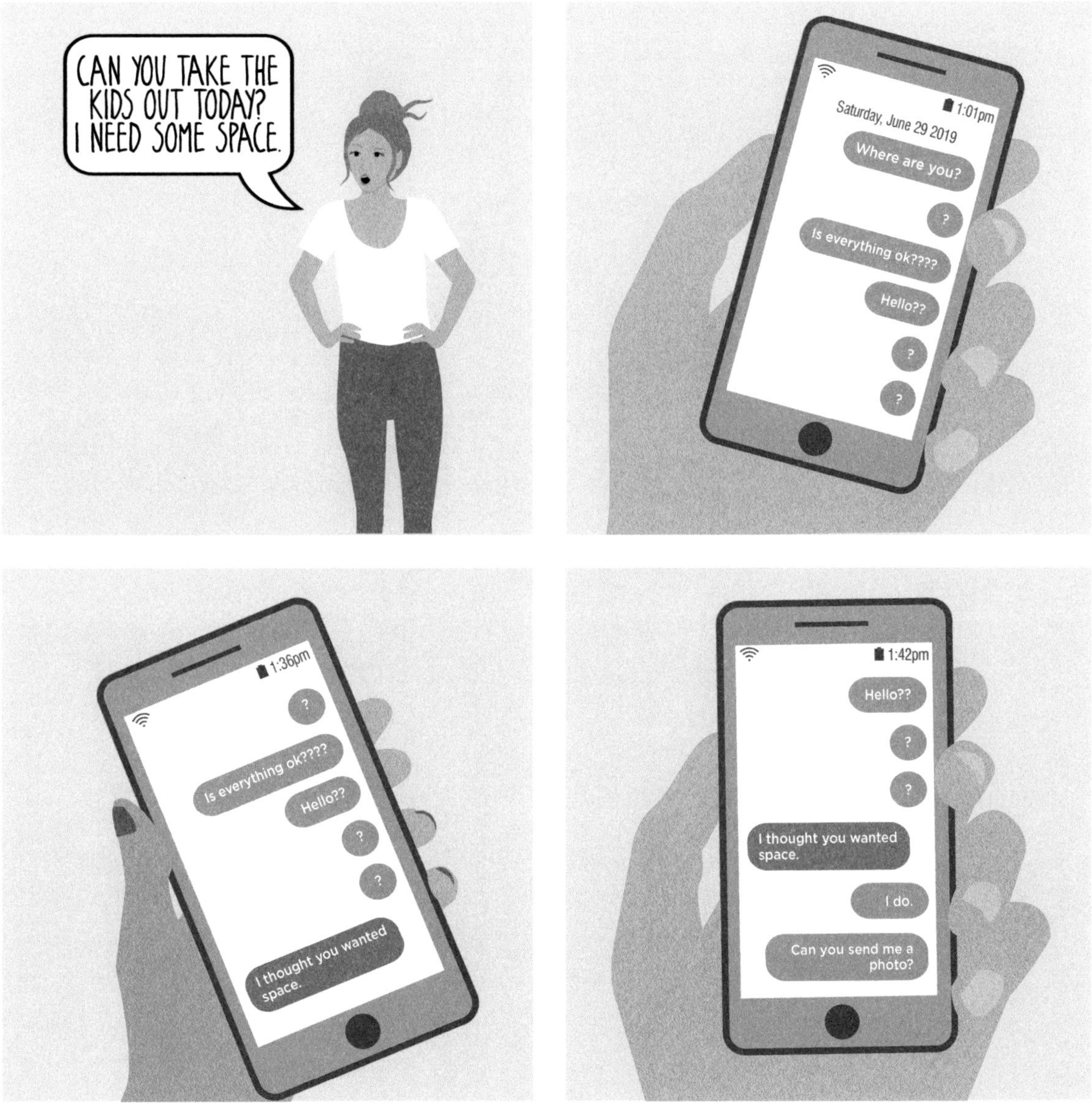
CAN YOU TAKE THE KIDS OUT TODAY? I NEED SOME SPACE.
1:01pm
Saturday, June 29 2019
Where are you?
?
Is everything ok????
Hello??
?
?
1:36pm
?
Is everything ok????
Hello??
?
?
I thought you wanted space.
1:42pm
Hello??
?
?
I thought you wanted space.
I do.
Can you send me a photo?

REAL "SUPERFOODS"

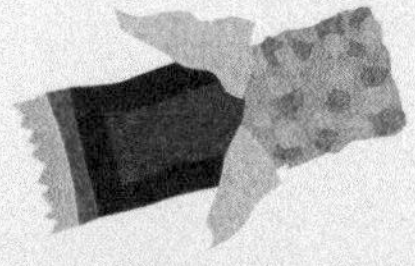

THE MUESLI BAR AT THE BOTTOM OF YOUR HANDBAG THAT YOU DISCOVER MOMENTS BEFORE A HUNGER-INDUCED MELTDOWN.

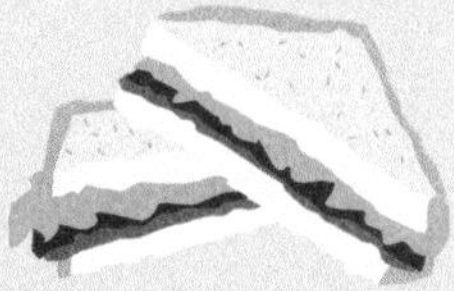

THE LUNCH THAT YOU MANAGE TO FINISH TEN GLORIOUS MINUTES BEFORE THE BABY WAKES UP.

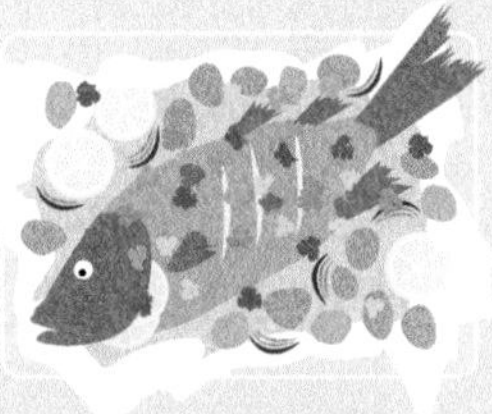

THE MEAL THAT MEETS EVERY SINGLE ONE OF YOUR EXTENDED FAMILIES' COMPLICATED DIETARY REQUIREMENTS.

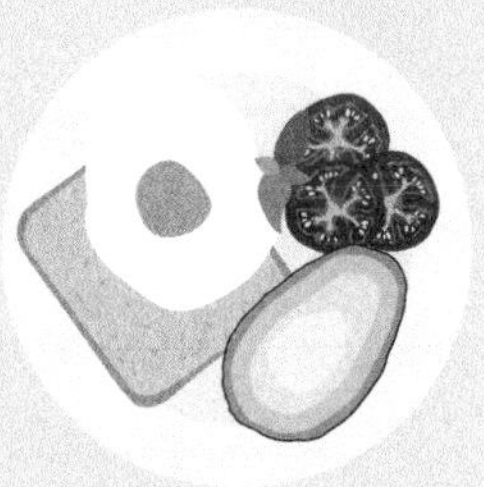

THE DINNER YOU CAN COOK FROM START TO FINISH IN SIX MINUTES.

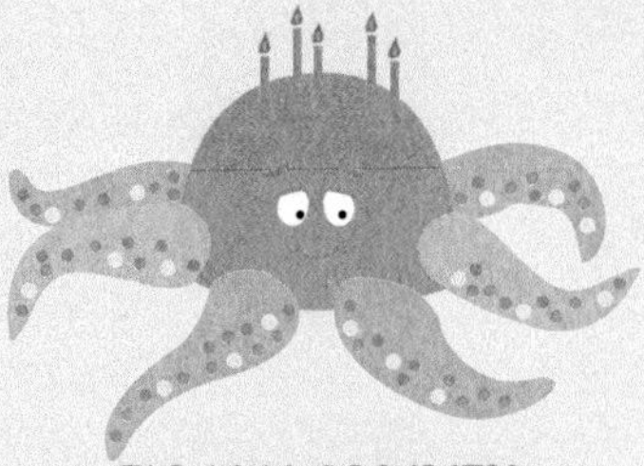

THE LONG-REQUESTED OBSCURELY THEMED BIRTHDAY CAKE THAT YOU MANAGE TO PULL OFF, RESULTING IN DELIGHTED SQUEALS.

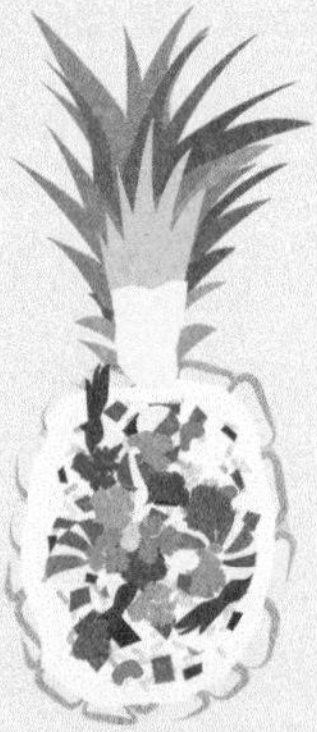

THE EXOTIC CUISINE YOU NEVER IN A MILLION YEARS THOUGHT YOUR KIDS WOULD EAT, BUT THEY DO.

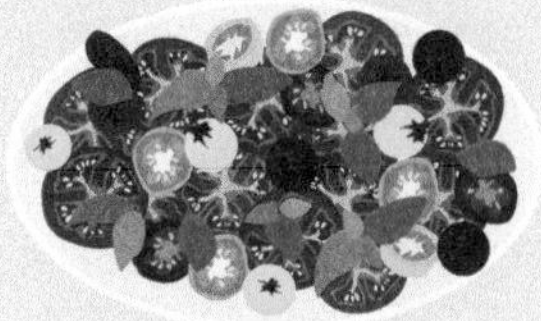

THE DISH YOU MADE USING INGREDIENTS YOU GREW YOURSELF.

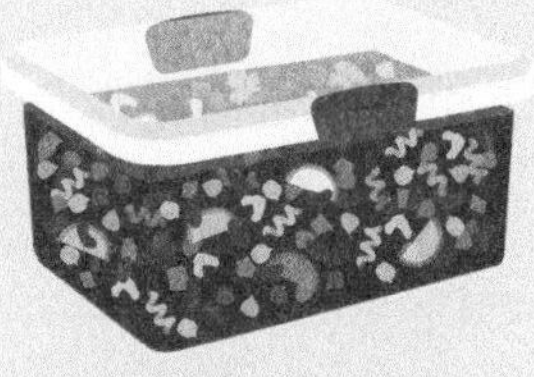

THE CONTAINER OF SOUP THAT APPEARS ON YOUR DOORSTEP WHEN YOUR FAMILY IS ALL SICK.

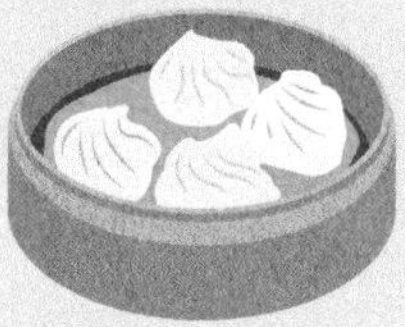

THE DINNER YOU HAVE WITH AN OLD FRIEND THAT REMINDS YOU OF THE CITY YOU MET IN.

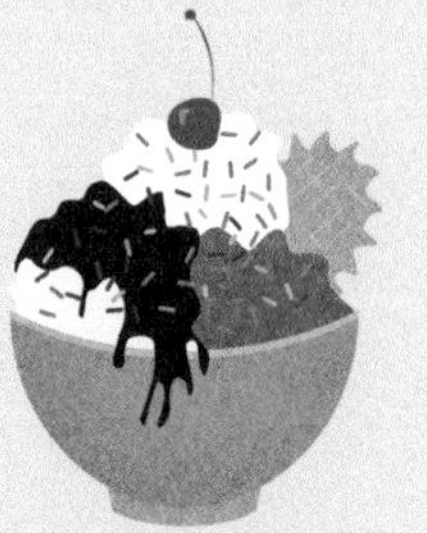

THE FOOD THAT IS JUST REALLY, REALLY DELICIOUS AND LIFTS AN AFTERNOON MOOD.

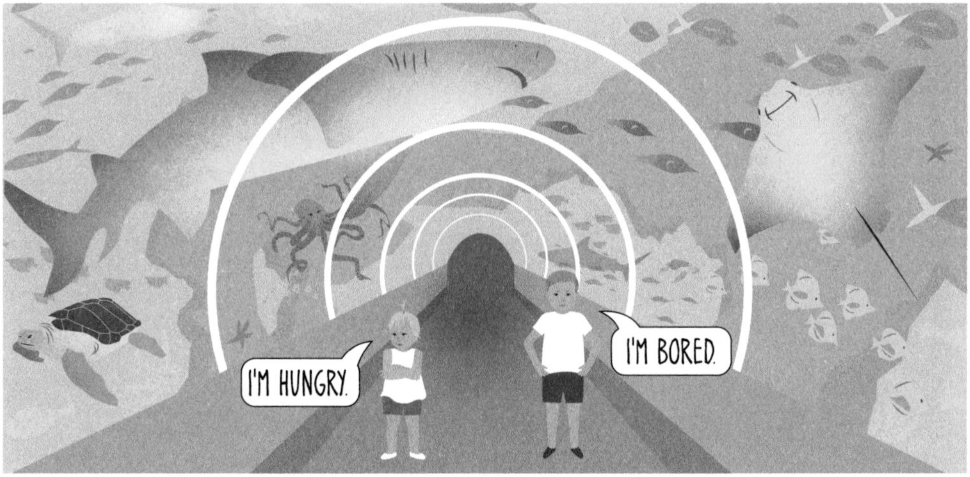
I'M HUNGRY.
I'M BORED.

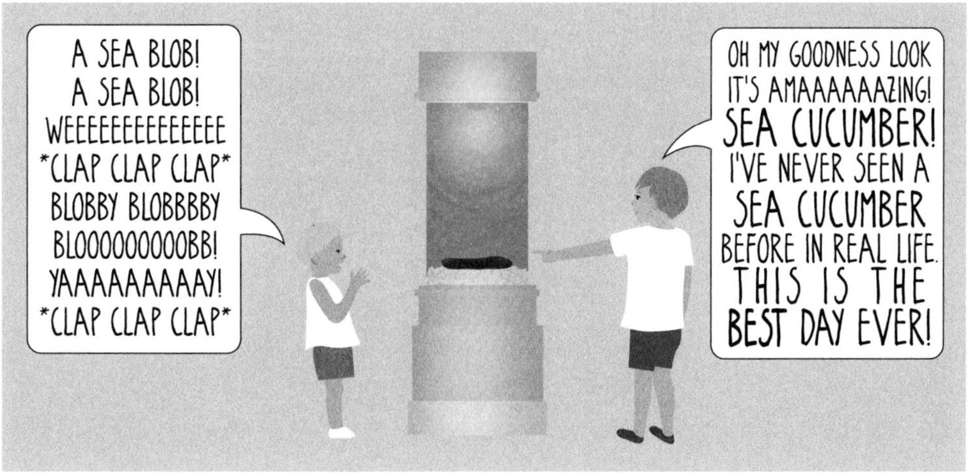
A SEA BLOB! A SEA BLOB! WEEEEEEEEEEEEEE *CLAP CLAP CLAP* BLOBBY BLOBBBBY BLOOOOOOOOOBB! YAAAAAAAAAY! *CLAP CLAP CLAP*
OH MY GOODNESS LOOK IT'S AMAAAAAAAZING! SEA CUCUMBER! I'VE NEVER SEEN A SEA CUCUMBER BEFORE IN REAL LIFE. THIS IS THE BEST DAY EVER!

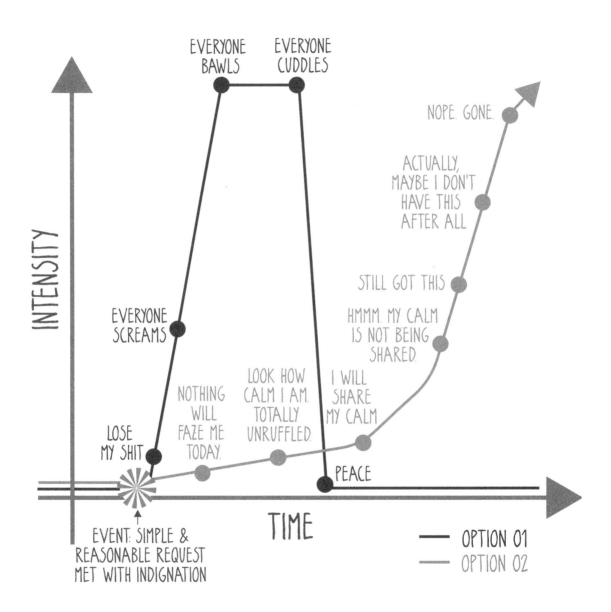

EVERYONE
BAWLS

EVERYONE
CUDDLES

NOPE. GONE.

ACTUALLY,
MAYBE I DON'T
HAVE THIS
AFTER ALL

STILL GOT THIS

HMMM. MY CALM
IS NOT BEING
SHARED.

EVERYONE
SCREAMS

LOOK HOW
CALM I AM.
TOTALLY
UNRUFFLED.

I WILL
SHARE
MY CALM

NOTHING
WILL
FAZE ME
TODAY.

LOSE
MY SHIT

PEACE

INTENSITY

EVENT: SIMPLE &
REASONABLE REQUEST
MET WITH INDIGNATION

TIME

OPTION 01
OPTION 02

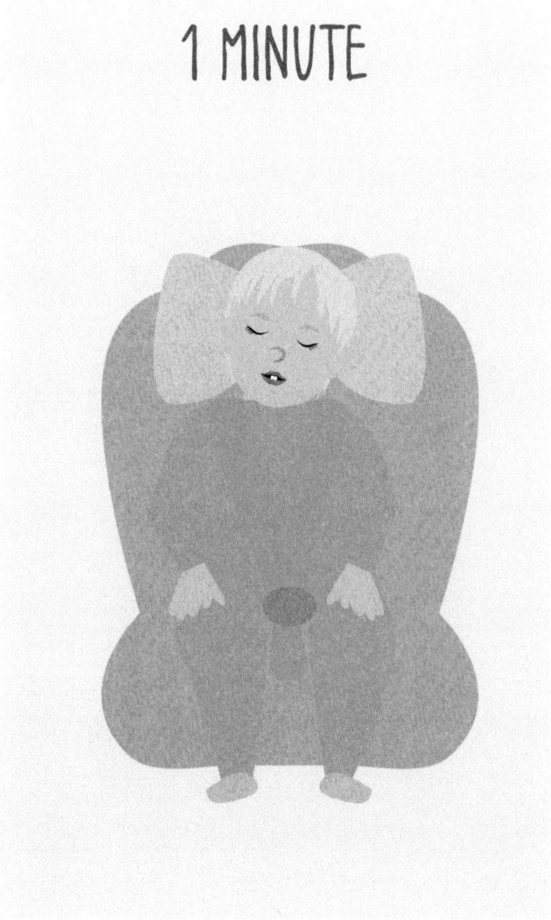
1 MINUTE

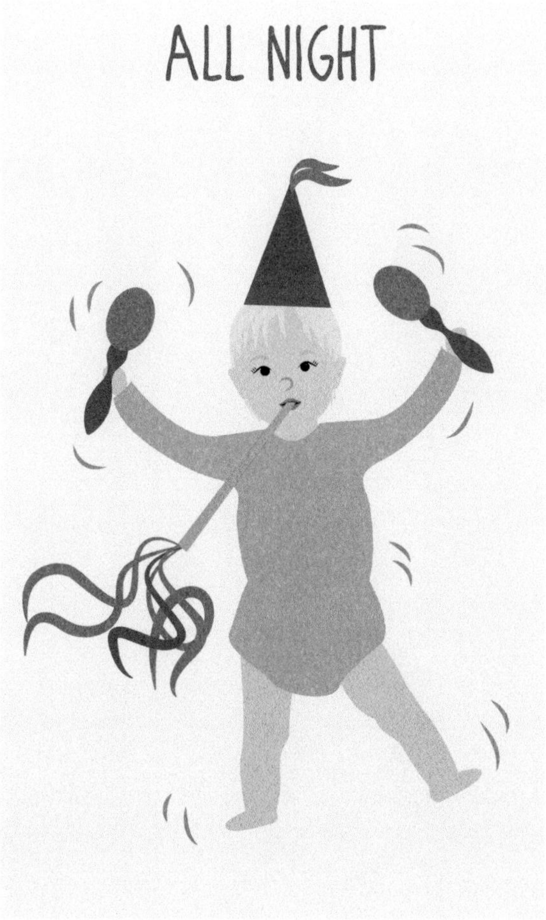
ALL NIGHT

MUM HACKS (THAT COMPLETELY BACKFIRE)

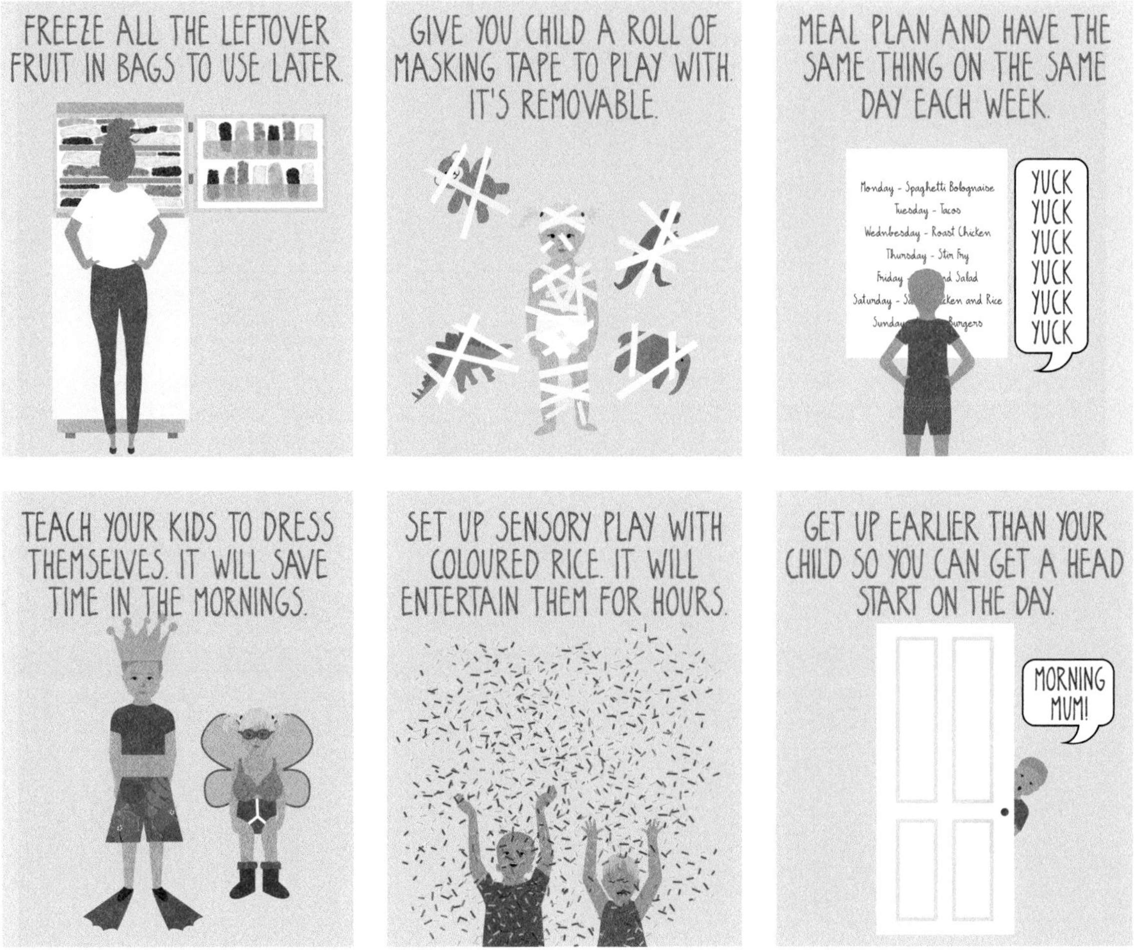
FREEZE ALL THE LEFTOVER FRUIT IN BAGS TO USE LATER.
GIVE YOU CHILD A ROLL OF MASKING TAPE TO PLAY WITH. IT'S REMOVABLE.
MEAL PLAN AND HAVE THE SAME THING ON THE SAME DAY EACH WEEK.
Monday - Spaghetti Bolognaise
Tuesday - Tacos
Wednbesday - Roast Chicken
Thursday - Stir Fry
YUCK YUCK YUCK YUCK YUCK YUCK
TEACH YOUR KIDS TO DRESS THEMSELVES. IT WILL SAVE TIME IN THE MORNINGS.
SET UP SENSORY PLAY WITH COLOURED RICE. IT WILL ENTERTAIN THEM FOR HOURS.
GET UP EARLIER THAN YOUR CHILD SO YOU CAN GET A HEAD START ON THE DAY.
MORNING MUM!

TALK TO YOURSELF THE WAY YOU WOULD TALK TO A CHILD

LOOK HOW MUCH YOU'VE GROWN!

Hide vegetables from yourself. Praise yourself for brushing your teeth, going to the toilet and washing your hands. Take some time to sit in the corner and have a good think. Squeeze and admire your glorious, squishy thighs. Congratulate yourself on using your inside voice and your very best manners. Marvel at the complete and utter wonder of the universe that you are here. And if you're still feeling a little bit cranky, it might be time for an early night.

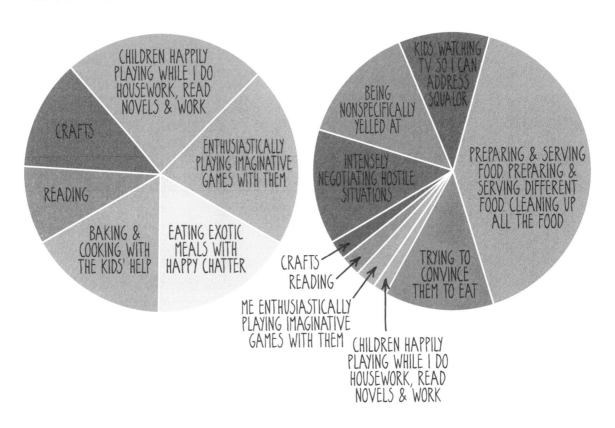

WHAT I THOUGHT A DAY PARENTING WOULD LOOK LIKE

CHILDREN HAPPILY PLAYING WHILE I DO HOUSEWORK, READ NOVELS & WORK

CRAFTS

READING

BAKING & COOKING WITH THE KIDS' HELP

EATING EXOTIC MEALS WITH HAPPY CHATTER

ENTHUSIASTICALLY PLAYING IMAGINATIVE GAMES WITH THEM

WHAT A DAY PARENTING ACTUALLY LOOKS LIKE

KIDS WATCHING TV SO I CAN ADDRESS SQUALOR

BEING NONSPECIFICALLY YELLED AT

INTENSELY NEGOTIATING HOSTILE SITUATIONS

PREPARING & SERVING FOOD. PREPARING & SERVING DIFFERENT FOOD. CLEANING UP ALL THE FOOD

CRAFTS
READING

ME ENTHUSIASTICALLY PLAYING IMAGINATIVE GAMES WITH THEM

TRYING TO CONVINCE THEM TO EAT

CHILDREN HAPPILY PLAYING WHILE I DO HOUSEWORK, READ NOVELS & WORK

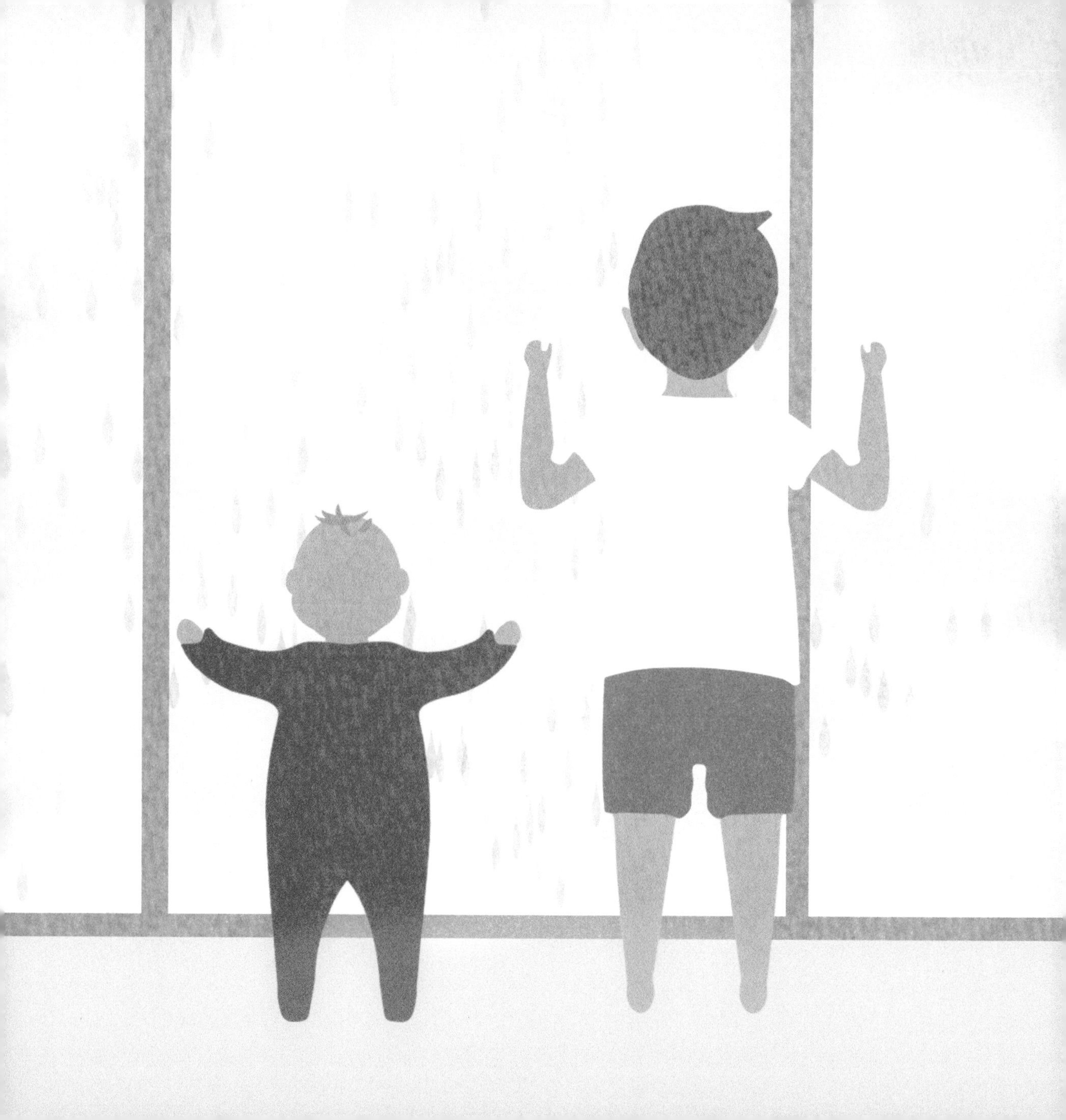

Some days I do have it all together. The kids eat well—colourful things, even. The house is in order. We make animals out of paper plates and toilet rolls. Other days it's a different story. The day is set to a soundtrack of whinging and bickering. I wonder if the clock battery is flat because time does not appear to be moving while we're playing. I resent them because I'm bone-achingly tired from being woken up numerous times the night before. I'm overwhelmingly frustrated that a disproportionate amount of my day is spent looking for shoes. On those days, the main thought running through my mind is that I mustn't be a very good mum.

Deep down, I know I'm a good mum. I know this because I really love my kids. Of course, at times I find them boring and slightly annoying.

But I also find them adorable and hilarious, and their inquisitive little minds set my heart alight. I know the fact I even question whether I'm doing a good enough job probably means I am.

There's a lot of guilt associated with wanting space from our children. It's very normal to feel this way. The part of me that needs space is a major part of my identity. I need space to create and think and draw and exercise and sometimes even have a shower.

For now, their love for me is uncomplicated and unconditional. As they grow, I know this will evolve. One day I'm sure that seeing me work hard on something I feel passionate about will make them proud and inspire them. And they will realise that I was better equipped to meet their needs when I was also meeting my own.

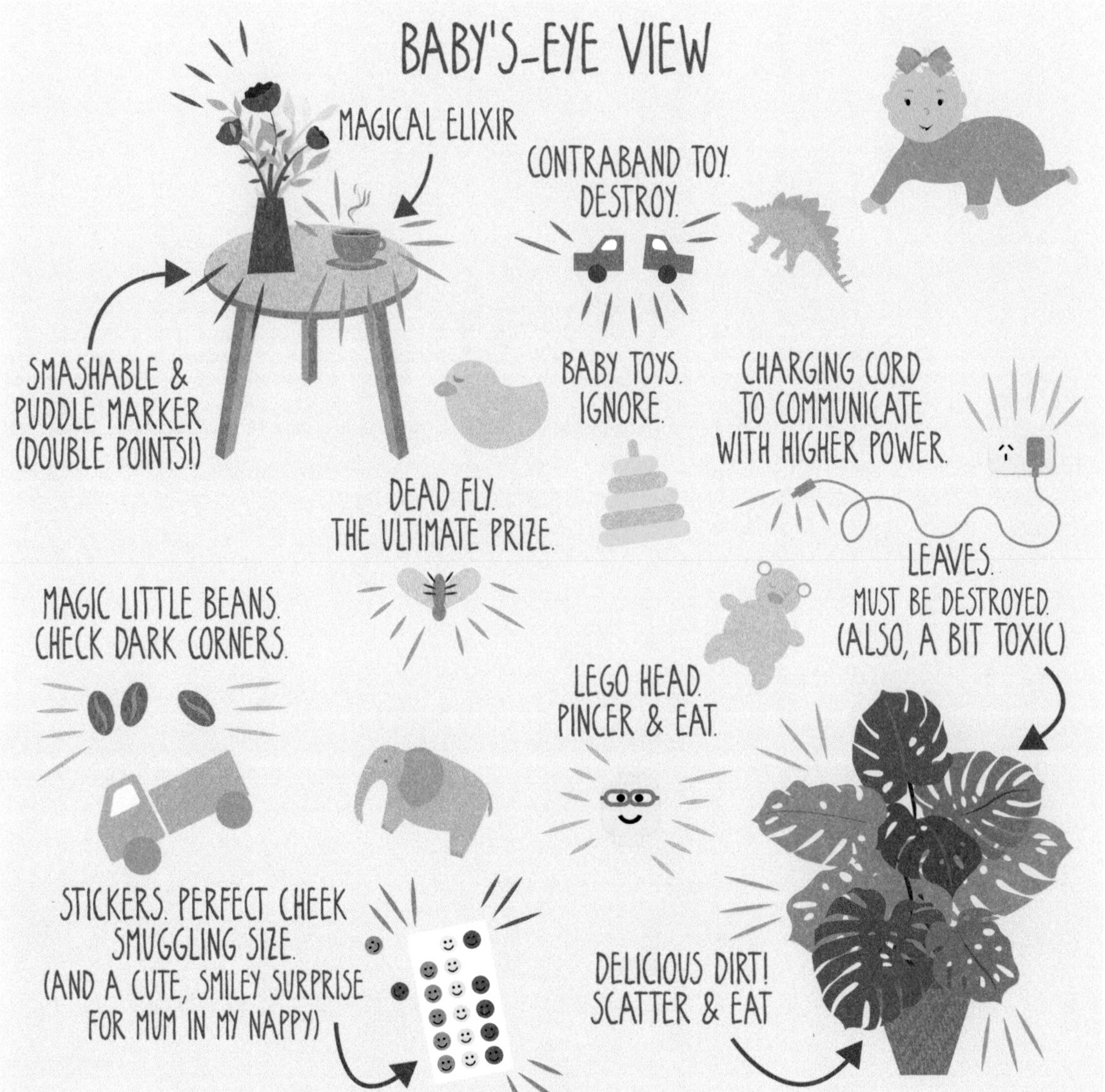
BABY'S-EYE VIEW
MAGICAL ELIXIR
CONTRABAND TOY. DESTROY.
SMASHABLE & PUDDLE MARKER (DOUBLE POINTS!)
BABY TOYS. IGNORE.
CHARGING CORD TO COMMUNICATE WITH HIGHER POWER.
DEAD FLY. THE ULTIMATE PRIZE.
LEAVES. MUST BE DESTROYED. (ALSO, A BIT TOXIC)
MAGIC LITTLE BEANS. CHECK DARK CORNERS.
LEGO HEAD. PINCER & EAT.
STICKERS. PERFECT CHEEK SMUGGLING SIZE. (AND A CUTE, SMILEY SURPRISE FOR MUM IN MY NAPPY)
DELICIOUS DIRT! SCATTER & EAT

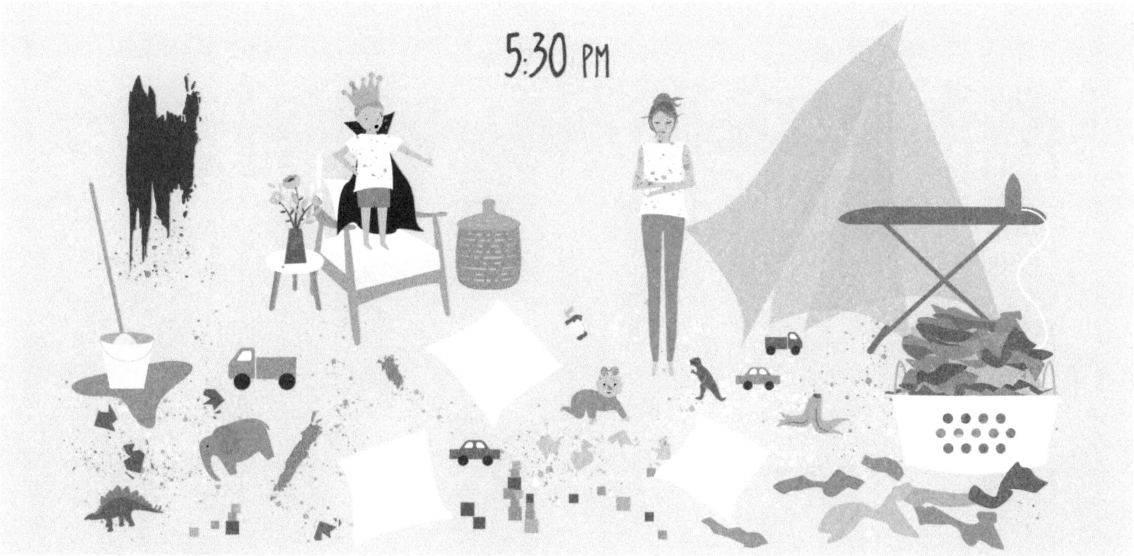
5:30 PM

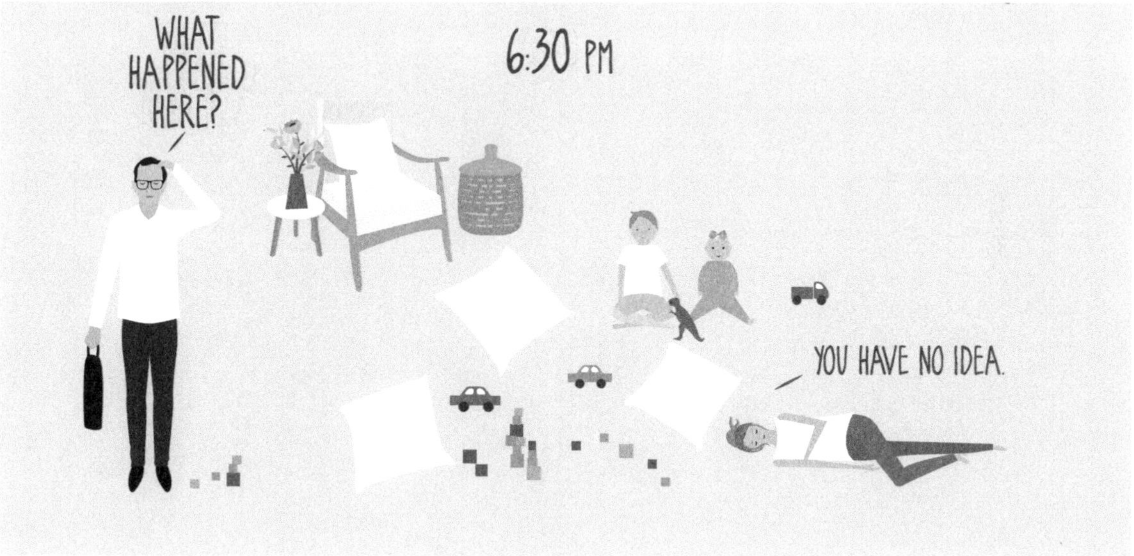
WHAT HAPPENED HERE?
6:30 PM
YOU HAVE NO IDEA.

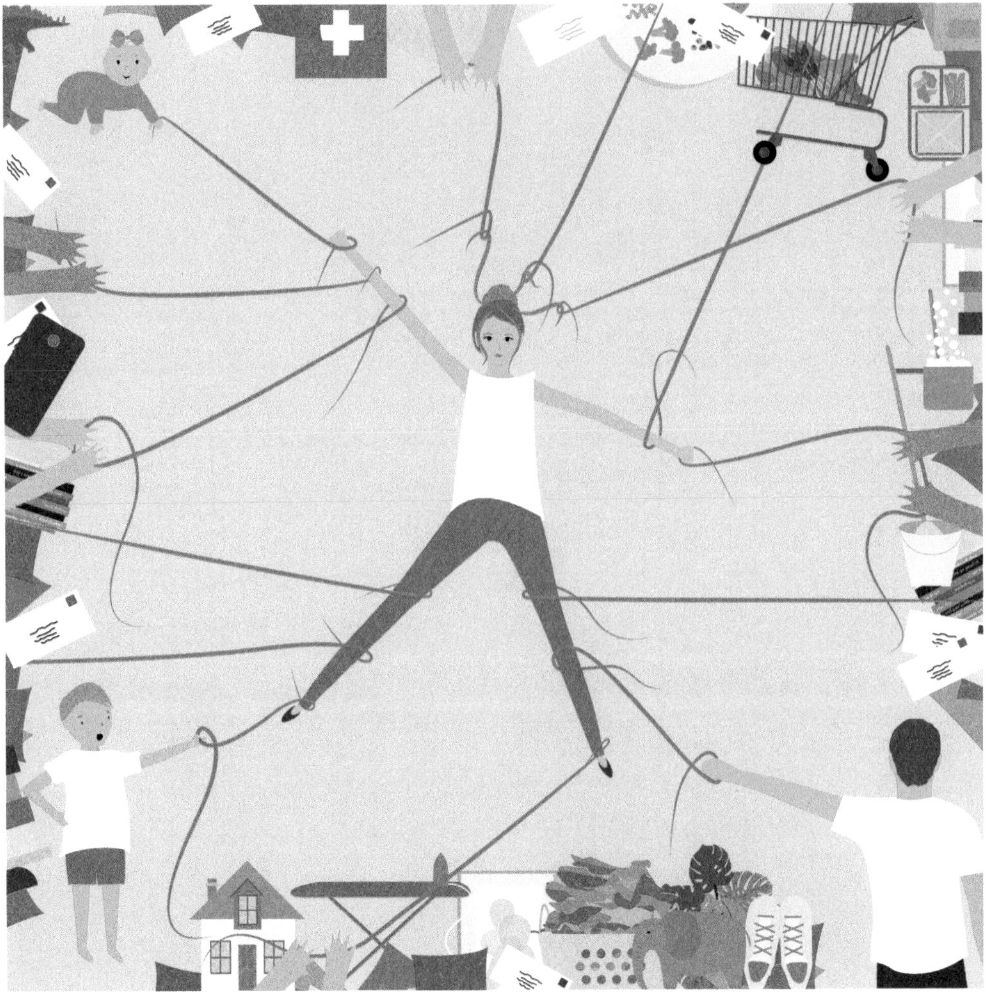

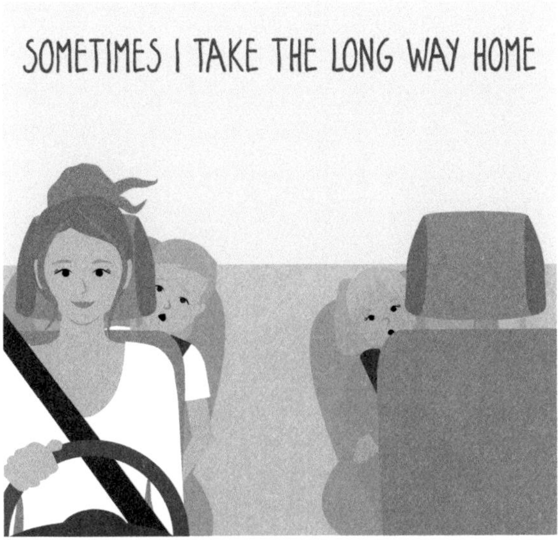
SOMETIMES I TAKE THE LONG WAY HOME

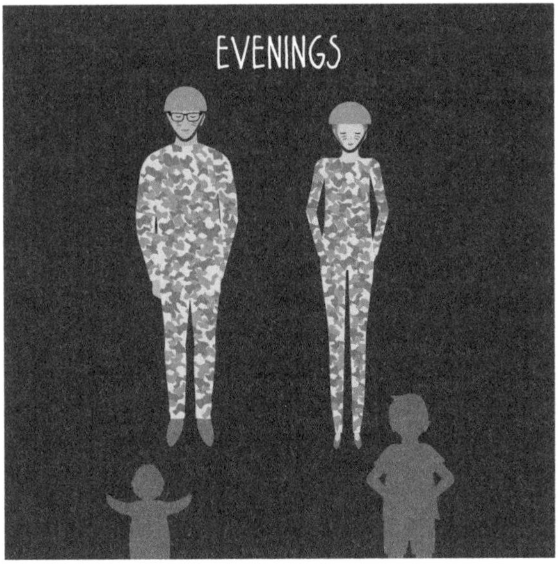
EVENINGS

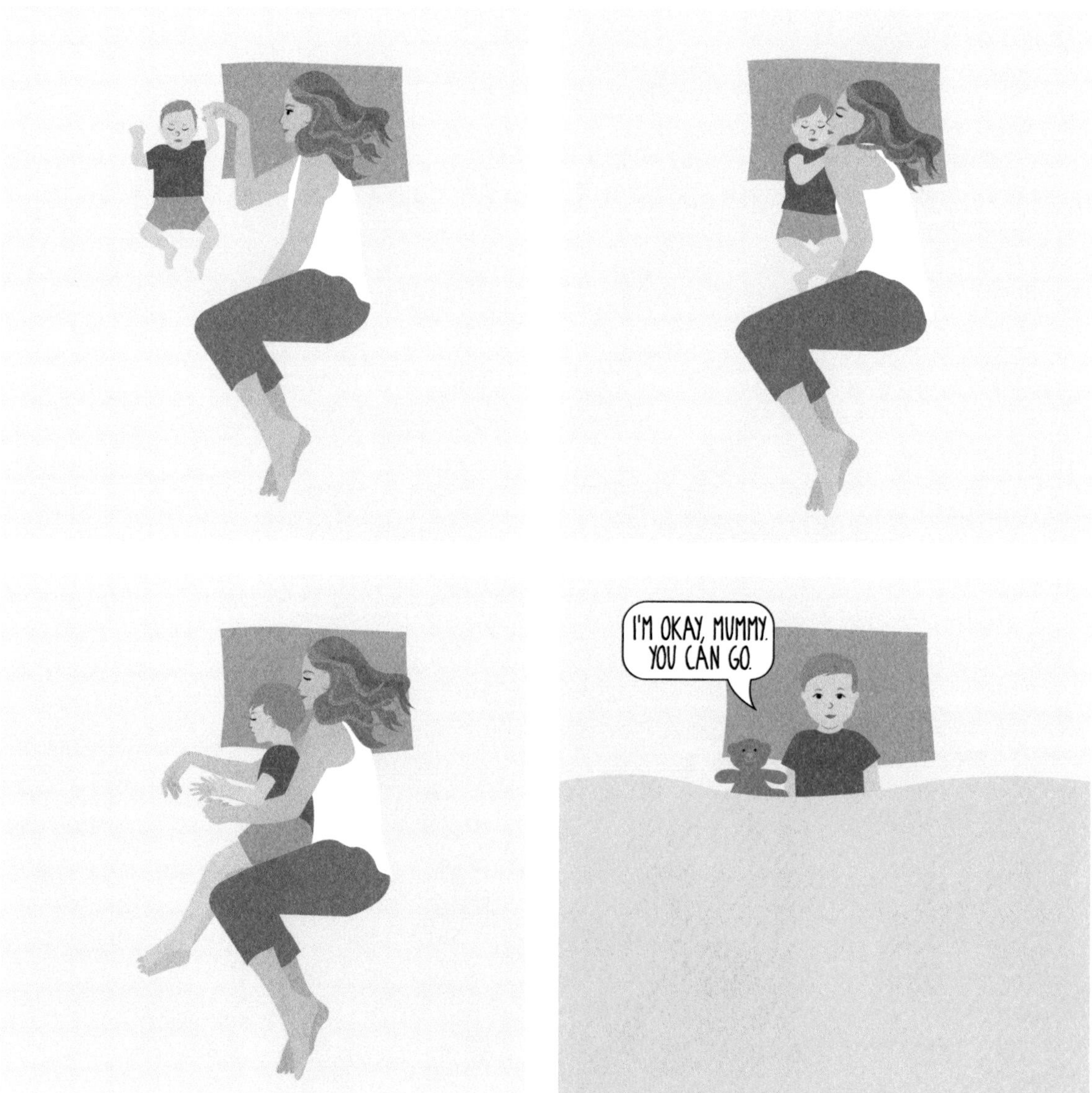
I'M OKAY, MUMMY. YOU CAN GO.

DRIFTING OFF TO SLEEP

As a work-at-home mum, my days are unpredictable and slightly chaotic. My children wake up, sleepy and bleary-eyed little bundles of cuddles. And then the day begins. We roll through the waves of endless snacks, giggling fits, nonsensical demands, sibling squabbling, sporadic outpouring of affection and inexplicable mess. Towards the evening, insatiable hunger and tiredness takes control of their mood, and the house looks like it was ransacked by wild monkeys. I yearn for the peace of bedtime. Somehow we survive dinner, and then the moment they are plunged into the bath I watch the chaos of the day slip away into the suds.

My son has always needed someone in the room with him while he falls asleep. When he was a newborn, I told a friend I had to hold his little hand till he was fast asleep, and she asked, "Aren't you worried you'll have to do it forever?" And while it is an amusing thought—me holding the hand of my future adult son while he sleeps—there were times when it felt like it might be forever. He quickly outgrew his bassinet and moved into a cot, and still we laid next to him, our hands awkwardly reaching through the bars, the sharp corners leaving indents on our wrists. And then he graduated to a single bed. Without fail, every night, one of us would be curled up next to him waiting to hear his breathing become slow and deep. More often than not, my husband would fall asleep in there and emerge hours later, squinting and disorientated.

Last week, just shy of his fifth birthday, as I went to lie next to him, he announced he was going to fall asleep on his own.

It was in the same week that my toddler daughter started sleeping through the night. Our midnight catch-ups were no more.

While I'm thoroughly enjoying catching up on sleep and Netflix, I can't help but feel my babies are slipping away from me. I'm proud of their independence, but I'm also terrified by it.

These milestones are bittersweet. For years you have longed for this moment. Some freedom. A semblance of your life before you had children. And then, just like that, your evenings belong to you again. And you long for one more night cuddled up in their bed.

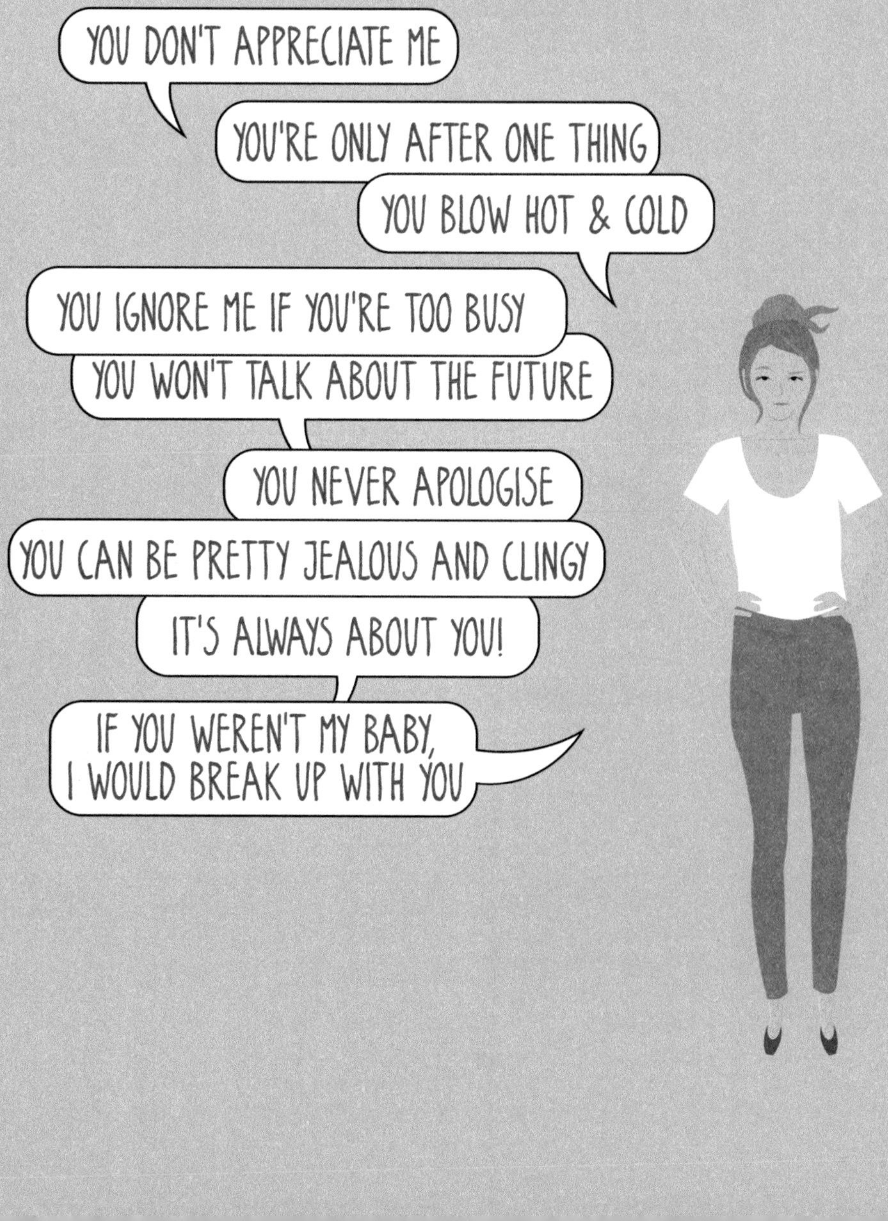
YOU DON'T APPRECIATE ME
YOU'RE ONLY AFTER ONE THING
YOU BLOW HOT & COLD
YOU IGNORE ME IF YOU'RE TOO BUSY
YOU WON'T TALK ABOUT THE FUTURE
YOU NEVER APOLOGISE
YOU CAN BE PRETTY JEALOUS AND CLINGY
IT'S ALWAYS ABOUT YOU!
IF YOU WEREN'T MY BABY, I WOULD BREAK UP WITH YOU

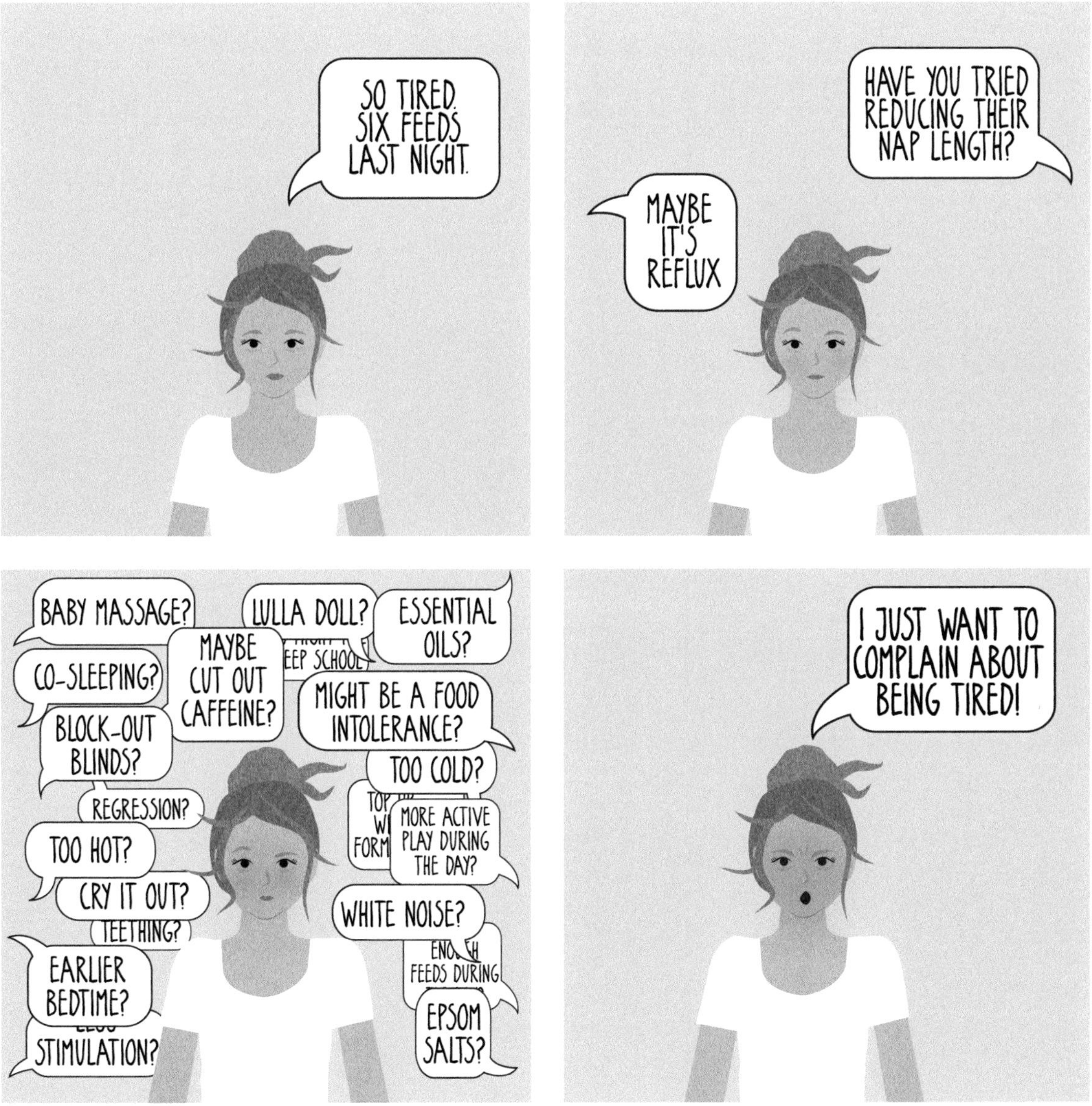
SO TIRED. SIX FEEDS LAST NIGHT.
HAVE YOU TRIED REDUCING THEIR NAP LENGTH?
MAYBE IT'S REFLUX
BABY MASSAGE?
LULLA DOLL?
ESSENTIAL OILS?
CO-SLEEPING?
MAYBE CUT OUT CAFFEINE?
MIGHT BE A FOOD INTOLERANCE?
BLOCK-OUT BLINDS?
TOO COLD?
REGRESSION?
MORE ACTIVE PLAY DURING THE DAY?
TOO HOT?
CRY IT OUT?
WHITE NOISE?
TEETHING?
EARLIER BEDTIME?
EPSOM SALTS?
STIMULATION?
I JUST WANT TO COMPLAIN ABOUT BEING TIRED!

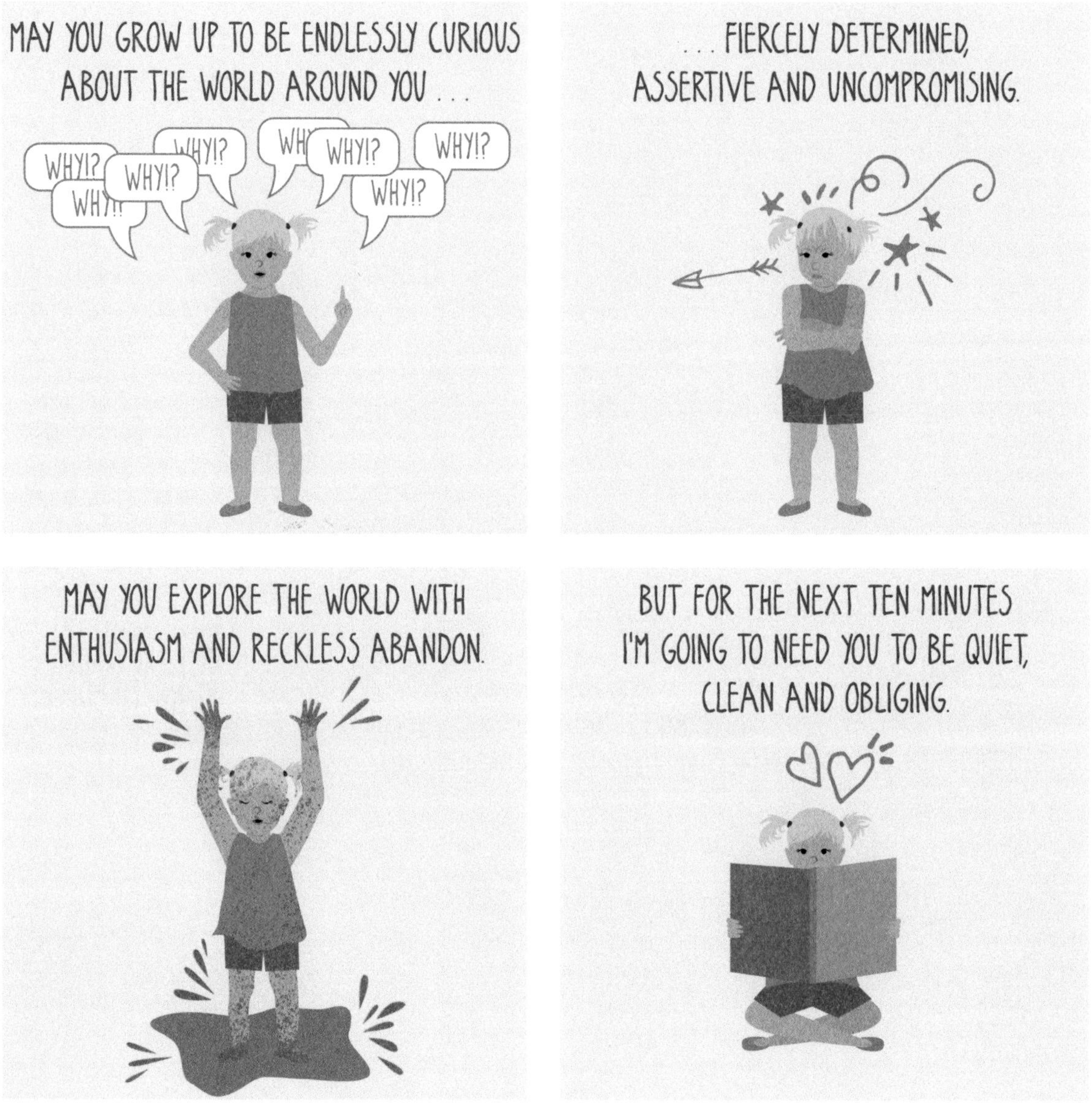
MAY YOU GROW UP TO BE ENDLESSLY CURIOUS ABOUT THE WORLD AROUND YOU . . .
WHY!?
WHY!?
WHY!?
WHY!?
WHY!?
. . . FIERCELY DETERMINED, ASSERTIVE AND UNCOMPROMISING.
MAY YOU EXPLORE THE WORLD WITH ENTHUSIASM AND RECKLESS ABANDON.
BUT FOR THE NEXT TEN MINUTES I'M GOING TO NEED YOU TO BE QUIET, CLEAN AND OBLIGING.

DEGREES OF FRIENDSHIP

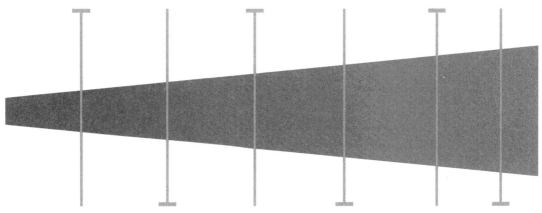

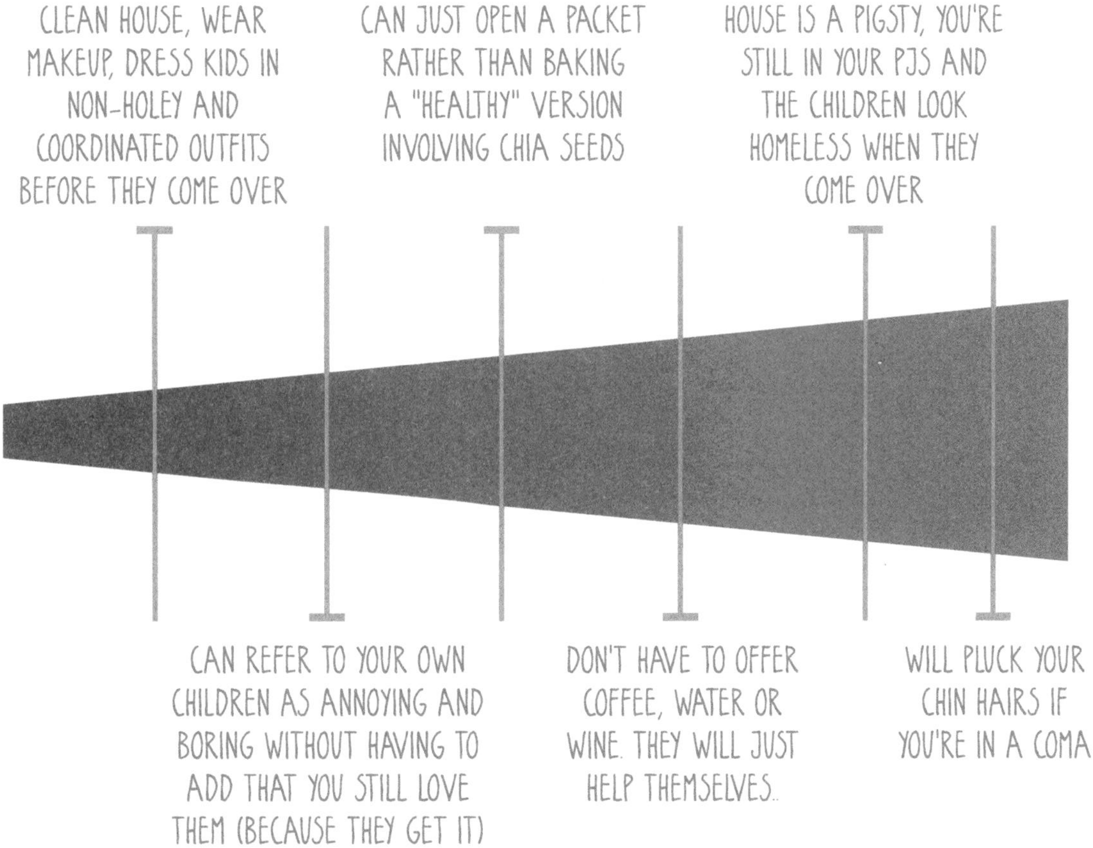

CLEAN HOUSE, WEAR MAKEUP, DRESS KIDS IN NON-HOLEY AND COORDINATED OUTFITS BEFORE THEY COME OVER

CAN JUST OPEN A PACKET RATHER THAN BAKING A "HEALTHY" VERSION INVOLVING CHIA SEEDS

HOUSE IS A PIGSTY, YOU'RE STILL IN YOUR PJS AND THE CHILDREN LOOK HOMELESS WHEN THEY COME OVER

CAN REFER TO YOUR OWN CHILDREN AS ANNOYING AND BORING WITHOUT HAVING TO ADD THAT YOU STILL LOVE THEM (BECAUSE THEY GET IT)

DON'T HAVE TO OFFER COFFEE, WATER OR WINE. THEY WILL JUST HELP THEMSELVES..

WILL PLUCK YOUR CHIN HAIRS IF YOU'RE IN A COMA

THIS AGE IS

TRICKY

THIS AGE IS

MAGIC

[ME, AT EVERY SINGLE AGE]

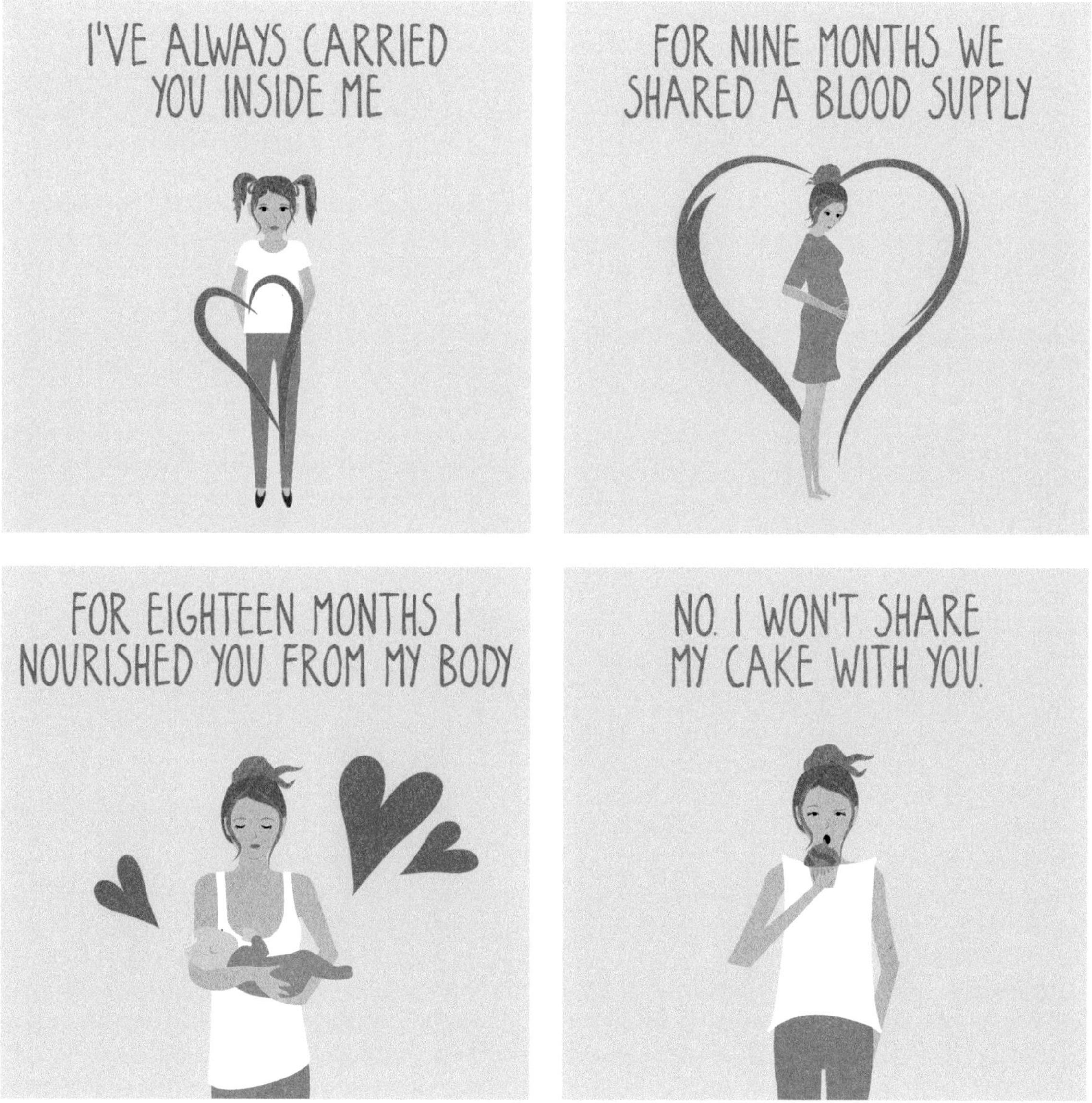
I'VE ALWAYS CARRIED YOU INSIDE ME
FOR NINE MONTHS WE SHARED A BLOOD SUPPLY
FOR EIGHTEEN MONTHS I NOURISHED YOU FROM MY BODY
NO. I WON'T SHARE MY CAKE WITH YOU.

ACKNOWLEDGMENTS

To the team at Tiller Press/Simon & Schuster who managed to turn my thoughts into a book while being at the epicentre of a global pandemic: I appreciate the faith you had in me in a very uncertain world. Thank you especially to Emily Carleton for finding me, giving me this incredible opportunity and holding my hand through an unfamiliar process, and to Samantha Lubash and Patrick Sullivan for bringing it to life.

To Ray: Sometimes you forget to thank me for cooking dinner, but I know I ALWAYS forget to thank you for all the sacrifices you've made for our family and how incredibly hard you work. Thank you for keeping me in check—grammatically and emotionally. And thank you for finally admitting I'm funnier than you.

To Mum: You made motherhood look so effortless, which, to be honest, was slightly misleading. Your unfaltering belief that I can achieve anything, while often undeserved, has shaped who I am and always given me the confidence to launch myself into new ventures and experiences. This book would not have been possible without our unlimited and free access to the exceptional Grannie Day Care, and I'm grateful for this every day.

To Dad: You have bestowed upon me the latest in technology, fine taste in wine, an unparalleled work ethic and the gift for spinning a yarn. Like everything you do, you've taken to your role as a grandparent with enthusiasm, thorough research and a tiny amount of bias (yes, yes, yes, I know your grandkids are the cleverest kids in the world).

To my sister, Elouise: I was lucky to have you growing up by my side, and I'm even luckier to have such a strong, loyal and compassionate woman riding this motherhood roller coaster with me. And, of course, thank you for the endless free legal advice.

To my wonderful parents-in-law: You smash all the in-law stereotypes and give me nothing but support and friendship. Thank you for never giving me parenting advice, even though I would probably take it from you; after all, I quite like the one you raised.

To my enduring friendships: Our group nicknames may be ridiculous, but our friendship is not. To my "Bunnikins," my "Womb" and my "Willows," thank you for decades of unbridled laughter, comforting conversation, reckless adventure and nightcaps that we most definitely didn't need.

To my children, Hugo and Leni: You turned me from someone who would head for the nearest exit when someone tried to pass me their newborn to someone who could skilfully breastfeed a baby while wiping a toddler's bum. You made me a mother. You have made me scared, besotted, tired, mesmerised, frustrated, protective and fulfilled, often all in the space of an hour. Keep being the perfect, hilarious, loving, emotional and strong little people you are (so we have enough material for a second book). I love you with all my heart.

To my amazing online community and everyone who has shared, liked and commented on my illustrations and reached out to me with your own tales of motherhood: Without you, this book wouldn't exist. You validated my experiences, amplified my voice and gave me a platform. As long as you continue to appreciate my work, I will continue to create it for you.